From Love Canal to Environmental Justice

From Love Canal to Environmental Justice

The Politics of Hazardous Waste on the Canada-U.S. Border

THOMAS H. FLETCHER

broadview press

National Library of Canada Cataloguing in Publication

Fletcher, Thomas H. (Thomas Hobbs), 1960–
    From Love Canal to environmental justice : the politics of hazardous waste on the Canada-U.S. border / Thomas H. Fletcher.

Includes bibliographical references and index.
ISBN 1-55111-434-8

    1. Hazardous waste sites—Environmental aspects—Canada. 2. Hazardous waste sites—Environmental aspects—United States. 3. Hazardous waste sites—Location—Canada. 4. Hazardous waste sites—Location—United States. 5. Environmental justice—Canada. 6. Environmental justice—United States. I. Title.

GE190.C3F54 2003   363.72'87'0971   C2003-901658-7

Broadview Press, Ltd. is an independent, international publishing house, incorporated in 1985.

North America	UK, Ireland, and Continental Europe	Australia and New Zealand
Post Office Box 1243,	Plymbridge	UNIREPS
Peterborough, Ontario,	Distributors, Ltd.	University of
Canada K9J 7H5	Estover Road	New South Wales
Tel: (705) 743-8990	Plymouth PL6 7PY	Sydney, NSW, 2052
Fax: (705) 743-8353	UK	Tel: + 61 2 96640999
	Tel: (01752) 202301	Fax: + 61 2 96645420
3576 California Road,	Fax: (01752) 202333	info.press@unsw.edu.au
Orchard Park, New York	orders@plymbridge.com	
USA 14127		

Broadview believes in shared ownership, both with its employees and with the general public; since the year 2000 Broadview shares have traded publicly on the Toronto Venture Exchange under the symbol BDP.

We welcome any comments and suggestions regarding any aspect of our publications—please feel free to contact us at the addresses below, or at broadview@broadviewpress.com / customerservice@broadviewpress.com / www.broadviewpress.com

Broadview Press Ltd. gratefully acknowledges the financial support of the Government of Canada through the Book Publishing Industry Development Program for our publishing activities.

Cover design and typeset by Zack Taylor, www.zacktaylor.com.

This book is printed on acid-free paper containing 30% post-consumer fibre.

Eco-Logo Certified.
30% Post.   Printed in Canada

Contents

Dedicated to the life and memory
of Marcy Noonan (1961-1999)

Acknowledgements

I would like to thank a number of people for their inspiration and support of the work that went into this book. The fieldwork and research could not have been possible without the kind efforts of many people who shared information with me, including archivists, community activists, and government and industry officials from the Niagara and Detroit-Windsor/Sarnia regions, as well as Albany, Lansing, Ottawa, Toronto, and Washington, DC. Though they are too numerous to list here, their support was critical to the realization of this project. I benefited tremendously from exposing myself to the diversity of their situations, knowledge, and perspectives. Though not all of them will agree with my interpretations, each provided important and useful input. Their stories reveal the difficulties that hazardous waste facilities present to communities and groups who want to promote economic affairs and protect the environment in ways that are socially just. If I could single out just one person, it would be Beth Miller who introduced me to Detroit as I was beginning the project.

Several people at Bishop's University, Department of Environmental Studies and Geography, have been supportive and encouraging. My colleagues, Darren Bardati, Derek Booth, Nicole Couture, Norm Jones, Curt Rose, and Meredith Watkins have created quite a pleasant working environment. I have learned a lot from several of my students in the Human Impact on the Environment course and in Environmental Policy for their insightful questions, comments, and overall reactions to much of the material presented on the following pages. One of them, Stephani Mustillo, assisted me with some of the research.

The research began as a study of environmental justice and hazardous waste at McGill University. Gordon Ewing, Thom Meredith, and Sherry Olson were particularly helpful. I am especially grateful to Sherry who was the first to suggest combining the dissertation with subsequent research to make this book. Several fellow graduate students also assisted in one way or another, especially Katie Pickles, now with the Department of History, University of Canterbury, who guided me through the publishing process from the proposal to the final revisions. John Hull, Karen Richardson, and many others helped during the initial project at McGill. I formulated the original ideas for the study while working for US EPA, thanks to the insights of former colleagues. Brian Gardner and Marie Howland honed my research skills while I was studying at University of Maryland as did K. Jill Kiecolt and many other professors when I was a student at Louisiana State University.

Several funding sources supported the work. The first financial assistance came in the form of a Fulbright scholarship (Canada-US program), followed by two Max Bell scholarships, a Hydro-Québec scholarship, and McGill research grants. For my post-doctoral research, I investigated the history of Love Canal and its impact on environmental policy, supported by a Larry J. Hackman research residency with the New York State Archives, sponsored by the Archives Partnership Trust. I would like to thank all of the archivists who helped me with that part of the project, as well as Kathleen DeLaney with the State University of New York at Buffalo Archives. A Bishop's University senate research grant allowed me to continue the work.

I gratefully acknowledge the contributions of The Against the Adams Mine Campaign for permission to reproduce Figure 1; the State University of New York at Buffalo Archives for permission to reproduce Figures 3, 4, 5, 6, 7, originally produced by the New York State Department of Health (1981); Atofina Chemicals Inc. for permission to reproduce Figure 10; and the Ontario Environmental Review Tribunal for permission to reproduce Figures 14 and 15, originally produced by the Ontario Waste Management Corporation (1988).

Broadview Press obviously has much to do with the results as shown here. Anne Brackenbury, senior publisher's representative and acquisitions editor, first encouraged me to submit a manuscript proposal to Broadview after listening to my ideas. Michael Harrison, vice-president and social sciences editor, was supportive and encouraging from beginning to end. The anonymous reviewers offered many helpful suggestions, as did the editorial board, especially for their idea to discuss the Toronto garbage crisis as a way of illustrating the social and spatial dimensions of hazardous waste disputes. Betsy Struthers, poet and editor, guided me through the copyedit process in addition to editing the book. Of course, I accept responsibility for any and all shortcomings.

I owe the greatest debt of gratitude to my family from Baton Rouge, Louisiana.

Preface

On January 27, 1999, the Heinz Foundation named Lois Gibbs and Florence Robinson winners of its prestigious Award for the Environment in memory of the late American Senator John Heinz. That the two will share this honor is symbolic of the 25-year history of environmental politics since Lois Gibbs led the drive to clean up a toxic waste dump in the Love Canal, New York. In 1998, Robinson and her mostly African American neighbors in Baton Rouge, Louisiana achieved final success in their struggle to have a controversial hazardous waste incinerator shut down and dismantled. Professor Robinson, who helped form this local activist group, also teaches biology at nearby Southern University and serves on the National Commission on Superfund, which oversees the federal program that Love Canal inspired. Her work builds on that of Gibbs who moved on from Love Canal to form an organization that has taken full part in the anti-toxics and environmental justice movements, the Citizens' Clearinghouse on Hazardous Waste, now known as the Center for Health, Environment and Justice.

NIMBY, or "not-in-my-backyard," has become more of a household word than a policy acronym and is an indication of considerable change in environmental politics. Moreover, issues related to hazardous waste and other forms of pollution have become increasingly important in economically marginalized communities, overlapping with the politics of race and class in ways reminiscent of the civil rights movement. Robinson and Gibbs exemplify both this struggle and its historical roots. In addition to honoring their admirable work, the Heinz award shows that the seminal moments of 1978 in Niagara Falls are as relevant to contemporary environmental politics as are the events of 1998 in Baton Rouge and other industrial communities. In the words of Teresa Heinz, Chairman of the Heinz Family Foundation (quoted in Dunne, 1999): "Lois Gibbs and Florence Robinson are heroes to everyone who cares about the ability of even the least power-ful among us to stand up and demand environmental justice."

So what is environmental justice? Both a contemporary social move-ment and a statement of what environmental policy should strive for, it is a term that many people have heard about, although it means different things to different people. As a form of social justice concerned with equity and fairness in environmental management, environmental justice has emerged as an important consideration in public policy, particularly in the United States where the movement originated during the early 1980s. A grow-ing body of evidence supports the hypothesis that hazardous waste and other industrial pollutants disproportionately burden many communities. Though this suggestion is hotly contested by industry groups who have commissioned their own studies with findings to the contrary, the envi-ronmental justice movement has found its place within (as well as outside) mainstream environmentalism where the concept was largely shunned only ten years ago.

Government policy has been nearly as slow to respond to environ-mental justice concerns though, to its credit, the American Environmental Protection Agency (EPA) initiated an Environmental Equity Work Group in July 1990 and created an Office of Environmental Justice in November 1992. President Clinton signed an Executive Order (12898) on environmental justice in February 1994, requiring all federal agencies to determine and remediate any environmental injustices subject to their jurisdiction. The impetus for EPA's efforts came not from environmental-ists, but from the Michigan Coalition, a group of activists and academics who sponsored a conference on Race and the Incidence of Environmental Hazards at the University of Michigan in January 1990. In March of that year, the conference panelists wrote a letter to William Reilly, the EPA administrator. Although initially reluctant, after meeting with some of the group members, Reilly appointed staff from several EPA offices to form the Environmental Equity Work Group.

A form of social justice, environmental justice is better described as an outgrowth of the civil rights agenda than as an extension of environmental-ism. While concerns about equal access to employment and education may seem far away from attempts to reduce technological risks, in practice these seemingly disparate struggles have proven to be quite comfortable with one another. This is due in large part to the fact that many of the founders of the environmental justice movement in the 1980s and 1990s were also involved in the civil rights movement during the 1960s and 1970s. In contrast, mainstream environmentalists are typically white and middle-class rather than low-income racial minorities. While environmentalists, like conservationists, have tended to treat natural resource and pollution issues as separate from social concerns, environmental justice activists are more likely to view environmental problems *as* social problems.

Despite the uniformity of general purpose behind environmental justice and social justice activism, the specific issues they deal with are substantially different. Yet, German sociologist Ulrich Beck suggests deeper linkages between wealth distributions (or inequality) and risk distributions:

> In advanced modernity the social production of *wealth* is systematically accompanied by the social production of *risks*. Accordingly, the problems and conflicts relating to distribution in a society of scarcity overlap with the problems and conflicts that arise from the production, definition and distribution of techno-scientifically produced risks.... The concepts of "industrial" or "class society", in the broadest sense of Marx or Weber, revolved around the issue of how socially produced wealth could be distributed in a socially unequal and also "legitimate" way. This overlaps with the new *paradigm of risk society* which is based on the solution of a similar and yet quite different problem. How can the risks and hazards systematically produced as a part of modernization be prevented, minimized, dramatized, or channeled? Where they do finally see the light of day in the shape of "latent side effects", how can they be limited and distributed away so that they neither hamper the modernization process nor exceed the limits of that which is "tolerable" — ecologically, medically, psychologically and socially? (Beck, 1986: 19; emphasis in original)

Environmental justice and social justice, then, are "similar and yet quite different problems" that overlap in much the same way as Beck describes regarding the connections between risk and wealth or, alternatively, between hazards and production. Moreover, just as concepts of social justice are relevant to the production and distribution of wealth, so too is environmental justice an important framework for understanding the production and distribution of hazards and risk. Hazardous waste, a common form of technological hazard, has become an increasingly complex and controversial problem during the last two decades, largely due to the potential risks it presents, but also and increasingly because of its inequitable and unjust distribution throughout society. Historically and to the present, industrial societies have "distributed away" what seem to be the worst of these technological hazards by localizing them and have attempted to "limit" the risks associated with them through containment in landfills and other kinds of facilities. As a result, the risks and other burdens associated with hazardous waste often are concentrated locally, at least in the present, and are intensified over time if facility containments begin to fail.

In general, the economic and other benefits of production are distributed more broadly across society, though far from evenly, as compared to the burden of waste. Industrial societies rely on the availability of numerous products that contribute to the generation of noxious by-products. Manufacturing provides economic benefits through commodity exchange, employment, and revenue generation, just as it improves standards of living with the creation of everything from time-saving appliances to life-saving pharmaceuticals. Yet toxic residuals generated during production processes present many negative consequences for the communities where they are transported, treated, stored, and disposed. These include increased public health and ecological risks from pollution in the environment, threats of accidents such as spills and explosions, and psychological distress over the perception of risks, among others.

The hazardous waste "life-cycle" begins with the generation of waste (or birth, to follow the analogy), through the many phases of and possibilities for its handling, and ending (or perhaps dying) with its management in a treatment, storage, or disposal facility (TSDF). The life-cycle analogy is somewhat synonymous to the cradle-to-grave hazardous waste management systems used, at least in theory, by many countries. Canada and the United States both have management systems of this type, again, at least in theory. I will explain, however, that hazardous waste regulatory programs tend to neglect the beginning phase of the life-cycle, generation, and pay most attention to the latter phase, management in a hazardous waste facility.

Another problem with the cradle-to-grave approach is that toxic threats from waste do not end (or die) with final placement in a landfill, for example. Rather, the potential for leaching remains for hundreds of years. Despite this, federal and state/provincial authorities in both countries have justified the siting of new facilities as a way to provide industry with what American environmental law regards as "capacity assurance" for hazardous waste disposal; thus, they have, in effect, promoted the generation of waste. With the rising cost of waste management services, industries have a direct incentive to minimize waste as an economic consideration, but only to the point that a company benefits financially. Federal and state/provincial policies fail to control or regulate the generation of waste at the point of production, since they come into effect only after its creation. Hazardous waste regulations are thus limited to standard setting, implementation, and enforcement of rules pertaining to hazardous waste facilities, transport methods, and the remediation of contaminated sites. Regulators promote pollution prevention to reduce the demand on existing facilities and the need for new ones, but do so largely through voluntary programs rather than specific requirements, except in isolated circumstances related to particular enforcement actions.

Government and industry support of proposals for new waste sites and expansions of existing ones have often resulted in contentious disputes in the communities where they are (or are to be) located. Environmental justice implications of the siting process are revealed especially in cases involving racial minority and low-income communities. But as the case studies reviewed in this book will show, questions about the fairness of hazardous waste policy figure prominently in disputes over hazardous waste facilities in all kinds of communities, not only in the United States but in Canada as well. I argue that the facility siting process and the environmental justice implications of hazardous waste that it reveals reflect a fundamental contradiction in policy between capacity assurance objectives (which largely benefit industry) and waste reduction or pollution prevention initiatives (which could benefit society and the environment). Both countries made this "end-of-pipe" choice to emphasize waste management over waste minimization beginning with their initial legislative and regulatory responses to the industrial waste problem in the late 1970s, and this emphasis is still largely in place.

The purpose of this book is to seek a greater understanding of the environmental justice implications of hazardous waste in North America, particularly matters related to distributive and procedural equity. Environmental justice is an important framework for understanding hazardous waste because questions of fairness and equity are often central to disputes over such decision-making as facility siting. Because the majority of studies in the field of environmental equity and justice have focused on the toxic waste problem in the United States, this research builds on that work to present a broader North American view of hazardous waste planning at the local and regional levels and in a binational setting. The result is a local, regional, national, and international representation of facility siting disputes from a range of perspectives including governments, industries, and communities. Moreover, while Canada and the United States regulate hazardous waste quite similarly in most respects, their differing policy styles and approaches to facility siting have resulted in some interesting contrasts in overall policy as well as controversies within the border regions.

We begin with an exploration of a waste management dispute that has received widespread media coverage in Canada: the Toronto garbage crisis. Though this case deals with municipal garbage rather than toxic waste, the issues it demonstrates have close parallels with the hazardous treatment and disposal controversies reviewed in the following chapters. In particular, the Toronto case demonstrates an all-too-typical desire on the part of some to ship waste long distances to communities that receive little or no economic benefit from the production associated with it. Instead, these host communities are asked to bear the majority of environmental burdens associated with facilities such as landfills, incinerators, and the like. The Toronto case involved a proposal to ship garbage by rail to a rural area of northern Ontario where most residents, including many First Nations people, clearly wanted nothing to do with it. These people exhibited what many would regard as a classic NIMBY response, but their grievances also involved numerous fairness issues that are consistent with the issue of environmental justice; this will be demonstrated in the following sections.

One could draw such parallels between the policies and cases reviewed in this book and other Canadian environmental crises as well. Proposed plans for long-term storage of nuclear waste at a centralized facility in the Canadian Shield have evoked many of the same concerns about spatial and intergenerational inequity as occur so often in the case of hazardous waste facility siting disputes. The American proposal to bury nuclear waste at Los Alamos, Nevada has faced similar opposition. Another Canadian case also harks back to the legacy of Love Canal, if not to the politics of facility siting exhibited in the Toronto case and the disputes reviewed in Part II. The Sydney Tar Ponds in Cape Breton, for example, are often referred to as the "Love Canal of Canada" due to the severity of contamination and the long-fought (but thus far unsuccessful) attempts by local residents to be relocated (Barlow & May, 2000). Elizabeth May, Executive Director, Sierra Club of Canada, recently went on a 17-day hunger strike to call attention to the matter. Because the focus of this book is on hazardous waste facility siting policy and cases, the Sydney Tar Ponds matter is not addressed. Nonetheless, it speaks to the lasting impression that Love Canal continues to make on environmental policy and politics.

In Part I: Themes, I examine the two issues most central to the study — hazardous waste and environmental justice — and their relationship to one another. Chapter 1: Love Canal and Hazardous Waste Policy tells the story of Love Canal in order to explain how the events of 1978 in Niagara Falls continue to shape environmental policy and politics in the new millennium. It describes the anti-toxics movement Love Canal generated and continues with the story of environmental justice in the early 1980s. The activism of this latter movement is shown as an outgrowth of the former, but with significant contributions from the civil rights movement of the 1960s. The chapter also reviews hazardous waste laws and regulations in the United States and Canada, most of which were enacted and implemented only after Love Canal. The Canadian government has established policies that are largely similar to those in the United States, in part to avoid becoming a "waste haven" for American industries. One of the biggest differences is that Canadian provinces have often used crown corporations for waste management services in order to promote public interest and fairness. While some American states have experimented with the use of public utilities for waste management (including New York State), this approach has generally been either abandoned or avoided altogether in the United States in favor of private-sector approaches.

Chapter 2: Environment and Social Justice sets the social context for the study by exploring what Beck refers to as risk society, the relationship between risk and wealth in the postwar era. I argue, following Beck and others, that the role of information is becoming increasingly important for our understanding of the overlap between hazards and production. Risk assessment pervades the field of environmental management yet generally evades the sensitivities of environmental justice. Cumulative risk, for example, is usually given scant attention in environmental assessments of development proposals of all kinds, including hazardous waste facilities. Cumulative equity, a fairness issue in heavily industrialized communities, is even further removed from the priorities of decision-making officials who must determine whether the risks or the benefits of a project have the most weight. Such is the case for other environmental equity and justice considerations as well.

Chapter 3: Environmental Justice and "Industrial Ecology" reviews empirical research on environmental justice. Much of this work has and continues to center on the question of whether race or class is more strongly associated with environmental injustice, if at all. Notwithstanding the importance of this issue, academics and activists alike have become concerned that it is time to get beyond the "race versus class trap" in order to devise practical, yet fair, environmental policies. To achieve such a reality, the generation of industrial waste must be given at least as much attention as the question of where it goes. After all, for every unit of hazardous waste avoided by industry through process and other changes within production, there is one less unit to distribute, however equitably or inequitably. Toward that end, this chapter also reviews the growing body of "industrial ecology" literature, mostly from the field of engineering, which is at the forefront of this technological movement. I demonstrate the significance of these developments for environmental justice concerns.

Part II: View Points presents a series of Canada-United States border regional case studies. Together, Chapter 4: The Niagara Region and Chapter 5: Detroit and Sarnia review hazardous waste facility siting disputes, which occurred in each of the two international border regions. The ten cases comprise the total of such incidents in both areas since the early 1980s when formal review procedures were established in all three jurisdictions. The case studies reflect diversity in the kinds of communities involved, as well as in the types of facilities proposed. Both chapters review three issues: the determination of facility need; the selection of facility locations, sizes, and types; and the promotion of fairness in facility siting. Siting boards were required by law to address each of these questions in their decision-making. Local opponents of the proposals often criticized the proceedings for emphasizing the first two questions at the expense of the last one. Such was the case in Ontario as well as in the United States in spite of the use of crown corporations designed to protect the public from the "vagaries" of the private sector. Also, the Ontario government joined local groups in officially opposing the Niagara, New York facilities.

Starting with Chapter 6: Towards Environmental Justice and Hazardous Waste, Part III: Interpretations analyzes the ten cases reviewed in Part II, drawing on their similarities and differences. It focuses on spatial and social equity (i.e., the geographic and socioeconomic distribution of benefits and burdens), cumulative and intergenerational equity (i.e., the accumulation of benefits and burdens in place and over time), and procedural equity and beyond (i.e., getting beyond distributive equity). This chapter demonstrates that equity and justice come in a variety of forms, each of which is important in its own right. Moreover, both the historical and geographical contexts are critical to understanding specific cases, which often differ in terms of the salience of particular categories of distributive and procedural justice. Also, individual disputes often reflect a wide diversity of opinion within communities over the relative importance of these issues.

Chapter 7: Conclusion considers the ten cases from Part II in terms of the themes set out in Part I. One of my arguments, drawing on Chapter 1, is that information has increasing importance for the environmental justice movement. As we enter the twenty-first century, pollutant release and transfer registries such as the Toxic Release Inventory in the United States and the National Pollutant Release Inventory in Canada are subject to the scrutiny of stakeholders on all sides of environmental issues. Pressure to increase the numbers of chemicals included in the databases, to lower the reporting thresholds, and to incorporate information on chemical usage (in addition to releases and transfers) has already begun and will only grow in the coming years. The EPA has reviewed public comments on proposed rules to deal with each of these issues. In spite of vehement industry opposition and a diversity of opinion within the scientific community, these kinds of measures are likely to become government policy in the early part of this century.

Consistent with Chapter 2, I argue that Love Canal and stories like it have and will continue to fuel the environmental justice movement. The NIMBY syndrome has not become a critical obstacle to hazardous waste siting across North America by chance. Rather, community struggles are preceded by the examples set forth through other local protests and their associated networks. Moreover, the increasing role of information overlaps these local issues, thus further enabling communities to "jump scales" and thereby contribute to national, and even international, environmental decision-making.

Finally, the environmental justice movement is likely to draw on advances made by academia, government, and industry within the industrial ecology movement. Such an approach is especially important with regard to persistent, bioaccumulative toxic substances, as well as carcinogens more generally, which present very high risks even at very low concentrations. In the twenty-first century, industries will have to demonstrate a commitment to preventing pollution, in addition to controlling it, if they are to maintain legitimacy in the face of the environmental justice movement, as well as with environmentalism more broadly. Such an approach will reduce demand on existing hazardous waste facilities and obviate a considerable degree of the need for new and expanded facilities. Likewise, the environmental justice movement will have to recognize the accomplishments of government and industry in this regard if it is to maintain its own legitimacy. Industrial ecology principles aimed at preventing pollution within production, rather than dealing with it after the fact, have great potential to reduce cumulative risk and equity concerns related to concentrations of existing facilities, which are critical matters for industrial communities, many of them poor and black.

List of Acronyms

CCPA	Canadian Chemical Producers Association
CEAG	Citizen's Environmental Action Group
CEC	Commission for Environmental Cooperation
CEPA	Canadian Environmental Protection Act
CERCLA	Comprehensive Environmental Response, Compensation, and Liability Act
CMA	Chemical Manufacturers Association
CMVA	Canadian Motor Vehicle Manufacturers Association
CWM	Chemical Waste Management
DEC	Department of Environmental Conservation
DNR	Department of Natural Resources
DOE	Department of Environment
EAA	Environmental Assessment Act
EAB	Environmental Assessment Board
ECA	Environmental Contaminants Act
EDS	Environmental Disposal Systems
EFC	Environmental Facilities Corporation
EMS	Environmental Management Systems
EPA	Environmental Protection Agency
ERES	Energy Recovery Systems
GAO	General Accounting Office
IJC	International Joint Commission
LAND	Lasalle and Niagara Demand
MI DEQ	Michigan Department of Environmental Quality
MI DNR	Michigan Department of Natural Resources
MOEE	Ministry of Environment and Energy

NAAEC	North American Agreement on Environmental Cooperation
NAFTA	North American Free Trade Agreement
NAS	National Academy of Sciences
NCS	National Chemical Services
NIABY	Not-in-anyone's-backyard
NIMBY	Not-in-my-backyard
NRC	National Research Council
NY DEC	New York Department of Environmental Conservation
OEPA	Ontario Environmental Protection Act
OTA	Office of Technology Assessment
OWMC	Ontario Waste Management Corporation
PTS	Persistent Toxic Substance
RCRA	Resource Conservation and Recovery Act
SRB	Site Review Board
TSCA	Toxic Substances Control Act
TSDF	Treatment Storage and Disposal Facility
UCCCRJ	United Church of Christ Commission for Racial Justice
UMass	University of Massachusetts

List of Figures

List of Tables

Introduction
From Toronto to
Kirkland Lake?

Toronto is in the midst of a municipal garbage crisis that has many parallels with the hazardous waste disputes reviewed in this book; the problem has been a long time in the making. The projected 2002 closure of the Keele Valley landfill and the booming population growth in southern Ontario provided clear evidence that a new waste management policy was necessary. Throughout the 1990s, the Metropolitan Toronto council (consisting of the City of Toronto and six regional municipalities) made it a priority to accomplish this with a new landfill, preferably with a location geographically distant from the population and the development pressures of the city itself. As early as 1989 Metro Toronto listed the Adams Mine abandoned quarry, 600 kilometers to the north, as a possible location and in 1990 selected it as its preferred site.

To city councilors, the Temiskaming region in northern Ontario had the benefit of distance from the population pressures of southern Ontario as well as an existing rail link that connected the two areas. The advantages of using the abandoned quarry were that the site was already excavated and had a long industrial history (see Figure 1). These facts, plus the region's need for new employment, seemed to make the selection ideal: southern Ontario's need for garbage disposal and northern Ontario's need for capital investment and jobs. The predictable NIMBY response also appeared more likely in urban and suburban communities of Metropolitan Toronto than in a remote rural locality. In fact, several possible landfill sites in and around Toronto had by then failed due to citizen protests (Ruryk, 2000).

In the early 1990s, Metro Toronto began efforts to secure Adams Mine as the ultimate site for its new plans. In 1990 the city negotiated financial

FIGURE I

Local Reaction to the Adams Mine Proposal

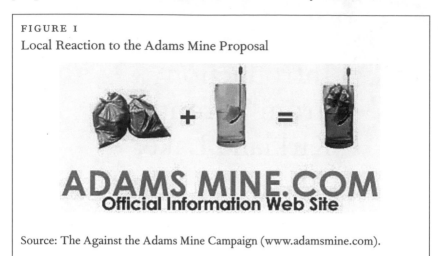

ADAMS MINE.COM
Official Information Web Site

Source: The Against the Adams Mine Campaign (www.adamsmine.com).

deals with neighboring municipalities and initiated enabling provincial legislation. By 1992, the Ontario government had passed legislation requiring Metro Toronto to include the larger Greater Toronto Area (which includes four neighboring regions) in its planning. The move was designed to achieve even greater economies of scale (e.g., a larger contract) and to extend the security of waste disposal capacity to a wider part of the southern Ontario region. The government's Interim Waste Authority spent $85 million examining potential landfill sites, most of which were located in municipalities outside of Metro Toronto, prompting an additional $15 million in spending by local officials who opposed the provincial policy (Davey, 1998). The dispute between Metro Toronto and other municipalities in the Greater Toronto Area amounted to a difference of opinion over the appropriate scale of spatial equity (i.e., local versus regional). During the same period, a similar controversy over spatial equity and spatial scale was also central to disagreements regarding a proposal by the Ontario Waste Management Corporation to site a hazardous waste facility on the Niagara Peninsula (reviewed in Chapter 4). The Adams Mine proposal seemed well on track until 1995 when Metro Toronto rejected the plan to develop the site as a provincially owned landfill because of financial as well as environmental considerations.

No sooner did the plan reach this apparent dead end, when private-sector options began to emerge. Such conflicts between public- and private-sector approaches are common in hazardous waste policy, as will be revealed in Part I of this book, and in facility siting disputes, reviewed in Part II. In

1996, Notre Development Corporation announced its own 65 million tonne landfill proposal for Adams Mine and initiated an environmental assessment (EA) process. By then, private-sector waste management was viewed as a necessary alternative to failed public-sector planning in the field of municipal as well as hazardous waste management. Government-owned and operated facility proposals were common in the 1980s but were viewed as unworkable for economic as well as social considerations by the mid-1990s. The new Harris Conservative government's environmental policy created an even greater incentive for a private-sector landfill in Kirkland Lake. In 1996, the Ontario government changed the Environmental Assessment Act (EAA), dropping the requirement to consider facility need (i.e., whether the landfill was necessary to provide disposal capacity) and, more importantly, alternatives to landfills (e.g., waste reduction and recycling).

Notre Development Corporation used this opportunity to secure its proposal and, in 1997, amended its request for a landfill approval. The new plan eliminated the recycling and transport provisions of the project previously required under EAA and the landfill itself was scaled back to one 20 million tonne pit rather than the three originally identified. Thus the new and downsized environmental assessment had fewer elements to consider, giving the request a greater chance of success than before. In 1998, the provincial government initiated a "fast-tracked" environmental assessment hearing that was to be completed in three months and that was based on one technical question associated with hydrogeology and the ability of the facility to prevent leaching and groundwater contamination. In June 1998, the three-person panel issued a split decision with two members recommending more tests to be assessed by the Ministry of Environment (MOE). The final decision-making authority to approve the request would therefore rest with MOE rather than the Environmental Assessment Board (EAB). The third member dissented and issued a minority opinion that the project be rejected outright, based on environmental and engineering concerns.

Dissenting opinion on the Notre proposal was not limited to minority opinion within EAB or even to Ontario more generally. In 1997, an additional review was commissioned by the Algonquin Nation Secretariat on the Algonquin-Temiskaming Reserve located just 20 kilometers from the Quebec border (Gallaugher & Lee, 1997). The Algonquin Nation comprises three First Nations communities including Wolf Lake, Temiskaming, and Barrière Lake. Each is situated on Lake Temiskaming, near the mouth of the Blanche River where the Adams Mine site drains. In addition to their land claim of the Adams Mine site itself, the Secretariat expressed concerns about the impacts of the proposed landfill on the waters, wildlife, lands, and people of their territory more generally.

The First Nations assessment of the Notre application and the environmental assessment concluded that the proposed leachate monitoring systems were inadequate to ensure safety during the 20-year projected operation of the facility (of the first cell, that is) and beyond. The operation of the facility, of course, would continue considerably longer with nearly certain construction of additional cells. Moreover, the possibility of future impacts would extend indefinitely. The potential contamination of fish and wildlife, the food sources of the people who live there, would pose considerable uncertainty for the region. Finally, an uncertain economic viability for the facility created concerns that the operator might abandon the operation prior to its projected lifetime and fail to provide adequate maintenance after its closure. The Algonquin Nation Secretariat recommended that MOE reject the Notre application unless the various uncertainties were clarified.

By this time, the Town of Kirkland Lake was also beginning to have doubts about the Notre plan. In 1997, Mayor Richard Denton was elected on an anti-dump platform, but an agreement between the corporation and the town council reached earlier that same year narrowed his options (Harris, 1999). The negotiated deal guaranteed municipal revenues in the form of a levy on tipping fees, an attractive financial arrangement for a town with 20 per cent unemployment. The region had been economically prosperous in the 1930s when the seven gold mines located there were among the richest in the world. Since their closure, however, few other economic prospects remained, yet the mine tailings continued to contaminate the waters of Kirkland Lake. Despite the potential for further contamination from municipal garbage, the town council voted in favor of Notre's plan and later warned the new mayor not to criticize the negotiated agreement for fear of forfeiting the benefits the town would receive if the facility were to be built.

Public sentiment for the deal continued to erode; an August 2000 poll of local residents found that 77 per cent were opposed to the Notre facility (Oracle, 2000). The random survey of 300 voting-age residents found that the principal concern was with the potential for ground water contamination (25 per cent). Numerous other reasons for opposition were also given, but a number of equity or justice concerns were even more important to Kirkland Lake residents. For example, 80 per cent stated that garbage should be disposed of where it is created (spatial equity), 79 per cent considered it unfair that future generations of local residents would have to maintain the facility (intergenerational equity), and 77 per cent were concerned that no local referendum had been held on the matter (procedural equity). Still, local opposition to the plan was and is not shared by all. Bill Enouy, a Kirkland Lake mayoral candidate, has argued that the project is necessary to revitalize the regional economy, given the estimated 80 full-time jobs and $1 million annual revenues it would bring to the town.

Public opinion in and around Toronto also fluctuated. Metro Council was clearly in favor of the Kirkland Lake proposal in one form or another throughout the 1990s. Bill Saundercook, the Toronto Works Committee Chairman, described it as having no alternative and argued for a speedy resolution (Honywill, 2000). By the year 2000, negative publicity had diffused the enthusiasm of even the politicians. In May of that year, few councilors even attended a hearing to decide on a $500 million contract with Notre. The loss of quorum necessary to make the decision official made for continuing uncertainty (Wanagas, 2000). By this point, widespread public protests in the Temiskaming region were diffusing Toronto area support for Adams Mine, but only to a point.

In July 2000, the city announced five possible replacements for the existing Keele Valley landfill, two of which were in Michigan, two in southern Ontario (one near London and the other near Windsor, just across the border from Detroit), and finally one in Kirkland Lake, still regarded as the best option by Metro Council. By this point, the alternatives to the Adams Mine were still considered worst-case scenario options (i.e., if Kirkland Lake fell through) and involved a complex mix of possibilities, including a four-way split for the garbage to two sites in southern Ontario and two in Michigan (Palmer, 2000). An extension of the closure date for Keele Valley to 2006 has been described by many as yet another possibility, although Ontario Minister of Environment Dan Newman has insisted that it will close sooner than that. Neighbors of the Keele Valley landfill in the southern Ontario Town of Vaughan have also insisted that the closure date not be extended (Demera & Moloney, 2000).

Still another twist on the Toronto garbage crisis was the possibility of using the Kirkland Lake proposal to embarrass the city over its now failed bid to host the 2008 Summer Olympics. In August 2000, ten Adams Mine activists flew to Lausanne, Switzerland to ask the International Olympic Committee to help them stop the plan and used the opportunity to initiate a letter-writing campaign, enlisting support from even the Pope (Prouta, 2000). In early October 2000, after a series of delays prompted by protests that blocked rail lines, the Metro Toronto Council voted to approve the Kirkland Lake proposal and related decisions such as a contract with Rail Cycle North, the company that would haul the waste by train 600 kilometers to the site. The rail contract was conditional and subsequently canceled over the unresolved issue of responsibility for potential future cost increases during the 12-year agreement (City of Toronto, 2000; Freeze & Abbate, 2000). Toronto Mayor Mel Lastman, perhaps the most vocal proponent of the plan, insisted the failed agreement had to do with "contract language" not environmental concerns, thus extending at least implicit hope that the Adams Mine proposal might ultimately prevail (Rusk & Bourette, 2000). However, only a few days after the Rail Cycle North contract failed, news reports from Michigan announced a five-year 300,000 to 500,000 tonne contract between the City of Toronto and Republic Services, Inc., a Florida-based company that owns a landfill in Sumpter Township, Michigan.

The decision to scrap the Kirkland Lake site (at least for now) in favor of shipping Toronto garbage to Michigan has created a decidedly negative response south of the border. American congressman Mike Rogers seemed to view Canadian waste imports as an assault on American patriotism when he charged that Toronto should keep its "dirty diapers and leftover Canadian bacon" in its own backyard (quoted in Shine, 2001a). Rogers, a Republican, represents the Brighton congressional district in Livingston County, northwest of metropolitan Detroit. He made the remark in May 2001 while introducing a bill in the House of Representatives that would give any American state the authority to restrict, and even prohibit, waste imports from other countries.

The bill is a tougher version of a similar one introduced in March 2001 by congressmen David Bonior and John Dingell that would stop short of banning imports, but would give state governments the power to place caps on out-of-state waste (Shine, 2001b). Both bills face steep obstacles in becoming law, not only because of the powerful waste management industry lobby in Washington but, more fundamentally, because the interstate commerce clause of the American Constitution does not allow outright bans on out-of-state waste. Nonetheless, congressmen Bonior and Dingell believe that capping such imports is constitutional, and Rogers skirts the interstate issue altogether by restricting the scope to international shipments. A newcomer to Washington, he stated: "I've done a lot of research and worked on this since I got here [in November 2000]." Although state-to-state shipments are clearly protected, at least to some degree, "you can ban foreign trash," Rogers asserted (quoted in Shine, 2001a).

Yet another, but less predictable, legal twist on the matter has originated in Ottawa. Environment Canada is considering a new regulation that would require municipalities to obtain the approval of American states before shipping municipal garbage to them. "It gives the opportunity for the receiving jurisdiction to approve or not approve shipments of waste," said Carl Chenier of Environment Canada (quoted in Shine, 2001c). The proposed rule is based on the "prior informed consent" provision of the Basel Convention, an international agreement respecting transboundary movements of hazardous waste. Grace Howland, also with Environment Canada, cautioned that nothing has yet been finalized but added that "the policy will likely include prior informed consent" (quoted in Shine, 2001c). Whatever the shape of the new waste export policy, it is expected to go into effect in 2003.

Although the Toronto garbage crisis involves municipal garbage, it has a number of implications for the focus of this book: hazardous waste. These include policy implications (discussed in Chapter 1), social justice implications (discussed in Chapter 2), and "industrial ecology" implications (discussed in Chapter 3). Moreover, the hazardous waste facility siting disputes reviewed in chapters 4 and 5 of Part II have many parallels with the controversies between Toronto and Kirkland Lake, as well as those that are emerging between the city and the state of Michigan. At present, it appears unlikely but far from certain that municipal garbage shipments from Toronto to Kirkland Lake will become reality. Instead, the Ontario government has traded an *intra*-provincial spatial equity problem for a cross-border and international spatial equity problem with Michigan, if only for the short-term. The lessons of hazardous waste facility siting disputes reveal similar problems and speak to the environmental justice implications of waste management more generally.

PART I

THEMES

Hazardous Waste and Environmental Justice

Introduction

This first section of the book introduces three broad themes that are critical to understanding the connections between hazardous waste and environmental justice. Chapter 1 examines North American hazardous waste policies and their connections to the history of Love Canal. When the Love Canal crisis emerged in 1978, Congress had recently enacted a new hazardous waste law that had yet to be implemented by the Environmental Protection Agency (EPA). This inaction changed quickly when the controversy prompted the agency to develop regulations pursuant to the new statute. This was the beginning of what are now known as cradle-to-grave management systems designed to track the movements of hazardous waste from generation to disposal and to toughen the standards for treatment and disposal facilities. Just two years after the Love Canal incident emerged, the United States developed another hazardous waste law that established the Superfund program. This ultimately $9-billion fund is used to finance the cleanup of contaminated sites like Love Canal and establishes tough liability provisions against the parties responsible for the pollution. The Superfund program is widely regarded as having been inspired by Love Canal. Also inspired were Canadian government officials at the federal and provincial levels who established their own hazardous waste laws. Canada's, particularly Ontario's, proximity to Love Canal was no doubt central to the response, as was the country's history of promulgating environmental policies in order to avoid becoming an American "pollution haven"; these began in the early 1970s, shortly after the establishment of Environment Canada and EPA.

Chapter 2 examines the connections between environment and social justice. As explained in the preface, the environmental justice movement views pollution as a matter of equity and fairness. The struggle is in one sense an outgrowth of the anti-toxics movement that Love Canal generated in the 1980s but it is equally the result of the civil rights movement of the 1960s. Ulrich Beck developed his concept of risk society as a device to understand the relationships between what he calls wealth distributions and risk distributions, which are central to problems associated with environmental injustice. Though Beck has generated considerable attention and praise, ironically, he has also been criticized for failing to understand the problem of environmental injustice. His work and the responses of his supporters and critics is nonetheless useful for understanding the environmental justice issue, as are broader theories of distributive and procedural social justice. The development of EPA's environmental justice programs is also illustrative when examining these connections.

Chapter 3 examines the connections between environmental justice and "industrial ecology" by reviewing the empirical research and evidence of two sets of academic literature that are generally regarded as separate matters. Empirical research into the issue of environmental justice addresses the extent to which particular groups and communities are burdened by pollution, especially hazardous waste. As such, this research uses demographics and spatial statistics to examine the extent to which environmental justice is associated with race or class, if at all. A statistical debate has ensued over methodological matters such as the appropriate geographic units of analysis in this type of research as well as matters of comparison groups. Nonetheless, many researchers and activists involved in the environmental justice issue have argued that it is time to get beyond these static questions and figure out how to reduce environmental injustices in all communities. This is where the industrial ecology literature comes in. Generated primarily by chemical, civil, and environmental engineers, this area of research examines pollution as part of product and chemical life-cycles and seeks to prevent it before it occurs through engineering solutions that obviate the need for waste treatment and disposal to the maximum extent possible. Government and corporate pollution prevention programs also set their sights on this problem and opportunity, mostly through voluntary programs that encourage rather than require industries to adopt particular practices. I argue that industrial ecology and environmental justice are not separate concerns, but rather that progress in each movement holds the promise of advancing the other.

I

Love Canal and
Hazardous Waste Policy

Introduction

North American governmental involvement in hazardous waste management begins with the enactment, implementation, and enforcement of
highly complex statutes and regulations operating at both the federal
and provincial/state levels. These laws and policies impose a number of
requirements on industries that generate hazardous waste as well as on
those in the business of waste treatment, storage, and disposal (TSD).
They apply to virtually all aspects of waste management from cradle to
grave, beginning with the point at which it is generated and ending with its
ultimate fate in a hazardous waste management facility.

Toxic waste programs define hazardous waste in a series of regulations
that make distinctions between wastes that are and are not to be regulated
as such. Other regulations impose restrictions on management methods
of land disposal such as "landfilling," incineration, deep-well injection,
and dilution and mixing. Further, "corrective action" programs clean
up abandoned or otherwise uncontrolled waste sites, often referred to as
"brownfields," presumably to distinguish them from "greenfield" sites,
which are previously undeveloped areas. Finally, facility siting proposals
are used to avoid the creation of future uncontrolled waste sites by assisting
waste generation and management industries in their attempts to build new
facilities or to expand existing ones.

Environment Canada and the US Environmental Protection Agency
have expressed concern about the large volumes of hazardous waste being
generated in both countries. Annually, the United States generates just over

40 million tonnes' of hazardous waste, and Canada generates approximately 6 million tonnes (EPA, 1999; Environment Canada, 2000; O'Neill, 2000). American hazardous waste generation has risen approximately 40 per cent since 1987, whereas Canada's generation rate is approximately the same as it was in 1986 (Environment Canada, 1988). The State of Michigan generates nearly one million tonnes of hazardous waste each year, the tenth highest amount of any American jurisdiction. New York State generates nearly 400,000 tonnes annually and ranks fifteenth. The Province of Ontario generates over 1.8 million tonnes annually, more than any other Canadian jurisdiction (Ontario Ministry of Environment, 2000).

From 1995 to 1999, the most recent years for which comparative data are available, the generation of hazardous wastes and other toxic releases has decreased by 3 per cent in North America, though there are some interesting differences with regard to various categories of toxins. These data are compiled by the Commission for Environmental Cooperation (CEC), an agency established pursuant to the North American Agreement on Environmental Cooperation, which began releasing comparative data in 1995 (CEC, 2002). Although air emissions of toxic chemicals have decreased by 25 per cent, toxic effluents released into surface waters have increased by 26 per cent, and land disposal (mainly in landfills) of hazardous wastes has increased by 25 per cent. Additionally, transfers of hazardous waste to off-site treatment and disposal facilities have increased by 33 per cent. With regard to types of hazardous wastes, there has been a 4 per cent decrease in off-site disposal of metal wastes, a 31 per cent increase in non-metal chemical waste, and a 1 per cent increase in transfers of hazardous waste to recycling facilities. The difference between Canada and the United States is most striking for on-site land disposal of hazardous wastes, which increased by 149 per cent in Canada and by 15 per cent in the United States. This suggests that North American industries are landfilling hazardous wastes at an increasing rate, especially in Canada. Another interesting comparison is that off-site releases of toxic waste increased by 3 per cent in Canada and by 40 per cent in the United States. This suggests that the NIMBY syndrome is prompting North American industries to shift the burden of toxic waste to external locations, especially in the United States.

The Canadian Green Plan (1990) and Environment Canada's Pollution Prevention Program promote life-cycle management of toxic substances in order to prevent waste before it occurs and funds research and development (R&D) to support technological innovations to reduce waste. Likewise,

EPA's Pollution Prevention Program seeks voluntary compliance from industries to decrease their use and emissions of toxic substances. What is common to both the Canadian and American waste reduction programs is that they are non-regulatory; rather than imposing specific requirements, they operate technical assistance, R&D, and other programs to promote voluntary reductions in pollution emissions by industry. In exchange for their efforts, industries participating in pollution prevention programs often receive favorable press as environmentally friendly industries. Also, many industries have reported cost savings due to more efficient use of costly toxic chemicals and lower pollution control fees (Gibson, 1999). Each of the American states and Canadian provinces have developed their own pollution prevention programs as well.

American and Canadian Hazardous Waste Policy and Politics

Hazardous waste regulations vary in style and content among North American jurisdictions, especially internationally. The American government uses strong federal statutes and regulations that specify requirements for nearly all conceivable circumstances. The Canadian government gives greater discretion to the provinces, which regulate industries based on federal science and guidance, but nonetheless rely on policies that are less explicit than those in the United States and which are often made explicit only as written into operating permits for particular facilities (Ilgen, 1985). The "spatial homogeneity" of American environmental policy has been fostered by Supreme Court interpretations of the Constitution, particularly of Article 1, Section 8, Clause 3, widely known as the Commerce Clause (Clark, 1981). Based on the interpretation that waste is technically a commodity, the Court has consistently denied states the ability to restrict access to their own treatment and disposal facilities by out-of-state generators (Lake & Johns, 1990). Canadian provinces, on the other hand, have the legal right to restrict the importation of waste.

Environmental disputes over locally unwanted land uses (LULUs) have become a common feature of community planning in North America (Lake, 1993, 1987; Popper, 1987). These locational conflicts between communities and higher levels of government (especially provincial/state) often amount to differing interpretations of local autonomy (Clark, 1984, 1985, 1986; Lake & Johns, 1990; Lake, 1994). They also arise from the "indeterminacy" of law as written and interpreted (Blomley, 1989; Clark, 1985, 1989). These indeterminacies greatly increase controversy and lengthen the time spent trying to site and permit new industrial facilities because of the varying interests and perspectives of "interpretative communities" (Blomley, 1989; Clark, 1985; Fish, 1980). These "communities" refer to not only local governments, but also to higher tiers of the state and with variation among branches (e.g., executive, legislative, judicial), as well as levels of government, depending on function (e.g., statutory and regulatory development, enforcement, and adjudication). Moreover, disagreements among interpretive communities highlight contradictions in policy and lead toward a "politics of interpretation" that exerts pressure on decision-making bodies, whether in the judiciary, legislature, or bureaucracy at any level of government.

Political scientists Harrison and Hoberg have found in both countries, but more recently in Canada, the rise of "legalism," an environmental policy style that has increased the role of the judiciary (Harrison & Hoberg, 1994; Hoberg, 1993). Also interest groups representing industry, the environment, and communities now enjoy greater access to policy-making processes. As the judiciary becomes more active in challenging administrative discretion, existing pro-environment decisions become more susceptible to challenges from industrial interests, and industrial projects become more vulnerable to community and environmental opposition. This complicates the problem of determinacy still further, often in conflicting and unpredictable directions. Nonetheless, community interests still face steep obstacles when government agencies and the courts narrowly interpret local autonomy in favor of state and provincial goals (Clark, 1985, 1986; Clark & Dear, 1984; Lake, 1994; Lake & Johns, 1990).

Both countries have made capacity assurance a central goal of their hazardous waste policies, especially the United States, which has the statutory authority to withhold Superfund cleanup monies from states that do not have existing or planned facilities in-state or an agreement with a nearby jurisdiction. Canada does not threaten its provinces with these kinds of restrictions on transfer payments; however, capacity assurance is an implicit feature of the country's hazardous waste policy, and it has been an important justification for facility siting as the Ontario case studies in Part II will demonstrate. This kind of governmental promotion of facility siting as an overall priority of hazardous waste policy places states and provinces in a strong position *vis-à-vis* local governments over decisions about whether and where to locate them. As well, state and provincial authorities exert control over administrative proceedings where facility locational decisions are made.

A related trend is the rise of "legal formalism," a doctrine used to justify American and Canadian judicial decision-making as based on noncontextual, neutral rules; that is, determinations made from universal (at least within the nation, province, or state) legal principles as opposed to contingent circumstances (Blomley, 1989; Clark, 1985, 1986, 1989). Clark (1985, 1986), in his comparative studies of urban law in Chicago and Toronto, and following the legal scholar Unger (1983), describes legal formalism as having two main characteristics: objectivism and formalism. Unger defined objectivism as "the belief that the authoritative legal materials—the system of statutes, cases, and accepted legal ideas—embody and sustain a defensible scheme of human association." He goes on to define the related concept of formalism as decision-making that "invokes impersonal purposes, policies, and principles as an indispensable component of legal reasoning" (quoted in Clark, 1986: 65).

Judicial bodies (including quasi-judicial facility siting boards) use the theoretical position of objectivism, along with the legal practice of formalism, to bolster their legitimacy as they attempt to "manufacture" determinacy from indeterminate rules stipulated in law. While policy makers (legislative and executive) and adjudicators, especially in higher tiers of the state, typically rely on abstract concepts to justify their actions and positions, enforcement officials, especially local government officials, often position themselves in opposition to abstraction by explaining their views in terms of social and spatial context as they attempt to respond to specific needs. Each extreme of this "interpretive continuum" (see Figure 2) has its own basis for internal validity, with proponents of abstract legal arguments relying on ideology to justify particular actions, and "immersed" local (and locally concerned) agents relying on instrumental forms of validity that are given meaning through lived communities. The result is a "territorial politics of location" that reflects a variety of perspectives on the role of the state at every level and on the territory of space (incorporating a variety of community and environmental interests and concerns), particularly at the local level (Cox, 1989). In terms of hazardous waste facility siting disputes, the outcome of this dialectic is often that environmental regulatory agencies at the federal and state/provincial levels will support proposals for

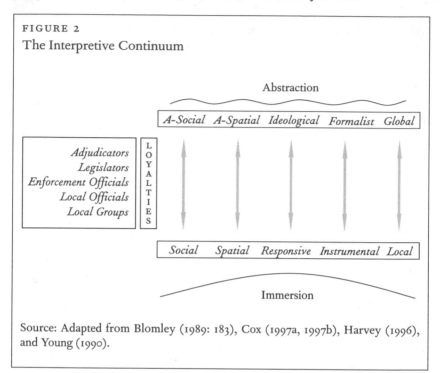

FIGURE 2
The Interpretive Continuum

Source: Adapted from Blomley (1989: 183), Cox (1997a, 1997b), Harvey (1996), and Young (1990).

additional capacity that are ultimately opposed by communities and local governments.

The relationship between local politics on the one hand and those representing larger spatial scales on the other can be conceptualized either in absolutist or relational terms. An absolutist view of the politics of scale is to make discrete distinctions among the local, the state/provincial, and the national. Such an approach is necessary to a point, if for nothing else than to remind ourselves of the real differences among these various levels of federalism and their associated constituencies at different scales. This is particularly important in Canada where competition between the federal and provincial governments over environmental matters makes it difficult to create national, much less federal, standards (VanNijnatten & Boardman, 2002). Alternatively, a relational approach treats the "local" and the "global" as competing forces that play out at various and shifting scales. Cox (1997a, 1997b), following Harvey (1982, 1985a, 1985b), argues in favor of this relational view in certain circumstances, some of which are directly relevant to hazardous waste disputes between communities and higher tiers of the state.

One example where Cox argues that a relational perspective is in order occurs when local government and other community agents are forced to engage in formal proceedings controlled by higher levels of government. In these instances, it probably matters less to local actors that provincial and state authorities make hazardous waste facility siting decisions in Canada and the US than the fact that environmental statutes and regulations in both countries are designed to promote industrial-environmental goals that are larger than local (e.g., capacity assurance, the US Commerce Clause), notwithstanding the numerous opportunities for community groups to participate in facility siting proceedings. Under such arrangements, local interests are subsumed to "spaces of dependence" whereby broader events and forces exert controlling influences (Cox, 1997a). The Ontario Environmental Protection Act (OEPA) and Environmental Assessment Act (EAA) are the most relevant Canadian statutes in this respect, at least with regard to the cases reviewed in Part II. The provision of intervenor funding for opposition groups helps to alleviate this problem by giving residents the ability to hire their own technical consultants, though they are still placed in the unenviable position of having to "prove their case."

Another instance where Cox argues that a relational view becomes useful occurs when local politics, through networks of various sorts, become interconnected among multiple communities. The NIMBY syndrome has not become a critical local obstacle to hazardous waste facility siting across North America by chance. Rather, these environmental struggles are preceded by the examples set forth by other local protests and their associated networks (e.g., the environmental justice movement, the anti-toxics movement). It is through these locally initiated but broadly applied arrangements that communities facing hazardous waste problems are able to transform their "spaces of dependence" into "spaces of engagement" with other communities facing similar obstacles. The result is that local land-use politics are enabled to "jump scales" and thereby address global environmental problems (Cox, 1997a).

Local stakeholders still face considerable obstacles when confronting spaces of dependence and engagement of the sort Cox describes. This is particularly true in cases where local interests are not coupled with and represented by local governments, the smallest, yet most numerous, of agencies in federal political systems such as Canada and the US (Judd, 1997). Additionally, in the absence of local and regional land-use planning corresponding to the goals of national or provincial/state environmental objectives, implementation remains "fractured" (Robertson & Judd, 1989; Willis & Powe, 1995) and also hindered by "structural constraints" (Lake & Disch, 1992; Lake & Johns, 1990) and a lack of democracy (Pulido, 1994) within the legal system, making spatial homogeneity of the sort Clark (1981) describes an elusive as well as indeterminate goal. Similarly, non-decision-making can be as powerful as decision-making at all spatial scales, so long as the issues surrounding these policies are kept out of the political arena (Bachrach & Baratz, 1962). A good example related to hazardous waste occurs when facility siting debates are restricted to the relative merits of various locations at the expense of discussing larger policy questions such as whether expanded pollution prevention could obviate the need for additional capacity. Similarly, while capacity assurance objectives are not required through statute in Canada, as is the case in the United States, provincial support for new and expanded facilities often have the same result: local opposition to top-down facility siting processes.

Local groups opposed to facility siting proposals face high hurdles when local politicians and bureaucracies in higher levels of government choose to either support the developments or offer no formal opinion about them. Alternatively, groups who support plans for new or expanded facilities are hindered in cases where local governments choose to formally oppose them. In either case, local governments facing hazardous waste facility siting proceedings must deal with external forces over which they have little direct control, while negotiating with various and often competing interests within their communities (e.g., economic competition, environmental protection, labor rights).

Love Canal: Historical Legacy and Locus for Action

Love Canal, located in Niagara Falls, New York on the Canadian border, is in many respects the birthplace of the anti-toxics and environmental justice movements as well as the beginning of hazardous waste policies as we know them today in North America. The now infamous environmental disaster dramatically illustrated the problems with disposal of toxic residuals from chemical production.[2] Moreover, it started a local grassroots protest that spread to countless other communities facing similar problems, especially in the US. The dispute also generated a national movement to reform hazardous waste policy with a Superfund to clean up contaminated communi-

FIGURE 3
Signage at Love Canal

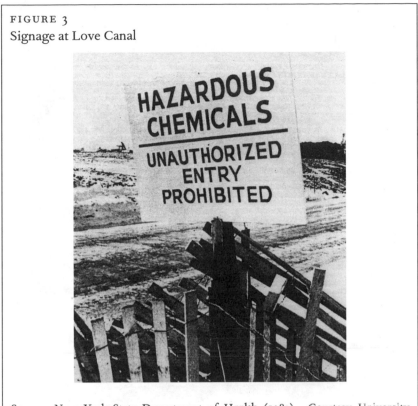

Source: New York State Department of Health (1981). Courtesy University Archives, State University of New York at Buffalo.

ties and the implementation of a long-delayed cradle-to-grave management system designed to prevent further problems (Silverman, 1989). Canadians took serious notice of Love Canal because of its proximity to the Canadian-American border and its contribution to the contamination of Lake Ontario, a major source of drinking water and recreational use for southern Ontarians. The controversies surrounding Love Canal continue, as do the effects on public environmental consciousness, especially in communities that have their own hazardous waste problems.

Hooker Chemical and Plastics Corporation, now Occidental Chemical Corporation, dumped approximately 22,000 tons of toxic wastes into Love Canal from 1942 to 1953 (see Figures 3 and 4). Also, the City of Niagara Falls used it as a municipal waste facility for many years. Originally disposed as liquids and solids in metal drums and other types of containers,

FIGURE 4
Location of Love Canal

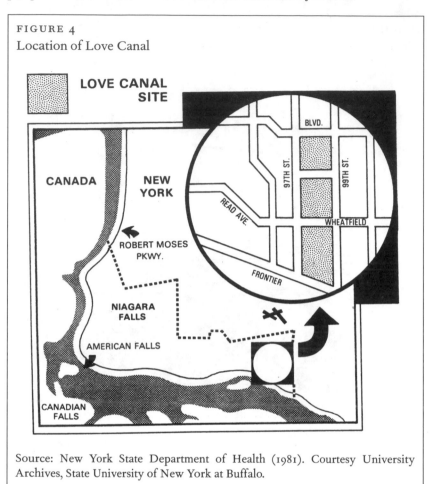

Source: New York State Department of Health (1981). Courtesy University Archives, State University of New York at Buffalo.

approximately 200 chemicals and chemical compounds have been identified there (Hennessey, 1978). Typical of the era, the dump site was unlined, used no leachate control or detection equipment, and, when completely filled, was capped with only a thin layer of clay. In 1953, Hooker sold the property to the Niagara Falls Board of Education for $1. The deed stipulated that chemical wastes were buried there and claimed to absolve the company of future liability related to the property. In 1954, the city built an elementary school on top of the canal and nearby home construction began to accelerate, even directly adjacent to the site. Throughout the 1960s, nearby residents complained of fumes and minor explosions, but the worst trouble began in the mid-1970s when heavy snowfalls, followed by spring

FIGURE 5
Aerial View of Love Canal

Source: New York State Department of Health (1981). Courtesy University Archives, State University of New York at Buffalo.

thaws and rain, caused the chemicals to seep first to the surface and then laterally through surface soils into yards and basements of nearby homes. The blizzard of 1978 produced an especially large amount of precipitation (DeLaney, 2000).

By 1978, the contamination reached a level of severity that forced New York's Commissioner of Health to declare a State of Emergency and recommend evacuation of local residents (see Figures 5, 6, and 7). The evacuations began with an initial recommendation for relocation of pregnant women and children under two years of age residing in homes adjacent to the canal. That same year, New York Governor Carey expanded the relocation order to include all residents of these same homes and later expanded the zone of relocation twice. President Carter eventually declared the site a federal emergency. The boundaries of the evacuation zone became a matter

FIGURE 6

Location of Love Canal Emergency Zones

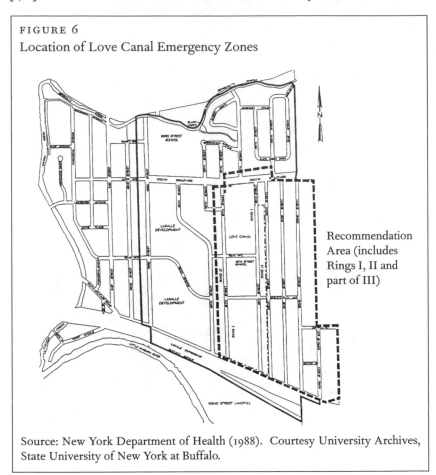

Recommendation Area (includes Rings I, II and part of III)

Source: New York Department of Health (1988). Courtesy University Archives, State University of New York at Buffalo.

of dispute from nearly the beginning. The first health orders applied only to so-called Rings I and II (the homes adjacent to and immediately across the street from the canal), while the last health order eventually included Ring III, indicated by the unbroken black border on Figure 6.

Local activism, especially under the leadership of Lois Gibbs, accounts for the expansion of the relocation borders, as well as for the larger significance of Love Canal to environmental politics (see Figure 6). After the decision was made to relocate residents of Rings I and II, Gibbs began mapping the incidence of illnesses in the area and eventually hypothesized that they were clustered around old streambeds (swales) and other "historically wet areas" that neighborhood developers had filled prior to home construction. She and Beverly Paigen, a biomedical geneticist, conducted a

FIGURE 7

Local Reaction to Love Canal

Source: New York State Department of Health (1981). Courtesy University Archives, State University of New York at Buffalo.

survey to determine the validity of the swales theory. The study was later discredited for being "unscientific," mainly because it failed to use a control group as is necessary in the design of experimental research. Nonetheless, the study was a major influence on the later decision to expand the permanent relocation of homes to Ring III. The swales theory combined with the fact that the remediation of the site was accomplished more through containment, rather than removal, of toxins has been central to criticisms of the most recent relocation to occur at Love Canal, the resettlement of part of the neighborhood now known as Black Creek Village (Fletcher, 2002).

FIGURE 8

US Willingness to Accept a Hazardous Waste Facility (1973 and 1980)

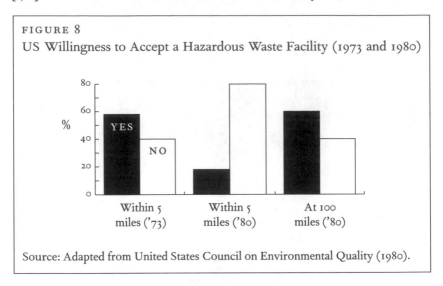

Source: Adapted from United States Council on Environmental Quality (1980).

Dumping chemical wastes into such a crudely designed landfill and then building schools and homes on and around it seem foolish and doomed to fail by today's environmental standards. But Love Canal was not at all atypical of industrial waste management practices of the chemicals, metals, and other heavy industries in the war and early postwar, years. As well, legal and administrative frameworks of the day were relatively new and insufficient for preventing disasters like Love Canal. As of 1926, only 13 American states, including New York State, had adopted "nuisance" laws specific to industrial wastes, and by 1939 the number had only grown to 31 (Colten & Skinner, 1996). This regulatory context, combined with dramatic increases in postwar industrialization, led to an increased incidence of ground water contamination throughout the United States. By 1958, virtually every industrialized American state had discovered cases of toxic contamination of ground water.

Love Canal's effect on public perception of hazardous waste has been remarkable. In 1973, before the disaster had been revealed, EPA conducted a survey of people's attitudes about living near a toxic waste facility. The results indicated little concern about such land uses. Sixty per cent of survey respondents reported to favor or strongly favor having a hazardous waste facility in their own county, and 58 per cent believed it would leave their property values unchanged or even increase them. Fifty-eight per cent also said they were willing to live within five miles of one (see Figure 8). By 1980, just two years after wide national publicity of Love Canal, public

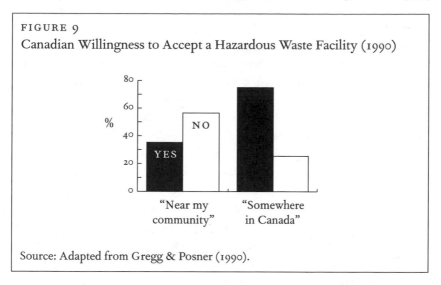

FIGURE 9

Canadian Willingness to Accept a Hazardous Waste Facility (1990)

Source: Adapted from Gregg & Posner (1990).

acceptance of hazardous waste facilities within five miles had dropped to 20 per cent (United States' Council on Environmental Quality, 1980; Mitchell & Carson, 1986). The 60 per cent acceptance level was reached only at the distance of 100 miles in the 1980 survey and again in a similar national survey conducted in 1989 (Kasperson, et al., 1992).

Canadian acceptance of toxic waste facilities is as low as in the United States. A 1985 poll of Canadian opinion on current events asked the public to respond to the following statement: "No matter what the circumstance or how safe they said it was, I am unwilling to have a hazardous waste disposal site located near my community" (Gregg & Posner, 1990). Sixty-eight per cent of respondents agreed with the statement, 27 per cent disagreed, and 5 per cent said "it depends" or had no opinion. When asked to respond to the same statement in a second poll conducted in 1989, Canadian opposition appeared to soften slightly. That time, 56 per cent agreed, 33 per cent disagreed, and 11 per cent said it depends or had no opinion (see Figure 9).

A much more remarkable difference of opinion was found between the level of acceptance for toxic waste sites at the national level, as compared to the notion of having a facility in or near one's own community. In addition to asking the public to respond to the locally oriented statement, the 1989 poll also asked: "Would you support the establishment of a facility for the disposal of toxic waste produced in Canada?" As shown in Figure 9, an overwhelming 75 per cent of respondents supported or strongly supported the idea (50 per cent and 25 per cent, respectively), while only 25 per cent were opposed or strongly opposed (15 per cent and 10 per cent, respectively).

Clearly, public concern about Love Canal and problems like it has "amplified"[3] North American concern about toxic waste significantly. Canadians as well as Americans have strong reservations about locating waste facilities in their own communities, but for the majority of Canadians, at least, the idea of placing one "somewhere" in their country seems to be desirable, provided it is not in their backyard. This pattern is at least roughly consistent with that of American public response shown in Figure 8. Partly, this contradiction reflects cost trade-offs inherent to waste management locational decisions. These occur somewhere between the disbenefits of proximity to waste facilities and the expense of moving wastes "elsewhere." Additionally, the concentration of risks and burdens near hazardous waste facilities, when compared with diffuse spatial patterns of benefits, leads to a particularly large degree of social distrust of siting proposals (Kasperson, et al., 1992), as well as a corresponding increase in risk concerns (Vaughan & Seifert, 1992) in local communities. These conditions have provided the necessary context for anti-toxics and environmental justice grassroots activism, especially among women (Brown & Ferguson, 1995).

The Environmental Protection Agency and Hazardous Waste Regulation

The creation of the Environmental Protection Agency on the heels of Earth Day in 1970 marks the beginning of the formalized environmental policies and regulations we see in America today. President Nixon created it as an independent agency[4] by merging several disparate programs dealing with water, air, and waste policy that had previously been located within various cabinet-level departments (Landy, et al., 1990). Still, the United States had no federal statute dealing with toxic waste until 1976 when Congress amended the Resource Conservation and Recovery Act (RCRA) to specifically address the issue. Coincidentally, this was about the same time that that New York State officials began inspecting the Love Canal site and collecting samples of chemical sludge from sewers and basement sump pumps in the area.

DEVELOPING RCRA: EPA, INDUSTRY, AND CONGRESS

The Resource Conservation and Recovery Act (RCRA) is a complex statute that deals with solid and hazardous waste management, theoretically from cradle to grave, or from the time at which it is generated until its ultimate and final treatment or disposal. The original version of the law, the Resource Recovery Act of 1970, dealt only with non-hazardous solid wastes. By the time the law was amended in 1976 to add a separate section (Subtitle C) respecting hazardous wastes, industry still managed its toxic residuals very informally. Most were kept on-site at the same industrial locations where they were generated and simply dumped on the land in lagoons or ponds, which is a practice that still holds true today, though with many more regulations in place to ensure better environmental protection.

While national attention to Love Canal was not to occur for a full two years, some environmentalists and legislators were very aware of the disasters waiting to happen as a result of the standard industrial hazardous waste practices of the day. In general, however, very little was known about the issue since industries never discussed it or publicly reported anything about it. Colten and Skinner (1996), using historical analysis of internal memoranda, have documented numerous instances when many chemical and other companies were well aware of the dangers. Nonetheless, the issue of hazardous waste had not yet become politically charged when the 1976 Subtitle C provisions were written into law.

One of the first and most crucial decisions to be made regarding RCRA was whether to regulate production or to regulate disposal; that is, should the government require industries to change their industrial processes so that less volume or toxicity is generated or simply develop rules regarding how and where to manage and dispose of toxic wastes. Congress was the first to deal with this fundamental choice in strategy during its many deliberations that started in 1974 and ended in 1976 when RCRA Subtitle C was enacted. In a critical report to Congress on hazardous waste, the EPA admitted that "control of toxic materials before they become toxic wastes could greatly reduce the size of the overall hazardous waste management problem," yet concluded that the Toxic Substances Control Act (TSCA), also pending Congressional action, would "dovetail neatly" with RCRA (EPA 1974, quoted in Szasz, 1994: 17). Such a strategy would separate the regulation of production, through TSCA, from the regulation of disposal, through RCRA.

Both Democrats and Republicans in the House and Senate agreed with EPA that RCRA should regulate disposal, but some Democrats introduced bills that would regulate certain hazardous or potentially hazardous products, thus, in effect, regulating production as well. Some proposals even went so far as to suggest requiring permits not only for waste treatment and disposal, but also for production processes that generate hazardous wastes. As Szasz demonstrates, industrial interests, particularly the chemical, oil, and plastics sectors, testified to Congress and EPA their adamant objections to the regulation of production or any other government control of private economic decision-making. The DuPont Corporation testified:

> We believe that the disposal of wastes ought to be regulated instead of regulating the nature and use of the product or the type of manufacturing process used ... greatest emphasis should be placed on establishing standards which assure that the ultimate disposal method is satisfactory.... [I]t is unreasonable in most instances to require the use of certain types of processes solely based on the waste generated.... [P]roduct standards could have severe economic effects ... [would] not be in the overall interest of the consumer ... [and may have] a detrimental effect on the development of new materials and innovative uses of existing materials. (Quoted in Szasz, 1994: 19)

With respect to the issue of generator permitting as compared to disposal permitting, Dow Chemical argued:

> The permit system for disposal facilities for hazardous waste seems appropriate. However, we strongly maintain that a permit system for generators of waste would unduly restrict American capacity to respond to needed changes by tending to "lock in" processes according to the technology available at the time the permit was issued ... The regulatory program should concentrate on standards for the actual disposal of wastes ... regulation of manufacturing processes must be avoided. (Quoted in Szasz, 1994: 20)

Union representatives at the time were very concerned about potential job losses, so they tended to agree with industrialists on the basic question of regulating production or disposal. One union official suggested that "the entire concept of source reduction ... may be premature at this time," and another testified:

> I object to any standardization of products or packaging if it is going to eliminate jobs ... We do not want to accept in any manner the elimination of our good jobs at the expense of the litter and solid waste problems, no matter how it comes about, whether it be standardization of products or what. We object to that. There have to be other ways and means in which we can do this without knocking our people out of work. (Quoted in Szasz, 1994: 19)

Ultimately, Congress was very sympathetic to these concerns in its decision regarding RCRA's regulatory focus. The House Commerce Committee concluded:

> Rather than place restrictions on the generation of hazardous waste, which in many instances would amount to interference with productive processes itself, the Committee has limited the responsibility of the generator for hazardous waste to one of providing information ... *there will be no requirement of the generator to modify the production process to reduce or eliminate the volume of hazardous waste.* (Quoted in Szasz, 1994: 21-22 [emphasis added])

With these and other important words of caution against what it regarded as over-regulation of industry, both houses of Congress passed the treatment and disposal bill with overwhelming majorities, and President Ford signed it into law in October 1976 (Kovacs & Klucsik, 1977). The decision also amounted to a statutory distinction between hazardous waste management and the regulation of hazardous waste facilities, on the one hand, and the regulation of toxic substances generated by manufacturers, on the other. In 1984, RCRA was amended to strengthen some of the existing provisions and to add new ones, most notably a requirement to pre-treat hazardous waste before landfilling (Mazmanian & Morell, 1992; Soesilo, 1995). RCRA still has no legal or regulatory basis for requiring industries to reduce their generation of waste.

RCRA AND SUPERFUND:
CRADLE-TO-GRAVE AND CAPACITY ASSURANCE

If EPA's and Congress's concerns about regulating industry too heavily were not apparent before the passage of RCRA, they became increasingly obvious during early attempts to implement the hazardous waste provisions of the statute. Despite EPA's statutory obligation to write new regulations pursuant to the law, the agency made little progress, and Congress failed to actively question this during oversight hearings until 1978 when an explosion at a Rollins Environmental hazardous waste facility in New Jersey received extensive news coverage (Szasz, 1994). Also in 1978 the Love Canal story began receiving widespread national attention, forever changing the way North Americans would think about toxic substances (Levine, 1982). In what seemed like an instant, the environmental community and Congress became keenly interested in EPA's progress at implementing a national hazardous waste program. The General Accounting Office (GAO), a Congressional investigatory agency, started a series of studies that were very critical of EPA's attempts to implement Subtitle C. In December 1978, the agency released its first draft hazardous waste rules, hoping finally to gain favor with its critics, only to receive 1,200 sets of highly critical comments from industry. In 1980, EPA finally issued its first set of formal hazardous waste regulations, four years after the new law had been enacted.

The RCRA Subtitle C hazardous waste program that emerged from these initial efforts involves a series of regulations and program elements given statutory authority through RCRA Sections 1004 and 3001 through 3005. This enabling legislation, in turn, gives EPA the authority to write specific regulations in the American *Code of Federal Regulations* (40 CFR Parts 260 through 265). 40 CFR Part 261, under statutory authority delineated in RCRA Section 3001, seeks to operationalize the definitions of "solid waste" and "hazardous waste," the latter being a subset of the former, which is itself defined in opposition to non-waste items such as products and industrial feedstocks. The regulation builds from Congress's basic definition of "solid waste" as:

> [A]ny garbage, refuse, sludge from a waste treatment plant,
> water supply treatment plant, or air pollution control facility
> and other discarded material, including solid, liquid, semi-

solid, or contained gaseous material resulting from industrial, commercial, mining, and agricultural operations, and from community activities. (RCRA Section 1004[27])

40 CFR Part 261 also uses the statutory definition of "hazardous waste" which includes:

> solid waste, or [a] combination of solid wastes, which because of its quantity, concentration, or physical, chemical, or infectious characteristics may:
> A. cause, or significantly contribute to an increase in mortality or an increase in serious irreversible, or incapacitating reversible, illness; or
> B. pose a substantial present or potential hazard to human health or the environment when improperly treated, stored, transported, or disposed of, or otherwise managed. (RCRA Section 1004[5])

Thus, "hazardous wastes," considered as a subset of "solid wastes," are to be specially regulated because of their dangerous characteristics. Any wastes displaying such characteristics (e.g., toxicity, reactivity, corrosivity, ignitability) are designated as "characteristic" hazardous wastes. As well, other wastes not necessarily exhibiting these characteristics are regulated as "listed" hazardous wastes by virtue of their inclusion in Subtitle C regulations.

RCRA also establishes a manifest system to track hazardous wastes destined for off-site treatment or disposal from the point of generation to the point of ultimate disposal, that is, from cradle to grave. Before transport can occur, hazardous waste generators are required to designate the permitted treatment, storage, or disposal facility (TSDF) that will receive any shipment. This information is specified on a uniform manifest document that is also used to track any and all movements of the shipment, including all modes of transport. For international shipments, generators must submit a notice of export to the receiving country and wait for a notice of consent from that country before transport can take place, according to the Basel Convention, the United Nations agreement which governs most of the world's international hazardous waste shipments (United Nations Environment Program, 1994). Since it is not a signatory to the

Basel Convention, the United States has developed bilateral agreements with Canada and Mexico, the two countries with which it conducts the vast majority of its trade (O'Neill, 2000). The Canada-United States agreement allows American and Canadian companies to ship hazardous wastes across the border without first receiving a prior notice of consent, making it one of the least regulated international trade routes for hazardous waste (Handley, 1989, 1990). The only limitation on such movements is with respect to PCBs (Environment Canada, 2001).

Management and siting of hazardous waste facilities are regulated under RCRA Sections 3004 and 3005, but the main statutory basis for their existence comes from 1986 amendments to the original Superfund law, the Comprehensive Environmental Response, Compensation and Liability Act (CERCLA) of 1980. CERCLA established a $1.6 billion[5] trust fund to clean up abandoned or uncontrolled hazardous waste sites like Love Canal. The program is unique in its liability and cost-recovery provisions. It uses the power of joint-and-severable liability to require that responsible parties (i.e., waste generators, facility operators) pay for as much as the full cost of cleanup. This gives EPA, through the Justice Department, a legal basis to sue companies or individuals for damages, even beyond those for which they are found to be personally responsible. As a result, if the evidence implicates only one of several responsible parties, the American government can sue that individual or firm for up to the full cost of cleanup.

The CERCLA amendments, known as the Superfund Amendments and Reauthorization Act of 1986 (SARA), increased the trust fund to $9 billion and added a number of new provisions, including a community right-to-know program, which allows the public to access a Toxic Release Inventory database on industrial discharges of certain chemicals. In addition, SARA imposed a requirement on states that would dramatically affect their implementation of RCRA generally and their use of hazardous waste facilities specifically. Pursuant to CERCLA, Section 104C9, the agency requires states to develop and submit capacity assurance plans (CAPs) that demonstrate an ability to safely dispose projected hazardous waste generation or risk losing federal Superfund dollars. This has been the prime justification for building new facilities in the United States and has given this responsibility to the states. At present, EPA considers all states to be in compliance with capacity assurance objectives and, therefore, eligible for funding (EPA, 2002). New and expanded facilities have made this possible at the state and national levels, though community resistance has obviously curtailed it at the local level in numerous instances (such as in the case studies reviewed in Part II). The agency recognizes this problem and has issued guidance to states, industries, and the public on the "social aspects of siting RCRA hazardous waste facilities" (EPA, 2000). It addresses quality of life and stakeholder communication issues, as well as the problem of environmental injustice.

The Superfund program has also had to face the question of how to treat communities, such as Love Canal, in which toxic contamination is discovered. Love Canal is an unusual Superfund site, not only for the fact that it preceded and inspired the Superfund program itself, but also because residents were evacuated permanently. Most people who find themselves residents of contaminated sites have no choice but to move back after the remediation, even though most "cleanup" strategies, including Love Canal, have involved the containment, rather than removal, of toxins. In 1993, this problem led EPA to issue a directive on "Land Use in the CERCLA Remedy Selection Process." It extended previously existing Superfund guidance to address a problem that the agency itself recognized, that "EPA has been criticized for too often assuming that future use will be residential" and that "[i]n many cases, residential use is the least restricted land use and where human activities are associated with the greatest potential for exposures" (EPA, 1993: 2). The directive specified that the general public and particularly local residents should be involved in the examination and choice of remediation goals and future land uses well before decisions are finalized. The agency's Brownfields Economic Development Initiative makes similar recommendations regarding future land uses and post-remediation, including environmental justice (Fletcher, 2002).

Canadian Hazardous Waste Policy: Ottawa and the Provinces

Ilgen (1985) has described Canada's approach to environmental management generally, and toxic waste regulation specifically, as being somewhere "between Europe and America." Historically, Canadian public officials have preferred to rely on British- and European-style case-by-case negotiations among government and industry to shape policy, but the country has increasingly begun to develop a more legalistic approach similar to the United States, complete with federal and provincial regulations as well as an expansion of the courts' powers at both governmental levels to resolve disputes (Harrison & Hoberg, 1994; Fafard & Harrison, 2000). Still, the federal role in environmental policy is much more limited in Canada than in the United States (Harrison, 1996; VanNijnatten & Boardman, 2002). Also, while volumes of American regulations are written to deal with nearly every conceivable environmental circumstance, Canada continues to keep its regulations at both the federal and provincial levels relatively general, often relying on operating permits for particular facilities to delineate specific standards and other requirements.

THE DEPARTMENT OF ENVIRONMENT AND CEPA

Canadian hazardous waste policy is governed most broadly by legislative provisions set out in the Canadian Environmental Protection Act of 1988 (CEPA). CEPA is a broad environmental statute based partly on the "peace, order, and good government" clause of the British North America Act of 1867 and is designed to deal with a "national concern over toxic substances and the environment" as well as to clarify federal/provincial authorities and responsibilities for environmental protection (Macdonald, 1991: 51-52). Historically, Canadian provinces have taken the lead on environmental protection because of their legal ownership of public lands and natural resources (particularly minerals and forests) within their own borders. But in the years following the creation of Environment Canada 1970, the provinces became increasingly concerned about a federal encroachment on their environmental and natural resource management rights.

CEPA AND THE ENVIRONMENTAL CONTAMINANTS ACT

CEPA reflected complex negotiations between Ottawa and the provinces that had become necessary because of jurisdictional disputes over natural resources and energy rights resulting from federal environmental legislation established during the early 1970s and leading up to the patriation of the Canadian Constitution in 1982. Among these statutes was the federal Environmental Contaminants Act (ECA) of 1975, which had been enacted because of the ongoing development of a similar American bill later passed into law as the Toxic Substances Control Act (TSCA) of 1976. Jack Davis, Canada's first Minister of the Environment, had proposed ECA in 1972, arguing that it was needed to prevent the country from becoming a pollution haven for multinational corporations based in both countries. The delay reflected a decline in environmental interest within Parliament (Harrison, 1996). All of the provisions originally written under ECA were incorporated into CEPA in 1988.

Notwithstanding the enactment of ECA, the Canadian federal government largely patterned its toxics policies on the American TSCA (toxic substances) and RCRA (hazardous waste) programs (Doern & Conway, 1994). The provinces became increasingly frustrated with this lack of implementation progress, yet they also feared federal encroachment into their own jurisdictional and statutory responsibilities, particularly if it were to hamper economic development (Harrison, 1996; Fafard & Harrison, 2000; Boardman & VanNijnatten, 2002). CEPA represented a compromise between the federal and provincial governments by establishing the concept of "equivalency." This provision holds that provincial regulations are to be considered equivalent to federal regulations, and thus to take precedence, unless Environment Canada finds a lack of provincial enforcement of environmental regulations. These kinds of federal-provincial power struggles over environmental policy continue to this day over the Harmonization Accord, which is aimed at producing national standards for a variety of pollution issues, including toxic substances and other matters related to hazardous waste management.

Still, Canadian toxic waste regulation at both levels of government has much in common with the American approach in the use of manifests to provide cradle-to-grave management, the development of siting and operation standards for hazardous waste facilities, and the allocation of funds for cleaning up uncontrolled or abandoned waste sites. Also, while there is no federal statutory requirement that the provinces build new facilities as is the case in the United States, the concept of capacity assurance has been promoted at both levels of government so as to allow industry continued access to disposal sites (as is demonstrated by the Canadian facility siting disputes reviewed in Part II).

In the year 2000, Canada imported 279,000 tonnes of hazardous waste from other countries, representing a 32 per cent reduction from 1999 when the figure was 394,000 tonnes (Environment Canada, 2001b). Canadian Environment Minister David Anderson commented on this development, saying that "While the decrease in imports from 1998 and 1999 takes us in the right direction, there is still more work to be done by governments and industry in Canada and in North America" (Environment Canada, 2001b: 1). He was referring in part to new Canadian pre-treatment standards implemented in 2000 that had been in effect since 1984 in the United States. Over 98 per cent of Canadian imports and exports of hazardous waste are with the United States (Environment Canada, 2000a). Canadian exports and imports add up to approximately 5 per cent and 10 per cent, respectively, of that generated domestically (Environment Canada 2000b). With regard to the room for improvement, he was referring to the fact that even with the recent decline, hazardous waste imports are over 150 per cent higher than they were in 1991 (Environment Canada, 2000b; Environment Canada, 2001b) and 400 per cent higher than they had been in 1994 (CEC, 2002). Canadian hazardous waste importing has become a "growth industry," particularly in Ontario (Canadian Institute for Environmental Law and Policy, 2000).

Controlling Toxics in Ontario

Ontario, Canada's largest and most industrial province, has traditionally been a leader in the development of environmental protection standards north of the border. It is also the country's most polluted province, exceeded in industrial pollution releases by only the American states of Texas and Ohio, according to a study of 1999 data conducted by the CEC (CEC, 2002). Moreover, its releases have increased more than any other jurisdiction in North America (19 per cent) during the five-year period for which the most recent comparative data are available, 1995 to 1999. The most significant increase occurred in the Sarnia area at one of the facilities examined in Part II, Chapter 5. Ontario's status as a "big" polluter and a proactive environmental regulator makes it an important jurisdiction to study in the Canadian context.

The province established its Ministry of Environment (MOE) in 1972, periodically merging it with the energy portfolio as the Ontario Ministry of Environment and Energy (MOEE), although they were separated again in August 2002. The agency's record of pollution control dates back to 1957, when it enacted the Ontario Water Resources Act to control air and water pollution; in 1967 it established Canada's first industrial discharge standards for particular pollutants under the Air Pollution Control Act. In 1972, the same year it created its MOE, the province passed the Ontario Environmental Protection Act (OEPA), which has been used as the statutory authority for a variety of rules, including Regulation 309 (General-Waste Management Regulation), which establishes requirements for waste (including hazardous) generators and hazardous waste facility operators. Regulation 309 also defines hazardous waste (in much the same way as the Americans do in RCRA) as either characteristic wastes (e.g., toxicity, reactivity, corrosivity, and ignitability) or listed wastes specified by either a chemical name or as a particular industrial process. The main distinction between the American and Ontarian definitions is that the latter includes PCBs whereas the former does not.[6] Regulation 309 of OEPA also has jurisdiction regarding hazardous waste facility siting, along with the Ontario Environmental Assessment Act (EAA).

Ontario is the only Canadian province that has developed a contamination cleanup program. In 1986, it established a $10 million Environmental Security Fund and increased it to $20 million the following year. The program is much more limited than the American Superfund program in that the provincial government has only made funds available on a case-by-case basis, rather than establishing a trust fund, and there are no cost-recovery or liability provisions to shift the financial burden onto responsible parties such as waste generators or hazardous waste facility operators. Nonetheless, it has been an important mechanism for initiating cleanups when responsible parties are not able or willing to do it themselves. Moreover, there are important hazardous waste regulatory changes in the works for Ontario. The Ontario and Quebec governments were quick to announce tougher standards in response to angry public reaction to a Canadian firm that had developed a marketing campaign aimed at American hazardous waste generators. The company vowed that it could assume "full responsibility and all liability" for hazardous waste disposed in Canada (CEC, 2002). In 2002, the government proposed a $50 registration fee for companies generating hazardous waste, a fee that will generate nearly $12 million in annual revenues. Other important proposed policy changes include pre-treatment of hazardous waste prior to landfilling and tougher mixing rules, which will regard as hazardous compounds produced by the combination of hazardous waste with non-hazardous substances (MOE, 2001). If they are instituted, such regulatory changes will go a long way toward harmonizing Ontario policy with that in place in the United States since 1984 (MOE, 2000).

The Limits to Hazardous Waste Regulation
in Canada and the United States

Governmental hazardous waste regulations have been criticized for their emphasis on hazardous waste management and their relative neglect of pollution prevention. Lake (1993) and Lake and Disch (1992) argue that the authority of these regulations begins when the waste is generated and thus fails to deal directly with the question of how industries might generate less. Further, Lake and Disch submit that governmental incentives to build new hazardous waste facilities (e.g., capacity assurance objectives) create disincentives for industries to invest in waste minimization or pollution prevention strategies. Rather than dealing with hazardous waste as an externality of production to be reduced wherever possible (whether cost-effective in the short-run or not), government policies take it as given that industries will generate increasing amounts of hazardous waste that will continue to require proper management somehow and some place. As it stands, the only direct incentive for industries to reduce the volume or toxicity of their waste is if they find it reduces their operating or capital costs, either through efficiencies in the use of chemicals or through lower waste management costs (Gordon, 1986; Gottlieb, et al., 1995; Mazurek, et al., 1995).

Another problem with facility siting as a means of achieving capacity assurance relates to the problem of NIMBY (not-in-my-backyard). While the debate continues as to whether NIMBY, or perhaps NIABY (not-in-anyone's-backyard), is a good or bad thing, it is increasingly clear that some degree of community opposition to hazardous waste facilities nearly always occurs (Heiman, 1990). Thus, it is a force to be reckoned with, whether or not one believes there is ever a fair or just way to decide which kinds of facilities should go where. Often, these decisions pit communities against one another and limit public discourse to the relative merits of facility sites rather than overall policy objectives (such as whether to regulate waste at the point of production or after the fact). Increasingly tougher air quality standards in both countries have resulted in a 25 per cent decrease in toxic air emissions, but land disposal of hazardous wastes has increased by 25 per cent, due in large part to the end-of-pipe approach to hazardous waste policy in the United States and Canada. In response to this paradox, the Commission for Environmental Cooperation has observed the following:

We have made progress in reducing toxic releases to air. Now, how can we do the same for water and land releases? Why are more substances being shipped off-site for management? Is this indicative of facilities' desire to send their wastes to locations that are better equipped to manage them effectively? Or does it signal that end-of-the-pipe approaches are still too frequently employed instead of preventing pollution at the source? How can the right mix of requirements, incentives and tools be brought to bear to foster a decisive shift to the use of preventive approaches that will safeguard our environment and the health of our populations? (CEC, 2002: v)

Still another issue for hazardous waste policy generally, as well as for facility siting decision-making specifically, relates to the problem of environmental inequity or injustice. I will demonstrate in the next chapter that a plethora of research has found that issues of race and class often are associated with hazardous waste facilities. As capacity assurance objectives often result in facility siting processes, and as facility siting tends to create locational conflicts, so too do these disputes often lead to debates about fairness. This is often the case when actual or proposed hazardous waste facilities are located in low-income or racial minority areas (social equity); or when communities with no economic ties to industries which manufacture or use toxic substances in large quantities are expected to bear the burden of waste disposal (spatial equity); or when industrial neighborhoods already overly burdened with toxic emissions are asked to put up with yet another dump in their midst (cumulative equity); or when past or present decision makers set policies which unnecessarily transfer risk to future generations (intergenerational equity); or when decision-making processes give preference to industrial interests over community or environmental interests (procedural equity).

Notes

1. Tonnages are shown in metric measurements (tonnes), unless otherwise noted in some of the examples from the United States (tons).

2. For first-hand accounts of the Love Canal story, see Lois Gibbs, *Love Canal: My Story* (1988) and *Love Canal: The Story Continues* (1998); Adeline Gordon Levine, *Love Canal: Science, Politics and People* (1982).

3. See Kasperson et al. (1988).

4. EPA's "independent" status distinguishes it from most federal agencies, which are administratively located within, and under the jurisdiction of, a specific cabinet-level department. The agency's structure was designed to give it a degree of autonomy over the environmental mission without granting its administrator the symbolic significance of cabinet secretary. For several years, Congress has discussed "elevating" the agency to departmental status.

5. American and Canadian funding examples are stated in their respective currencies without further notation.

6. Instead, the United States regulates PCBs as a toxic substance through TSCA rather than as a toxic waste through RCRA.

2
Environment and Social Justice

Introduction

The struggle for environmental equity and justice has emerged from a combination of local activism and academic research in the context of the environmental justice movement. It has become a strong political force in the United States, arising out of grassroots struggles over hazardous waste sites, especially in African American and other marginalized communities. Much of this activism and research has focused on the distributional and procedural equity considerations of hazardous waste management. The United States government has attempted to meet these demands by creating an Office of Environmental Justice within the Environmental Protection Agency (EPA) and a National Environmental Justice Advisory Council. In 1994, President Clinton issued an executive order (12898) affirming the importance of the issue in environmental management decisions. Canada has not generated its own politics of environmental justice explicitly, though distributive and procedural equity concerns are often central to environmental disputes in this country.

Recent achievements toward addressing environmental injustices have been a long time coming. Goldman (1996) cites the 1982 civil disobedience in Warren County, North Carolina over the siting of a PCB landfill in a black community as a seminal moment in the environmental justice movement and an important impetus for this area of research. The protest involved hundreds of people, including prominent civil rights leaders, and led to the first study on environmental equity and hazardous waste. William Fontroy, former Congressional Delegate to the District of Columbia, commissioned the United States General Accounting Office (GAO) to conduct the investigation, which found that of the four commercial toxic waste landfills in the southeastern United States, three were located in poor black areas (GAO, 1983). In 1987, the United Church of Christ Commission for Racial Justice (UCCCRJ) released its own study, which addressed the issue at the national level (UCCCRJ, 1987). It found that race was the strongest predictive factor in the location of commercial hazardous waste disposal and treatment facilities as compared to income and other measures. Since these initial studies were released, a rapidly growing body of research on the issue has emerged, prompting a heated debate over the question of whether race or class is the most predictive factor in waste location, among other issues (see Anderton, et al., 1994; Goldman & Fitton, 1994; GAO, 1995). Chapter 3 reviews these and other empirical studies on environmental equity in detail.

This chapter attempts to make the link between environmental problems and social justice as a theoretical basis for environmental justice. Beginning with an examination of the environmental theories of Ulrich Beck, particularly his notion of "risk society," the chapter proceeds with a discussion of theories of social justice, starting with a discussion of utilitarian notions of efficiency, which form the basis of many cost-benefit or risk-benefit approaches to environmental policy analysis and which tend to ignore or underestimate problems of inequity. The following sections describe various theories of distributive and procedural justice generally, and environmental justice in particular. The chapter continues with discussions of EPA activities on environmental equity, as well as how the particular problem of hazardous waste intersects with environmental justice issues.

Beck's Risk Society

Ulrich Beck's writing on the environment, in many respects, speaks more directly to questions of environmental justice and hazardous waste than perhaps that of any other social theorist. His popular 1986 publication, *Risikogesellschaft* was translated into English by Mark Ritter in 1992 as *Risk Society* (Beck, 1992). Beck has since expanded on his original concept with *Ecological Enlightenment: Essays on the Politics of the Risk Society* (1995) and *World Risk Society* (1999). He has continued to elaborate on the idea, partly because the term itself has become so widely used, but especially because he has not always liked the way people have used it:

> When I was experimenting with the concept of a "risk society" in 1984, it was a test-tube product from my desk and aroused general skepticism. Since then, the term has entered the general discourse, and many people use it as if they know what it means. Yet there is still something prickly about it.... The debate has stirred up a lot of controversy. Some find the concept of risk society too tame, too actuarial, too closely attached to the monumental error it seeks to combat, too German in its prosperous pessimism: We've had the lobster, now please pass the disaster. (Beck, 1995: 1)

As this quote makes obvious, Beck's writing style is one of the more notable aspects of his work, leading to both the allure of and objection to his ideas. Goldblatt has referred to Beck's writing as "books of monstrous metaphors, testing and probing social conundrums and facing them with a black wit. They are not so much rigorous analytical accounts as surveys of the institutional bases of the fears and paradoxes of modern societies" (Goldblatt, 1996:154). Similarly, Bronner's take on Beck's books is that "Each is marked by an extraordinarily lively style, a provocative way of raising questions, and a genuinely experimental sensibility" (Bronner, 1995: 67).

At least part of Beck's inspiration for the idea of a risk society came from his observations about the 1986 Chernobyl nuclear meltdown; however, incidents such as that are only part of the story. In a nutshell, Beck argues that we are entering an age where concerns over the distribution of technological risks are becoming at least as important as concerns over distributions of wealth. As is indicated in the quote from his book *Risk Society* included here in the preface, wealth distributions are traditionally the most important political problem facing democratic societies. As we enter a risk society, concerns about chemical and nuclear hazards begin to predominate over economic concerns. His theory is not so much that we have entered the risk society as it is that we appear to be approaching it. Over and over, Beck refers to changes that are "emerging" more so than he references the changes that have occurred. On that point, Bronner describes him as "one of the very few thinkers capable of envisioning a different world on the horizon. He is unconcerned with the failed radical undertakings of the past. His environmental and sociological enterprise evidences a profound enthusiasm for the *novum*. A new risk society is emerging in large part due to the problems, not the least of which is environmental devastation, wrought by its predecessor" (Bronner, 1995: 67-68).

The predecessor of the risk society is the industrial revolution itself, according to Beck, but it has even earlier roots. The changes we are witnessing have been a long time in the making. Natural and early technological hazards have historically been obvious to the human senses. In medieval cities, buildings crumbled from contamination with urine, and garbage problems were as foul to the nostrils as to the eyes. The most unchecked period of industrialization and urbanization was the late nineteenth century when coal was as widely used for home heating as it was for commercial production. This was the period when the term "acid rain" was first coined to characterize the acrid smog that consumed London (Goudie, 2000; Meyer, 1996). Up to the early postwar period and even beyond, the environmental impacts of industrial activity were fairly obvious to the average person through casual observation of the air and water.

In the period following World War II, mass production of chemicals for military purposes gave way to the creation and expansion of markets for chemicals and a variety of products derived from synthetic chemicals. The growth of the petrochemical industry, in fact, resulted from the creation of "downstream" markets for residuals of chemical processes. The social effect was a faith in the promise of chemicals that seemed to have no limits (see Figure 10). Another of many significant societal shifts to occur during the postwar period also related to industrialization but had nothing to do with the environment. This change, the rise of the welfare state, came about because of concerns about the distribution of wealth and facilitated the rapid rise of the middle class. As a result, the distribution of goods and the class implications thereof have dominated most domestic politics until relatively recently.

As we approach risk society, according to Beck, we are increasingly confronted with environmental threats that make us concerned with the distribution of "bads." There are many dimensions to this shift, the most fundamental of which relates to what Kasperson, et al. (1988) have described as the "social amplification of risks" brought about by technological disasters like Love Canal or, more recently, Chernobyl. Both incidents had elements of the "old" distribution of bads (similar to early industrial

FIGURE 10
Early Post-War Advertising for DDT

Source: *Time Magazine* 1947. Used with permission from Atofina Chemicals.

society, that is) in that danger increases with proximity to the problem. Both, particularly Chernobyl, also introduced new elements of risk, since chemical and nuclear threats are not necessarily obvious to the human senses. And both required risk experts to explain the severity of danger associated with them, with quantities in the parts-per-billion. Beck describes this phenomenon as the "boomerang effect" (see Figure 11) whereby previously local risks become regional and global by virtue of transport, both natural (e.g., air and water currents) and anthropogenic (e.g., international trade). A good example of the former is the continued application of DDT in tropical countries that makes its way to the arctic environment, while a good example of the latter is the Canadian import of produce grown with pesticides outlawed domestically.

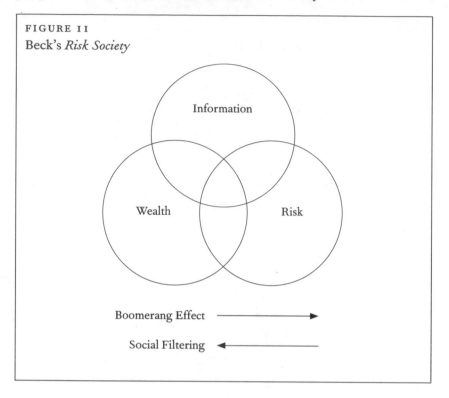

FIGURE II
Beck's *Risk Society*

This aspect of the emerging risk society also involves a shift in the role of information. As environmental and human health risks become less and less obvious to the average person, risk expertise becomes that much more important. Risk analysis and risk assessment are growth fields, providing important employment opportunities in industry and government alike. Along with the growth in risks that require such expertise to understand them comes concern with control of and access to information. Community right-to-know laws in Europe and North America have come about precisely because of chemical disasters in Seveso, Italy and at Love Canal. Nonetheless, Beck and others are still concerned about government and industry control of information about chemical risks to local communities.

Beck's critics often describe his framework as overly general, lacking in precision, and even flawed in that risk distributions have not, and are unlikely to, override concerns about wealth distributions (Goldblatt, 1996; Leiss, 1994). Indeed, the politics of environmental justice provide vivid evidence that low-income and other marginalized peoples (e.g., racial minorities) often are more likely to live in degraded environments than people who can afford to escape pollution. Beck acknowledges this and incorporates it into his framework through a "social filtering effect" whereby the poor continue to be disproportionately burdened by pollution in the form of class-specific technological risks. Nonetheless, he argues that such traditional distributions of risk are becoming increasingly undermined by the global reach of the boomerang effect described previously. Beck's use of the social filtering effect to temper the impact of the boomerang is nonetheless insufficient to please his critics, at least on this point. As Bronner argues: "none of this justifies essentially ignoring questions dealing with structural imbalances of power or the systemic ways in which interests are organized, wealth is distributed, and grievances are adjudicated."

It is for these reasons that some of the more general connections between social justice and the environment are elaborated in subsequent sections of this chapter. Nonetheless, Beck's work has made an enormous impact on environmental thought and is most relevant to questions of environmental justice and hazardous waste not only for its strengths but, paradoxically, also because of what may be its weaknesses. As Bronner concludes:

> For all of its problems, the work of Ulrich Beck retains an electric quality. Idea after idea jumps off the pages of his work. Some lack precision, others never receive justification, and still others contradict one another. Qualifications sit on top of one another; arguments disappear only to appear once again; fuzzy slogans compete with claims of common sense. But then come the golden nuggets of dazzling insight.... The sheer number of his ideas is surely what makes for the misunderstandings, the controversy and also the allure of his work.... The risk society offers a general framework with which to understand the trajectory of modernity without offering linkages to the constitution of particular events. It tries to deal with everyday life and perhaps it sacrifices history in the process. Nevertheless, paradoxically, its very strengths are probably generated by its indeterminate categories and its inability to confront structural imbalances of power. Beck's aim is, after all, less a confrontation with the present than an analysis of how the present is giving rise to a new future. (Bronner, 1995: 85-86)

Social Justice and the Environment

Environmental equity and justice issues have a number of wide-ranging theoretical implications for the study of industrial activity and its impacts on ecology. These implications include moral questions about what constitutes fairness and justice in both a distributive sense as well as in relation to process. They also include legal and political concerns about the role of government in regulating industry and in fostering public participation in planning. Further, environmental equity involves institutional questions about the role of industry in responding to governmental and public pressures and in implementing waste management programs. To study such widely ranging dimensions of environmental equity requires a similarly broad selection of social theories. In this chapter, I attempt to develop a theoretical framework based on theories of social justice and theories of environmental justice in order to discuss the complex interactions between industrial activities, the environment, the public, the state, political and policy processes, and value judgments inherent to questions of equity or fairness in environmental management. The result is a perspective that is both state-centered and society-centered (Clark & Dear, 1984; Dear, 1981). Following Lake, et al. (1990, 1992) I incorporate the role of the state at various levels of federalism as a part of structural relations of capitalism (i.e., the relationship between state and capital). Following Cox (1989, 1997a, 1997b) I also seek to integrate the role of local agents and other stakeholders representing industry, the environment, and social justice.

THEORIES OF SOCIAL JUSTICE

Social justice is a moral issue fundamental to the determination of fairness and equity. It has been explored by philosophers and social scientists in several ways, with some concluding that the distribution of social welfare, however defined, must be determined by perfectly competitive market economies. The chief responsibility of national governments in terms of maintaining social welfare, according to this libertarian or utilitarian view, is to maintain free and open markets. The result is that, generally speaking, benefits as well as burdens in society are distributed according to supply and demand (Fischhoff, 1977). Utilitarians do not necessarily object to all forms of "social programs" (e.g., public schools, unemployment insurance) so long as they are seen to allocate benefits broadly across society and not to reinforce "welfare dependency." Recent movements in the United States and Canada to replace welfare with "workfare" reflects this concern.

The opposing extreme to the utilitarian view is the notion that social justice is achieved only by distributing society's benefits as equally as possible. This egalitarian view holds that governments, rather than relying on market mechanisms, must establish planning authorities to distribute goods and services. The result of this arrangement is that society's benefits and harms are allocated according to normative principles, particularly need. There are, as well, many other concepts of social justice that fall between the extremes of utilitarianism and egalitarianism. Rather than focusing completely on either open competition or need, most politicians and social scientists seek balance through a combination of market forces and government programs, including regulation of the private sector. Many additional criteria for determining social justice come into play as well. There is perhaps an endless, though not mutually exclusive, list of options, as Harvey (1973, 1996) has shown in his writings on social justice.

Social justice is, in some respects, synonymous with equity, depending on one's view towards a just distribution. The concept of equity signifies a balancing of benefits and burdens between individuals as well as among groups or communities of people. So a concept of social justice that includes equity considerations will, by definition, seek to balance benefits and burdens in some way. In this respect, only the most purely utilitarian concepts of social justice exclude equity considerations completely, as they seek no active balancing role for governments. The more egalitarian the concept, the more important and salient this balance becomes.

Utilitarian notions of social justice are rooted in neoclassical welfare economics. The main principle of this perspective is "the greatest good for the greatest number" (Enbar, 1983: 6). Its conclusion is that the most efficient distribution of goods is achieved through market mechanisms. Utilitarianism, in its purest form, is most clearly reflected in the standard usage of cost-benefit analysis, which seeks only the most efficient distribution with little or no regard for equity. Cost-benefit analysis is, of course, not a theory in itself, but rather a method that tends to reflect utilitarian principles. Fischhoff (1977) has suggested that it may be possible to incorporate equity considerations into cost-benefit analyses of environmental and other issues by valuing equity as a benefit, though determining how to value equity quantitatively relative to other factors is a formidable problem. Consistent with this is the concept of just compensation whereby communities negotiate benefits in return for accepting noxious facilities (Rabe, 1994; Rabe, et al., 1996). Similarly, Daly and Cobb (1989) have argued against the use of discounting environmental costs in cost-benefit analysis, or at least to discount at lower rates. The problem with discounting, they argue, is that, first, it unnecessarily abstracts the reality of environmental costs, a "misplaced concreteness" that often leads policy makers to assume environmental degradation will be minimal and, second, that it undervalues the full cost of the degradation.

Robert Nozick (1974) has rejected utilitarian notions of social justice for their lack of attention to equity, among other reasons. His theory does not, however, move very far toward egalitarianism, because of the importance he places on minimal government involvement in people's lives and on "liberty, freedom, and self-determination." Nozick uses historical principles to determine how a distribution has come to be and, therefore, whether it is socially just. He argues in favor of rectification and compensation in situations where distributions are historically unjust. He criticizes utilitarians and egalitarians alike for using "current time-slice principles" to determine whether a distribution is just (Nozick, 1974: 153).

Nozick develops an entitlement theory of "acquisition and transfer" in order to illustrate his historically-centered arguments about social justice. Despite his preference for open markets and maximum freedom of choice, he expresses grave concerns about the "holding" of social goods through unjust means and the distribution of social goods (benefits) that are the result of the originally unjust holdings. He uses perhaps universally accepted examples such as theft, fraud, slavery, and also pollution, among others, to illustrate what he means by an unjust acquisition or transfer of economic benefits. He also includes less universally accepted examples such as "lack of open competition" and less clear examples such as "preventing [people] from living as they choose" (Nozick, 1974: 152). Nozick sees no universal theory for determining social justice, but simply stresses the importance of questioning the historical processes that lead to particular distributions in the determination of whether they are in fact socially just.

John Rawls (1967, 1971) moves further toward egalitarianism than does Nozick with his theory of justice, though it deliberately stops short of such an ideal. Rawls's ultimate concern is with inequality in the distribution of social goods. He puts forth two central principles of justice:

[F]irst, each person engaged in an institution or affected by it has an equal right to the most extensive liberty compatible with a like liberty for all. [S]econd, inequalities as defined by the institutional structure or fostered by it are arbitrary unless it is reasonable to expect that they will work out to everyone's advantage and provided that the positions and offices to which they attach or from which they may be gained are open to all. (Rawls, 1967: 61)

The basic positions that Rawls articulates here is that everyone should be granted the same liberties, that inequalities should only be acceptable if they are advantageous to everyone (what he calls the "difference principle"), and that there should be equality of opportunity in seeking positions in society. His theory is built on the assumption that these principles would govern the distribution of social goods by incorporating them into a political constitution and applying them through legislation.

To achieve his two principles of justice, Rawls proposes systems of savings and taxation. He develops a "just savings principle" in order to redistribute social welfare to future generations. Rawls finds the concept important to ensure a degree of intergenerational equity, and it corresponds very closely to the concept of sustainable development (Norton, 1989; Penn, 1990), "development which meets the needs of the present without compromising the ability of future generations to meet their needs" as defined by the Brundtland Commission (World Commission on Environment and Sustainable Development, 1987). Rawls argues for a proportional expenditure tax, rather than an income tax, to impose levies according to how much a person "takes out of the common store of goods and not according to how much he contributes" (Rawls, 1967: 72). He adds that his system of taxation could be based on a progressive scale in order not to burden the poor disproportionately, but only if it is necessary to "preserve the justice of the system as a whole" (Rawls, 1967: 72). As long as one includes natural resources in the definition of "goods," Rawls's proposal for taxation is consistent with conserving natural resources for the benefit of present and future generations (Penn, 1990).

David Harvey's early work on social justice (1973) is based largely on Rawls's distributive and procedural principles of social justice, even though it moves considerably further toward egalitarianism than Rawls does. While Rawls proposed to maintain a capitalist system with open and competitive markets regulated by government to redistribute social goods, Harvey argued in favor of "alternatives to the market mechanism ... in which the market is replaced (probably by a decentralized planning process)" (Harvey, 1973: 115). He argued that decentralized planning is generally preferable because unless a country has a "benevolent bureaucracy," its more advantaged areas are likely to exploit less advantaged areas. With decentralized planning, each region or territory would have some degree of autonomy when it comes to determining the distribution of benefits and harms. In addition, he contrasts Rawls's proposal for social justice with a Marxian interpretation that posits that, in order to achieve the difference principle, the least fortunate must have greater economic and political power.

In more recent work Harvey (1992, 1996) has returned to questions of social justice, primarily as they relate to questions of nature, environment, and difference. He draws heavily on the work of Iris M. Young (1990) who, like him, attempts to build a theory of justice that incorporates the distributive conceptions of Rawls and Nozick. Young recognizes the value of balancing benefits and burdens in society, including the distribution of social positions (i.e., class) as Rawls emphasizes. She also observes, however, that the distribution of positions is only one of many procedural factors regarding equity. She outlines five "faces of oppression" to describe various reasons for and processes of injustice: exploitation, marginalization, powerlessness, cultural imperialism, and violence. With respect to oppression and hazardous waste, she points to inadequate community involvement (Young, 1983). Even in cases where the local public and community officials are involved, they are generally limited to participation in facility siting processes rather than ongoing waste management. Furthermore, by the time public hearings and other community proceedings have begun, state environmental officials usually have already granted preliminary approvals of the proposals.

Harvey concurs with Young's observations on procedural justice and its consequences, and he offers a sixth principle or face of oppression, "that all social projects are ecological projects and vice versa" (Harvey, 1992: 600). He argues that:

> just planning and policy practices will clearly recognize that
> the necessary ecological consequences of all social projects
> have impacts on future generations as well as upon distant

peoples and take steps to ensure a reasonable mitigation of negative impacts. (Harvey, 1992: 600)

Social justice, then, is not restricted to distributions and procedures relating to political-economic goods or positions. In fact, economic development is a primary cause of environmental degradation in industrial societies. Thus, it is imperative that theories of social justice incorporate ecological principles and the human right to a clean environment into concepts of fairness.

THEORIES OF ENVIRONMENT AND JUSTICE

Industries that generate pollution from their production processes are subject to environmental pressures from concerned interest groups and governments. These pressures and the state of environmental problems they represent for present and future societies have been described as a form of "crisis" by Lipietz (1992a, 1992b). The environmental crisis is but one of many other challenges facing industry during what some have described as a fundamental global shift from mass production and consumption associated with Fordism to more flexible practices associated with post-Fordism (Piore & Sabel, 1984; Scott, 1988; Schoenberger, 1988; Dicken, 1998). These other crises relate to not only production and consumption practices, but also to inter-firm linkages, global competition, government regulation, and labor relations.

Concerns about environmental equity add to the complexity of environmental pressures by pitting social groups based on class, race, ethnicity, and ultimately, community against one another (EPA ,1992; Kasperson & Dow, 1991; Bullard, 1990; United Church of Christ, 1987; Kasperson, 1983). O'Connor (1981), while not referring to environmental conflict specifically, has described such class conflict as a form of crisis facing industry as well. Tickell and Peck identify as one form of crisis, "[s]tructural crises [which] occur when the mode of social regulation is no longer suited to the accumulation system" (Tickell & Peck, 1992: 193). This mode is a "regulation" theory category which refers to "the role of political and social relations (state action and legislature, social institutions, behavioral norms and habits, and political practices)" (Tickell & Peck, 1992: 192). Environmental problems also fit this category, considering the social and political implications of natural resource exploitation, industrial production, and product consumption in capitalist economies. Environmental pressures include:

1. ecological concerns regarding global environmental degradation caused by industry;

2. community concerns about how industrial activity affects local environments; and

3. social conflict over environmental quality and natural resources more generally.

In his most recent work on social justice, Harvey (1996) specifically addresses the problem of environmental injustice. By weaving together widely ranging discussions of space and time, nature and environment, and justice and difference, he further develops his Marxist approach to social justice. A central and recurring theme throughout the book is the question of "loyalties" and the highly related problem of "militant particularisms." The issue of loyalties arises in the context of labor struggles especially, based on Raymond Williams's observations on the subject in his novel titled *Loyalties* (Williams, 1985). Through various examples, Harvey shows how individuals engaged in political struggles can virtually never avoid expressing loyalties to one side or another of an issue or set of issues. When local communities are involved, as is often the case, the divisions tend to occur between local concerns and larger interests (e.g., provincial/state, national, or even global issues). Harvey, following Williams, illustrates the point by explaining how "[e]ven the language changes, shifting from words like 'our community,' and 'our people' ... to the 'organized working class,' the 'proletariate' and the 'masses' when one compares local interpretations to institutional responses" (Harvey, 1996: 33). The local terminology is highly personal and quite clear about loyalty to community, sometimes at nearly any cost (i.e., a "militant particularism"), whereas the broader political and institutional language is abstract and rational.

The chief weakness of the "traditional" environmental movement,[1] according to Harvey, is its tendency largely to avoid the politics of class and race even with respect to local ecological issues. Conversely, he finds strength in the environmental justice movement for its ability to face these problems head on. Pulido (1996a) makes this point as well, relating the struggle against environmental racism, in particular, to the politics of "subaltern" movements, by which she refers to the struggles of subordinated groups in response to economic and political marginalization, cultural identity issues, and quality of life problems, including environmental degradation. She argues that "mainstream" environmentalism has failed to address these concerns because of its tendency to isolate environmental issues from related social and cultural problems.

Hazardous Waste and Social Justice

Hazardous waste regulation is conducted according to both structural constraints as defined by the state and also pluralist politics. Structural constraints include laws, regulations, and policies as written and implemented by governments. The resulting structural or regulatory framework designates what industry can and cannot do with respect to hazardous waste. Also, any important and relevant issues missing from, or at least written too vaguely within, the regulatory framework become in effect sanctioned by the state, resulting in structural limitations. Further limitations result from a lack of government enforcement of environmental laws and regulations, as well as insufficient public and community involvement in environmental decision-making.

As indicated previously, Lake (1993) and Lake and Disch (1992) see structural limitations in the lack of attention paid to hazardous waste minimization and pollution prevention in American laws and regulations. Additionally, they contend that American policy makes five critical assumptions about hazardous waste that ignore waste minimization and perhaps promote waste generation:

Assumption 1: Private industry will, and should, continue to generate hazardous waste.

Assumption 2: Private generators will, and should, continue to externalize the costs of hazardous waste disposal and treatment.

Assumption 3: Providing facilities needed to treat and dispose of these wastes is a public-sector (specifically, a state-level) responsibility.

Assumption 4: By providing the needed treatment capacity, the state is fulfilling its responsibility for protecting the health and safety of the people in the state.

Assumption 5:   The scale and technology of needed facilities are dictated by the size and composition of the waste stream. (Lake & Disch, 1992: 667-71)

These assumptions deflect public discourse away from questions of how and why industry generates hazardous waste and toward the more immediate conflict over the location of facilities. The state's approach, according to Lake and Disch, is to "devise a strategy for waste regulation that fends off the impending legitimation crisis while allowing production (accumulation) to continue virtually unabated." In addition, the state argues for new hazardous waste disposal and treatment facilities to provide "safe" handling of increasing volumes of hazardous waste generated by industry, facilities that are necessary to provide sufficient capacity assurance. American law, in fact, requires states to develop capacity assurance plans that virtually mandate the siting of new facilities. Rather than dealing with the structural aspect of waste as an investment problem for capital (i.e., the need to limit amounts of pollution generated during production processes), the state instead develops a siting strategy that shifts the debate from structure to location. Geographically specific communities representing differences in race, ethnicity, and class are pitted against one another for the location of hazardous waste facilities. Typically, communities fight to keep them as far away as possible, though in many instances some community members support industrial facilities, however noxious, for the purpose of local or regional economic development through tax revenues and job creation.

Industries that generate hazardous waste respond to these crises by developing environmental management programs to comply with regulations, to facilitate public and community relations, and sometimes even to increase the cost-efficiency of production by preventing pollution by way of efficiencies in the use of feedstocks. These waste management methods clearly vary in terms of their benefit (or detriment) to the environment. All hazardous waste producing firms have to comply with regulations, though some clearly fail to do even that. Beyond that, industries develop voluntary pollution prevention strategies, often in concert with trade associations, such as the Canadian Chemical Producers Association and the American Chemical Manufacturers Association, to reduce operating costs. These prevention strategies include waste minimization, the treatment of waste to reduce toxicity; source reduction, decreases in toxic production feedstocks; and waste reduction, decreases in waste through reuse and recycling.

Industries have found such approaches as appealing as environmentalists do in that they have often resulted in efficiencies that reduce pollution control costs. The task ahead for industrialists and environmentalists alike is to achieve more results from pollution prevention.

EPA and Environmental Equity and Justice

EPA's first efforts regarding equity and justice began in July 1990 when the agency established an Environmental Equity Workgroup to review evidence that racial minority and low-income communities bear higher environmental risk burdens than the general American population and to consider how the agency might address these disparities. As described in the Preface, the initiative resulted most directly from a January 1990 Conference on Race and the Incidence of Environmental Hazards sponsored by the University of Michigan School of Natural Resources. A group of social scientists and civil rights leaders organized the meeting and shared research findings regarding environmental inequities. The panelists named themselves the Michigan Coalition and wrote a letter to the EPA administrator, William Reilly, in March 1990 requesting a meeting to discuss the group's findings, which resulted in the formation of the Workgroup.

After nearly two years of deliberations, the Workgroup issued its final report, *Environmental Equity: Reducing Risk for All Communities*, in June 1992. The report distinguished its emphasis on environmental equity, which addresses distributions of benefits associated with industrial activity and their corresponding environmental burdens, from the related but broader concepts of environmental justice and environmental racism. Environmental racism refers to the various ways in which racial minority groups have been marginalized historically and how they are affected by processes of social inequality and uneven development resulting in environmental inequities. Environmental justice is a still broader term, addressing not only the problems of inequity and racism but also how they relate to procedural and structural aspects of public policy.

EPA's equity report made a number of findings in support of the hypothesis that racial minorities and low-income people face disproportionate health and environmental problems. The agency observed that rates of exposure to air pollution, hazardous waste facilities, contaminated fish, and agricultural pesticides in the workplace are all higher for these groups as compared to the overall population. Another finding was that these groups also have higher rates of disease and death, though insufficient data were available to establish the environmental contribution to the difference since environmental and public health statistics are not routinely collected by race or income. The one exception is lead poisoning for which data have been collected and analyzed by race, indicating higher rates of unacceptably high blood lead levels in black children as compared to white children. The Workgroup concluded in its report that the agency should increase its priority on environmental equity by incorporating it into risk assessment, regulatory development, permitting, enforcement, and communication.

A variety of groups and individuals submitted public comments regarding the report's recommendations, including the Michigan Coalition. In general, the reactions reflected encouragement that EPA had finally addressed and admitted to the problem. After all, having the nation's environmental regulatory agency document the existence of environmental inequity was a crucial first step toward addressing the problem through public policy, even though it was already well documented and even if the recommendations were insufficient. The commentators were especially concerned that the language seemed tentative with its use of phrases like "where appropriate" and "to the degree feasible" as well as its lack of time tables (EPA, 1992). Some also criticized the report's focus on equity (as opposed to racism or justice), especially its explicit connection to risk, on the grounds that risk assessment is more of a political process than a scientific exercise and that inadequate data make the links difficult to prove.

In November 1992, EPA created the Office of Environmental Equity, later renamed the Office of Environmental Justice during the Clinton administration, with a broad mandate to serve as a focal point for ensuring that racial minority and low-income populations receive full protection under environmental laws. The office is charged with providing oversight on these concerns to all parts of the agency (EPA, 1993a). This involves reviewing how EPA conducts its business and recommending changes where necessary. The Office of Environmental Justice director advises the EPA administrator on the impact of environmental risks, programs, regulations, and legislation on socio-economically and politically disadvantaged communities. The Office of Environmental Justice also serves as a clearinghouse and dissemination point for environmental justice information to the public, other federal agencies, and EPA staff, consistent with President

Clinton's executive order on environmental justice issued in February 1994.

In April 1994, EPA's solid and hazardous waste program released its own report on environmental justice in which it announced initiatives aimed at addressing environmental justice problems. Much of their focus was the establishment of guidelines for dealing with communities in disputes over hazardous waste facilities. Part of this effort is on "brownfields" issues related to cleaning up contaminated sites. Through its Brownfields Action Agenda established in January 1995, EPA grant funds are now available to assist community groups in redeveloping sites upon the completion of cleanup activities and to work with investors, lenders, developers, and other affected parties. The agency's Brownfields Economic Development Initiative provides state and local governments with guidance on future land uses for brownfields redevelopment, as it had done since 1993 through the Superfund program (Fletcher, 2002; EPA, 1993b, 1998, 2000).

Another part of EPA's environmental justice and waste agenda addresses the question of hazardous waste facility siting. Building on the Combustion and Waste Minimization Strategy established in 1993, EPA has encouraged states to develop community participation strategies in efforts to reduce emissions at existing facilities (especially incinerators and other boilers and industrial furnaces that burn hazardous waste) and to examine alternative facility sites when issues of equity and justice arise (EPA, 1993). The agency clearly recognizes the need to address distributive equity, particularly with regard to racial minorities and low-income groups, as well as procedural equity to some extent. But its concept of procedural issues is still largely limited to community involvement in the location of facilities and the control of their emissions.

To be sure, although these are important items highly relevant to environmental equity, broader environmental justice questions are left unanswered. In a procedural sense, these community participation strategies fail to address land uses other than waste facilities that might be more acceptable to local residents. Instead, EPA's environmental justice strategy for siting is to address community concerns about equity only in the context of specific proposals in particular locations. This is understandable given the typical reality of local government control over land-use zoning and corporate ownership of industrial properties. What more, then, should EPA and other environmental regulatory agencies do to promote environmental justice in the context of hazardous waste policy? Part of the answer is in the reformulation of federal capacity assurance requirements that lead state governments repeatedly toward the siting of new and expanded facili- . ties. This is also true for the Canadian context, if only implicitly, given that this particular policy element has no statutory basis at either the federal or provincial level. Nonetheless, communities facing the prospect of hosting a new incinerator or landfill must either prove the site to be unfit for such a land use (e.g., hydrogeological problems) or demonstrate enough political opposition such that decision makers will be convinced to try an alternate path of least resistance (i.e., another location). Also, the fact remains that unless and until hazardous waste policies directly address pollution prevention through the regulation of waste generation within the production process, ideally with as much regulatory "teeth" as existing capacity assurance provisions, the issue of where to locate waste sites, however equitably, will not go away.

Distributive Justice and Hazardous Waste

Environmental equity research has found that hazardous waste is often generated in one community and transported to facilities in other communities (Lake, 1993; Lake & Disch, 1992; Lake & Johns, 1990; Bullard, 1990; Waldo, 1985). One of the chief reasons for this is that hazardous waste regulations and disposal fees vary among jurisdictions. Also, not all communities that generate hazardous waste have the capacity to manage it. Waste generators will often ship their wastes off-site, even across international borders, to minimize their costs. This phenomenon has implications for geographical equity, the physical or spatial location of benefits and burdens. The case studies presented in Part II will demonstrate that geographical equity is central to disputes over hazardous waste facilities when industrial waste generators in locations other than the host community are expected to benefit most from the additional capacity. This occurred in five of the ten cases presented, three of which involved proposals to expand existing facilities so as to attract larger and more geographically dispersed markets. Two of the cases involved non-industrial "greenfield" sites.

A second finding in equity research is that waste facilities tend to be located in communities inhabited by racial minorities and low income groups (Bryant & Mohai, 1992; Bullard, 1990; United Church of Christ, 1987; GAO, 1983, 1995). Like the industries it serves, the hazardous waste industry attempts to lower its costs wherever possible. As a result, firms often choose areas with low property values and residents who are less likely to launch protests. These findings have implications for social equity, the distribution of benefits and burdens among social groups. Only three of the ten facility siting cases presented in Part II occurred in black or poor communities, whereas the remaining seven cases occurred in white middle-class suburban areas. This research provides no evidence to suggest or refute the possibility that proposals for new sites may have been driven by racism or class discrimination in either of the two border regions investigated; nonetheless, each of the communities involved were concerned about becoming victims of failed hazardous waste policies.

A third aspect of hazardous waste management is that our society's reliance on products that contribute to the hazardous waste stream disproportionately burdens communities which currently have hazardous waste facilities (cumulative equity). This is particularly a problem given the many difficulties in siting hazardous waste facilities in non-industrial or greenfield locations. The result is that hazardous waste facility siting proposals are often for either expansions of existing facilities or new facilities in areas already heavily industrialized. As was the case with spatial equity concerns, cumulative equity issues were raised in five of the ten cases presented in Part II. They emphasize how environmental risks accrue over time in particular industrialized communities.

Another temporal dimension of environmental equity has to do with the environmental burden that present industrial activities and waste management decisions will have on future generations (intergenerational equity). This concern is especially present with regard to landfills, since they have the potential to leak and possibly contaminate ground and surface waters in perpetuity. Likewise, underground injection facilities, which pump liquid wastes into deep subsurface caverns, are criticized for the same reasons. In each of the five cases involving landfills and the one underground injection proposal presented in Part II, community residents expressed concern about the likelihood that the "natural" (e.g., geological) or "engineered" (e.g., synthetic liners) containments would eventually fail to contain the wastes *in situ*.

A fifth aspect of hazardous waste relates to procedural equity questions of how political and policy processes affect the aforementioned distributions of economic benefits and environmental burdens. Research on hazardous waste equity issues has often found that inequitable access to decision-making processes, and also inequitable power and authority among interest groups, leads to inequitable distributions of benefits and burdens (Goldman, 1996; Goldman & Fitton, 1994; EPA, 1992; Bullard, 1990; United Church of Christ, 1987). These studies have concluded that individual communities typically have relatively little input and even less power and authority with respect to issues of hazardous waste planning (including not only hazardous waste siting, but also issues of waste reduction and pollution prevention that relate more to production processes than waste facilities).

One way to overcome local opposition is to provide financial support to host communities so that they can hire legal and/or technical advisors, as was done in one of the cases presented in Part II. A voluntary process that leads to facility proposals only in communities that agree to them up-front is far preferable and less likely to receive local opposition (Rabe, 1994; Rabe, et al., 1996; Richards, 1996, Kunreuther, 1996; Zeiss, 1996). None of the cases reviewed in Part II involved such an approach, and they are relatively rare in any event. The siting of a hazardous waste incinerator in Swan Hills, Alberta is probably the best example of voluntary siting (Rabe, 1994) in that the community fought for rather than against the facility, though it too came to face local opposition once it was in place and operating. The facility's neighbors became particularly irked when it expanded to import out-of-province waste previously banned by the Alberta government and especially after a series of accidents (Westell, 1994; Marsden & Westell, 1997).

Regarding hazardous waste generators, EPA has worked with the states to develop a Combustion and Waste Minimization Strategy that emphasizes the reduction of emissions from existing hazardous waste facilities over the siting of new ones, as well as more explicit waste reduction standards for industries (EPA, 1993). Yet, despite these reforms, communities face steep obstacles in attempting local control because of American constitutional interpretations that waste is little more than a commodity with its own rights to free interstate movement (Lake & Johns, 1990). In Canada, there has been little political or academic interest in the issue of environmental justice as defined by Americans, perhaps because of historic national differences from the United States in the relationship between race and class and because provinces have the legal right to ban waste imports. Nonetheless, the case studies reviewed in Part II will show that principles of equity are prominent concerns of community and environmental activists as well as government regulators in Canada as well as the United States.

Beyond Distributive Justice

Environmental justice research is by no means uniformly concerned with distributive justice and equity issues such as the race *versus* class debate. Pulido (1996b) cautions that the question, while important, is but one of many related to an extremely complex and pervasive problem. The specific focus on proving and disproving the significance of race and class as demographic variables, she argues, promotes a "monolithic understanding of racism" that fails to account for its relationship with socioeconomic forces such as "relations of production" and "regimes of accumulation" that are themselves responsible for creating oppression in various forms (Pulido, 1996: 148). Robert Bullard, who has written more extensively on this subject than perhaps any other social scientist, has argued similarly that we must get "beyond the race versus class trap," suggesting that the issue can backfire in either direction if it is the only one the movement makes salient (Bullard, 1993). With respect to the question of environmental justice and its relationship to NIMBY, Lake (1996), following Young (1983, 1990), has argued for a broader conception of equity that "entails full democratic participation not only in decisions affecting distributive outcomes but also, and more importantly, in the gamut of prior decisions affecting the production of costs and benefits to be distributed" (Lake, 1996: 165).

Procedural equity, then, must not be narrowly conceived as the opportunity for targeted communities to participate in facility siting hearings. Instead, we must strive to "transcend the siting debates and participate in a prior process that eliminates the production of environmental problems" (Lake, 1996). With respect to hazardous waste facilities specifically, policies are limited by a number of "structural constraints" that serve to perpetuate an unnecessary emphasis on capacity assurance, leading to a discourse on toxics as a locational problem for communities and a site review process problem for state and provincial governments rather than an investment problem for capital (Lake, 1993; Lake & Disch, 1992; Heiman, 1990). In other words, the regulatory emphasis on waste management after the source, rather than during the production process, prioritizes the siting of facilities over the internalization of waste through recycling and recovery.

The relative emphasis on waste management structures the various distributive equity problems associated with toxics; while industrial waste generators and waste management firms reap the profits of their production, state and provincial governments, as well as communities, must absorb the costs. State and provincial governments subsidize with public funds what are often long, controversial and costly siting processes. Local governments and non-governmental groups that choose to fight against facility proposals, or at least involve themselves in the process in order to ensure community or environmental interests are represented, often have to absorb the associated legal and administrative costs on their own. Some local governments prefer to support the projects in order to take a larger share of the economic benefits, particularly through tax revenues.

In either case, local governments involved in siting processes must deal with external forces directed from higher tiers of the state over which they have little direct control, while balancing varying interests within their communities. These differing "loyalties" can lead to a number of reactions to waste facilities, but the strongest protests tend to come from people who live nearest them, while community support is more typical among those who may anticipate personal benefits. Still others may remain indecisive or simply apathetic if they foresee no particular stake. The case studies presented in Part II tell a series of these kinds of stories involving ten facility siting cases in Canada and the United States.

Note

1. By the term "traditional" environmental movement, Harvey refers to the leadership of the "Big Ten" environmental groups: Friends of the Earth, Sierra Club, Environmental Defense Fund, Natural Resources Defense Council, etc.

3

Environmental Justice and "Industrial Ecology"

Introduction

Hazardous waste management is a complex and multi-dimensional problem, as indicated by the regulatory frameworks described in Chapter 1 and their social justice implications illustrated in Chapter 2. Distributive equity, though it is not entirely representative of the connections between hazardous waste and environmental justice, is an important aspect of the overall problem. The social, spatial, and temporal array of hazardous waste facilities and their associated benefits and burdens, described conceptually in Chapters 1 and 2, set much of the context for how and why communities and groups react to siting proposals. This chapter reviews, in detail, the findings of a number of empirical studies on hazardous waste and distributive equity in order to more fully establish this background to the relations between toxics, facilities, and communities.

I have argued that distributive inequities and injustices are not the only important aspects of the hazardous waste problem. Structural limitations of environmental regulatory frameworks in Canada and the United States also influence many of the differences of opinion over facility siting. Capacity assurance objectives at the national and provincial/state levels lead to proposals for new and expanded facilities. In the United States, this is driven by federal legislation, and in Canada it has occurred implicitly through governmental support for particular facility proposals. Moreover, the lack of integration of such policies and proposals with local land-use planning, combined with the distribution of existing waste facilities, often bolsters community opposition.

These underlying factors in the relations between governments at all levels with companies that generate or manage hazardous wastes reflect what has been termed an "industrial ecology" in recent literature in the field of environmental engineering. Rather than emphasizing the location and character of wastes and facilities, as is typical in environmental equity and justice research, "industrial ecology" or "green design" research seeks to address the problem from within production processes that generate hazardous waste. This chapter describes some of the conceptual arguments and empirical findings of this emerging body of research in order to further develop the background for the case studies presented in Part II, Chapters 4 and 5. But first, I will present empirical findings from a variety of studies on distributive justice and hazardous waste.

Race, Class, and Scale

A variety of empirical studies have investigated the distributive equity dimensions of hazardous waste and toxic releases. Some of the research has focused on Superfund cleanup sites (Hird, 1993; Greenberg, 1993) while others have examined Toxic Release Inventory sites (Cutter & Solecki, 1996; McMaster, Leitner, & Sheppard, 1997). The studies on off-site hazardous waste treatment, storage, and disposal facilities (TSDFs) are the most relevant to the focus of this research. In general, the research on environmental justice and hazardous waste facilities has examined the extent to which the location of the latter is associated with race and class. A sometimes heated debate has ensued from the question of which factor is most predictive of facility location. Matters of spatial and temporal scale have factored heavily in the methods employed as well as the research findings.

Spatial scale is important because the results differ depending on the geographic units used in the analysis. Studies using American five-digit zip code areas have found class, and especially race, to be strongly associated with waste facility location (UCCCRJ, 1987; Goldman & Fitton, 1994), whereas studies using census tracts found neither variable to be a significant factor (Anderson, et al., 1994; Anderton, et al., 1994a, 1994b). Temporal scale is relevant to the degree that demographic changes occur in communities with hazardous waste facilities, particularly if the racial or class structure of an area changes after new facilities are sited. A "chicken or egg" debate has thus emerged as to whether hazardous waste facilities are attracted to racial minority and low-income areas, or whether minorities and the poor tend to move to locations near these land uses.

The first study to find the relationship between race, class, and the location of hazardous waste facilities was conducted by the United States General Accounting Office (GAO). It found that of the four commercial hazardous waste facilities in the southeastern United States, three were located in areas with mostly poor black residents, and all four had lower than average incomes (GAO, 1983). Without a larger sample size, or a comparison between the four communities and others with no sites, it is hard to determine the broader national significance of the findings (Cutter, 1995). Despite its limitations, however, the GAO study was an important starting point for empirical research into the distributive equity dimensions of hazardous waste. Together with Robert Bullard's research on the politics of waste siting in African American communities (Bullard, 1983, 1990; Bullard & Wright, 1986) problems of environmental equity and racism have been established for well over a decade, at least for the southern United States.

THE UNITED CHURCH OF CHRIST COMMISSION FOR RACIAL JUSTICE STUDIES

The United Church of Christ Commission for Racial Justice (UCCCRJ) conducted the first national study to investigate environmental inequities associated with hazardous waste in the United States (UCCCRJ, 1987). It compared communities (defined as five-digit zip code areas) with commercial (off-site) hazardous waste treatment, storage, or disposal facilities (the same kinds of facilities examined in Part II) in terms of their racial and socioeconomic compositions based on 1980 census data. The Center for Policy Alternatives, the National Association for the Advancement of Colored People, and UCCCRJ updated the original study in 1994 using 1990 census data (Goldman & Fitton, 1994).

The first UCCCRJ study found that communities with two or more commercial hazardous waste facilities or one of the five largest American commercial hazardous waste landfills had minority[1] populations of 37.6 per cent on average (UCCCRJ, 1987) compared to 12.3 per cent of communities with no such sites. Zip code areas with one facility had between 22 and 24 per cent minority residents on average, depending on the type of facility involved. The study found that racial differences between the communities with and without hazardous waste facilities were statistically significant at the .01 level. The report concluded that race was a stronger and more predictive factor than income, though it did not present data to substantiate this claim.

The second UCCCRJ-sponsored study found an even stronger relationship between facility location and race, at least partly because it looked at communities with larger numbers of sites than did the first study (Goldman & Fitton, 1994). The research compared communities with three commercial hazardous waste facilities, an incinerator, or one of the largest American landfills (45.6 per cent minorities) with other communities (14.4 per cent minorities), a statistically significant difference at the .01 level. Zip code areas with one or more facilities had 30.8 per cent minorities. Poverty rates in the communities with such facilities were found to be 35 per cent higher and income levels 19 per cent lower than the American average, though the differences were not statistically significant. Again, the study found race to be a stronger predictive factor than class in determining hazardous waste facility location.

The University of Massachusetts Studies

Anderton, et al. (1994a, 1994b) and Anderson, et al. (1994) published findings from a second set of national studies of race, class, and hazardous waste in the US, sponsored and funded by Waste Management, Incorporated and the Institute for Chemical Waste Management, whose loyalties clearly are to industry. The study was inspired and conceived from quite a different perspective than that of the UCCCRJ, whose loyalties are to civil rights. These differing points of view are made clear by comparing the methodologies — the size of geographic units and the definition of comparison groups — employed by the two groups. The industry-funded researchers, based at the University of Massachusetts-Amherst (UMass) Social and Demographic Research Institute, used census tracts, smaller geographic units of analysis than zip code areas, to reduce the "ecological fallacy" problem which increases with spatial scale generally. They also used different comparison groups. Instead of comparing all areas of the United States with and without commercial hazardous waste facilities as did UCCCRJ, the UMass group compared census tracts with facilities to those without, but only if they were within a metropolitan area with at least one facility within its borders (Anderton, et al., 1994b).

The UMass group found no statistically significant association between race, class, and waste at even the 0.10 level. Blacks and Hispanics represented 23.9 per cent of the population in census tracts with facilities as compared to 22.9 per cent in the control areas, a rather small difference. Similarly, mean poverty rates were only slightly higher in tracts with hazardous waste facilities (14.5 per cent) compared to those without (13.9 per cent). The only variable found to have a strong relationship with facility location was the number of persons employed in manufacturing and industry, or what the United States Census Bureau terms Precision Manufacturing Occupations. In the tracts with facilities, 38.6 per cent of employed persons age 16 and over worked in Precision Manufacturing, as compared to 30.6 per cent in tracts with no facility, a statistically significant association at the .01 level.

The UMass research also investigated the relationship between race, class, and waste in larger geographic units or "surrounding areas" by aggregating clusters of census tracts within a 2.5 mile radius of commercial hazardous waste facilities. Blacks and Hispanics in these areas were 35.4 per cent of the population on average as compared to 20.9 per cent in other census tracts. The percentage of families below the poverty line was 19.0 per cent on average within a 2.5 mile radius of a facility as compared to 13.1 per cent in other areas. These patterns are more similar to the UCCCRJ results than to the UMass census tract findings. Average employment in Precision Manufacturing was again higher in the cluster areas surrounding facilities (35.7 per cent) as compared to other areas (29.9 per cent), similar to the census tract results.

THE UMASS AND UCCCRJ STUDIES COMPARED

The UMass and UCCCRJ researchers interpreted their results very differently despite the similarities between the zip code area and geographic cluster findings. Anderton, et al. concluded that census tracts were a more appropriate unit of analysis than larger spatial scales such as zip codes or aggregated census tract clusters:

> [The] aggregated results are very similar to those reported from prior analyses of zip code areas.... If one could find some clear rationale (that is, an epidemiological demonstration that a particular hazard is characteristically distributed over

> a particular, larger area), perhaps these larger areas could be accepted as a more appropriate unit of analysis than census tracts. To this point, however, the proof is lacking. (Anderton, et al.1994a: 238-39)

This proof is lacking for two principal reasons. One is that environmental and health statistics are not routinely collected by race, income, or census tract in the United States in such a way that they can be correlated with pollution (EPA, 1992). The other has to do with scientific debate about the relative contribution of environmental and behavioral factors of public health problems among various racial and income groups (Colborn, et al., 1990, 1996; Gibbons, 1991; Gladwell, 1990; Okie, 1991). As a result, an epidemiological connection between waste location, public health, and socioeconomics is hard to demonstrate.

Goldman, one of the researchers on both UCCCRJ studies, emphasizes the similarities between their findings and those of the UMass group. Even the UMass census tract analysis (which found lower minority percentages than the aggregated cluster analysis) indicated that black and Hispanic populations were, on average, at 23.9 per cent in tracts with commercial hazardous waste facilities. Census tract clusters with facilities had average black and Hispanic populations of 35.4 per cent. These results are not dissimilar to the UCCCRJ findings which ranged from 22 per cent to 45.6 per cent for all racial minority groups (a somewhat larger demographic category), depending on the number, size, and type of facility. In response to the UMass research Goldman submits:

> So where's the beef? They doubled the percentage of people of color in their comparison group. Always watch a magician's other hand!... Instead of comparing their waste site tracts to the 12 per cent people of color average for the country, they compared them only to other tracts in metropolitan areas with commercial toxic waste sites, which, on average, have roughly 26 per cent people of color (eliminating the disparity). (Goldman 1996: 134)

In other words, the difference in results between the UCCCRJ and UMass studies has more to do with comparison groups than with units of analysis, according to Goldman.

Certainly, the UMass group's decision to count census tracts without commercial hazardous waste facilities only if there were at least one such facility in the same metropolitan area biases the results toward comparisons among industrialized urban and suburban areas. Their methodology ignores all rural tracts except for those where at least one facility is located. On average, this also makes for a comparison group with more than double the minority population than the United States as a whole (Goldman, 1996). Moreover, while the two sets of studies are roughly similar with regard to their findings on average minority populations in areas with facilities, depending on geographic scale and the types of facilities counted, the findings for the comparison groups are quite dissimilar. The result is that the UCCCRJ studies indicated large racial and socioeconomic differences between areas with and without hazardous waste facilities, whereas the UMass group found more similarities between the two groups.

The question, then, is whether comparisons of areas with hazardous waste facilities at any scale of analysis should be made with all other areas or only those in metropolitan areas with at least one facility. The first approach, advocated by UCCCRJ, seems more reasonable for a national comparison. The second approach, advocated by the UMass group, could be a useful way of exploring urban/rural differences, but only if the areas with facilities were compared to those without facilities separately for metropolitan and non-metropolitan areas. As it stands, the UMass approach seems to compare apples with oranges by including all areas with commercial hazardous waste facilities on the one hand, while counting only certain kinds of areas without facilities on the other.

DISTRIBUTIVE EQUITY AND HAZARDOUS WASTE IN THE DETROIT AREA

Mohai and Bryant (1992) have empirically measured environmental inequities related to commercial hazardous waste facilities in the three counties of metropolitan Detroit, Michigan. The Detroit area is part of the regional focus of Part II, Chapter 5 in this book. Mohai and Bryant compared white, minority, and low-income populations at various distances from commercial facilities and found that racial differences were statistically significant at the .01 level whereas socioeconomic differences were not significant at even the .05 level.

They examined the demographics of waste within metropolitan Detroit, the City of Detroit, and suburban Detroit by comparing racial and income breakdowns at three distances from hazardous waste facilities: less than 1 mile away, 1 to 1.5 miles away, and greater than 1.5 miles away. The average percentage of minorities increased consistently with proximity to facilities in the central city, the suburbs, and in the region as a whole, whereas the trend for white populations was consistently the opposite. The average percentage of persons below the poverty line also increased with proximity to facilities in the metropolitan area as a whole, but the results were mixed for central and suburban Detroit.

DISTRIBUTIVE EQUITY AND TOXICS IN ONTARIO

Jerrett, et al. (1997) conducted an empirical study of distributive environmental equity in Ontario using Canadian National Pollutant Release Inventory (NPRI) data on industry emissions and transfers (including hazardous waste generation) of 178 toxic substances. The analysis differs from the others because it is based on industrial pollution emissions, including hazardous waste generation, rather than hazardous waste sites. The study used census divisions as geographic units of analysis, generally delineated along county borders, though in some cases the boundaries correspond to regional municipalities or districts. Canadian census data do not allow for the kinds of racial comparisons seen in empirical studies of environmental equity in the United States, so the researchers restricted their analysis to socioeconomic factors such as income, dwelling values, manufacturing employment, and population. Environmental inequities are likely to be less racialized in Canada than in the United States because of the differences in minority residential patterns between the two countries. Race composition is one of the most significant differences between Canadian and American cities (Ewing, 1992; Goldberg & Mercer, 1986). Additionally, 75 per cent of blacks in the United States live in census tracts that are 30 per cent white, whereas about 70 per cent of Canadian blacks live in neighborhoods that are 40 to 70 per cent white (Fong, 1994).

The findings of Jerrett and associates corresponded more to the UMass studies than the UCCCRJ research. They found a positive relationship between pollution emissions and three factors: total population, median household income, and manufacturing employment. Only one variable, dwelling value, had a negative relationship with pollution emissions. This indicates that industrial pollution emissions are higher in areas with larger populations, higher household incomes, greater employment in manufacturing, and lower dwelling values. Together, these factors accounted for 62.6 per cent of the variation in pollution levels at the .01 level, and, individually, each was statistically significant at the .05 level. The researchers estimated that the positive relationship between total population and pollution emissions accounted for most of the variation (23.4 per cent), followed by the negative relationship with dwelling value (16.7 per cent), and the positive relationships with income (12.2 per cent) and employment (10 per cent).

The model held true for most of the census division areas when measured individually. Forty-five of 49 such regions in Ontario were within the range of −1.5 to 1.5 variation (standardized regression residuals) from the mean values predicted by the model. Two census divisions were below this range, suggesting that the model overestimated the relationship between the four variables and pollution levels, whereas two other areas were above the range, indicating the model underestimated the relationships. Lambton County was the most extreme case in the latter category. This area is just across the border from Michigan and, like metropolitan Detroit, is also part of the regional focus of Part II, Chapter 5 in this book. The researchers concluded that the large number of pollution sources in Lambton County, mostly in the Sarnia area, accounted for the deviation from predicted values. Each of the four areas that differed most from the model had among the highest or lowest pollution emissions, depending on whether the model underestimated or overestimated the strength of the relationships. Another Ontario community of interest in this book, the Regional Municipality of Niagara (from Part II, Chapter 4), followed the model as well as any other census division area, falling between −1.0 to 1.0 variation from the mean values. This is consistent with the fact that the emissions rate for the region was roughly the same as the provincial average (about 450 tonnes annually), the vast majority of which is generated in the city of Niagara Falls. The finding is also consistent with the concerns of rural Niagara, Ontario residents who opposed the construction of a facility for off-site treatment, incineration, and disposal of hazardous waste, given that their community (West Lincoln) generates little in the way of NPRI pollution, hazardous waste, or other.

DISTRIBUTIVE JUSTICE AND HAZARDOUS WASTE:
ASSESSING THE RESULTS

The distributive environmental justice implications of hazardous waste are revealed in a number of ways by the research presented here. Three of the four national American studies found race to be strongly related to hazardous waste facility location, though the relative strength of each varies with methodology. The UCCCRJ and UMass researchers used different geographic units of analysis and comparison groups. They found fairly similar average minority populations in areas with commercial hazardous waste facilities, but rather dissimilar racial compositions in areas without them. The UCCCRJ studies concluded that racial minorities and low-income groups are more likely to live in areas with hazardous waste facilities. They further concluded that race is a stronger predictive factor of waste location than class since the differences between communities with and without facilities were statistically significant in the first instance but not the second.

The two regional studies differed from one another as well. Consistent with the UCCCRJ research, Mohai and Bryant found race to be strongly associated with facility location in the Detroit metropolitan area. Income differences showed the same general trend, though the relationship was not statistically significant. Jerrett, et al. found no relationships between income and pollution in the province of Ontario, similar to the UMass research findings. The Ontario study differed from the others in that it did not look at race and it used toxic emissions data rather than waste facility location data. Another unique aspect of the research was that it used counties as geographic units of analysis, a larger spatial scale than was used in the other studies.

Been (1993, 1994) has criticized these kinds of studies as "snapshots" in time that fail to incorporate demographic changes that might occur after facilities are sited. Without incorporating a temporal dimension to distributive environmental equity research, she argues, there is no proof that siting processes are discriminatory. Been (1994) took the GAO findings, based on the 1980 census, and compared them to population data from 1970 and 1990. She found that African American populations decreased in each of the four southern communities with commercial hazardous waste facilities studied by GAO. In two of the cases, this decrease was considerable — about one-third. Been conducted a similar re-analysis of research conducted by Bullard (1983) in Houston, Texas and found exactly the opposite findings.

The percentage of African Americans in nine of ten Houston neighborhoods with facilities increased from 1970 to 1990, and the percentage of persons below the poverty line increased in seven of the ten cases over the same period. She concluded that while the results of her analysis are mixed, the Houston findings suggest that low property values in neighborhoods with facilities may attract racial minorities and poor people as much as facility siting proposals are drawn to minority and low-income areas.

Bullard (1994b) and Pulido (1996b) have both argued that the "chicken or egg" debate (i.e., which came first, the facilities or the racial minorities) is "irrelevant" since a strong spatial relationship between race and waste adds up to a discriminatory pattern, whatever demographic changes may occur subsequent to the siting of a facility. But for Pulido, at least, the arguments of Been and others are symptomatic of a narrow conception of racism that incorporates only intentionally racist acts:

> While I concur with Bullard from an activist perspective that the ["chicken or egg"] question is moot, it is important for what it reveals in terms of conceptualizations of racism as a specific, conscious act of discrimination, which much of the [distributive environmental equity] literature presumes. According to this reasoning, only conscious targeting constitutes racism. Taking this a step further, if residents came to the nuisance voluntarily, does this mean that a racist act did not occur? Does it mean that no corrective action need be taken? (Pulido, 1996b: 148)

These forceful statements reveal the importance of tackling problems of environmental racism, injustice, and inequity, regardless of whether they result from discriminatory intent. Similarly, Pulido (2000) and Bullard (2000) have also stressed the importance of understanding environmental justice issues, particularly social equity concerns among racial minorities, as a function of broader social and political forces that reinforce racism and racial segregation (e.g., "white flight" and "white privilege"). Following this line of reasoning, I argue that distributive environmental inequities in all forms (distributive and procedural) should be remedied to the degree possible, regardless of whether the patterns were intentional. Much of this work falls within the domain of contaminated site remediation to transform derelict industrial properties ("brownfields") into useful community spaces, as well as geographically targeted enforcement to deal with locally concentrated accumulations of toxic risks. This is not meant to suggest that a perfectly equitable distribution of environmental hazards is either achievable or necessarily desirable. Simply spreading the waste around is hardly the answer, particularly when pollution prevention can reduce the overall volume and toxicity of hazardous waste through production changes. Thus, it is important that we also get beyond distributive and procedural equity considerations of hazardous waste and resolve the various structural constraints of existing legal and regulatory frameworks. The next section examines these issues within the context of the "industrial ecology" of hazardous waste.

The "Industrial Ecology" of Hazardous Waste: Getting Beyond Distributions

In recent years, the Canadian and American governments have put increasing emphasis on voluntary pollution prevention programs that encourage industries to reduce hazardous waste and other environmental contaminants at the source rather than after the fact. Both countries, as well as several industry groups, subscribe to a preferred management hierarchy that emphasizes the substitution of toxics, source reduction, reuse, and recycling over treatment and disposal. This emphasis is consistent with the concept of "industrial ecology" which draws its analogy from natural ecosystems to describe the relationships between industrial production, the generation of residuals, and waste treatment and disposal (Allenby & Richards, 1994; Frosch, 1994a; Bradshaw, et al., 1992; Jelenski, et al., 1992). The concept illustrates the importance of internalizing pollution within production both because of the environmental effects of uncontrolled emissions and because of the economic inefficiencies in materials usage that waste represents. This section is based on environmental engineering literature and government reports on pollution prevention.

INDUSTRIAL ECOLOGY

In 1991, the United States National Academy of Sciences convened a colloquium entitled "Industrial Ecology" in Washington, DC at which environmental engineers and scientists from academia and industry presented papers and shared ideas on a "new approach to the industrial design of products and processes and the implementation of sustainable manufacturing strategies" (Jelenski, et al., 1992: 793). Patel (1992), the conference organizer, described the concept as a cradle-to-reincarnation production philosophy in which the cradle is considered as beginning within production and design, rather than after a waste stream is already generated, as is the case with cradle-to-grave hazardous waste management. Obviously, recycling is a key element in the "reincarnation" of production residuals into feedstocks (thus avoiding waste disposal), but the idea also includes a more fundamental rethinking of manufacturing based on six elements:

1. materials that have the desired properties and [that] are less harmful to the environment during their extraction or formulation stages;

2. use of just-in-time materials philosophy that would obviate the necessity of storage (and perhaps long-term degradation) of hazardous or nonhazardous feedstock materials;

3. process substitution that eliminates toxic feedstock;

4. process modification to contain, remove, and treat toxic materials;

5. engineering controls to assure robust and reliable processes; and

6. the end-of-life recyclability consideration. (Patel, 1992: 798)

INDUSTRIAL ECOSYSTEMS

Richards, et al. (1994) have developed a typology of "industrial ecosystems" with three categories representing the history, present, and desired future of manufacturing processes. Type I is completely linear, reflecting historic and many current industrial processes, with one-way flows of materials and energy and no recycling in production, use, or disposal. Many present industries have advanced to Type II by adopting some internal reuse and recovery strategies, but they still require virgin material inputs and emit pollution and wastes. As a hypothetical ideal, Type III industrial ecosystems would completely, or nearly completely, internally cycle all materials, thereby avoiding the problem of waste generation and management.

TABLE 1
Metal Recovery Potential in US Hazardous Waste Streams

Metal	Per cent of Metal Economically Recoverable	Per cent Recycled
Antimony	74–87	32
Arsenic	98–99	3
Barium	95–98	4
Beryllium	54–84	31
Cadmium	82–97	7
Chromium	68–89	8
Copper	85–92	10
Lead	84–95	56
Mercury	99	41
Nickel	100	0.1
Selenium	93–95	16
Silver	99–100	1
Thallium	97–99	1
Vanadium	74–98	1
Zinc	96–98	13

Source: Adapted from Allen & Behmanesh (1994: 80)

Though Type III industrial ecosystems are ideals impossible to attain across the board, there are indications that industry could do a much better job of recovering materials for the purpose of reuse as manufacturing inputs that presently end up in hazardous waste facilities. Allen and Behmanesh (1994) studied correlations between the market value of various metals and their concentration in available ores and hazardous waste streams. They found that industries frequently discard wastes with higher metals concentrations than are found in virgin supplies. Based on a Sherwood Plot, which has been used to calculate the price of metal based on its concentration in commercial virgin ore since the 1950s (Frosch, 1994b), Allen and Behmanesh compared the percentage of metal recycling in the United States to that which is economically recoverable from typical American hazardous waste streams (see Table 1). Of the 15 metal wastes included in the analysis, about 15 per cent were recycled, but over 90 per

TABLE 2

Worldwide Atmospheric Emissions of Trace Metals
(1,000 tonnes per year)

Element	Energy	Smelting, Refining, & Manufacturing	Manufacturing Processes	Waste Incineration & Transport	Total Anthropogenic
Antimony	1.3	1.5	—	0.7	3.5
Arsenic	2.2	12.4	2.0	2.3	18.9
Cadmium	0.8	5.4	0.6	0.8	7.6
Chromium	12.7	—	17.0	0.8	30.5
Copper	8.0	23.6	2.0	1.6	35.2
Lead	12.7	49.1	15.7	254.9	332.4
Manganese	12.1	3.2	14.7	8.3	38.3
Mercury	2.3	0.1	—	1.2	3.6
Nickel	42.0	4.8	4.5	0.4	51.7
Selenium	3.9	2.3	—	0.1	6.3
Thallium	1.1	—	4.0	—	5.1
Tin	3.3	1.1	—	0.8	5.2
Vanadium	84.0	0.1	0.7	1.2	86.0
Zinc	16.8	72.5	33.4	9.2	131.9
Totals	203.2	176.1	94.6	282.3	756.2

Source: Adapted from Ayres (1994: 30)

cent could have been recovered given that the percentage of metal within the waste was nearly as high as that found in ores (Allen, 1995).

As shown in Table 2, most of the same elements are found in worldwide atmospheric emissions from a variety of industrial activities, including waste incineration (Ayres, 1994). Allen and Behmanesh's and Ayres's results, published by the United States National Academy of Engineering, show that considerable progress is still necessary to achieve even a Type II industrial ecosystem nationally or internationally. Moreover, movement toward a Type III ideal, where manufacturing and processing industries recover or recycle higher proportions of metals and other toxic substances on-site, could produce several forms of environmental benefit. Not only can a Type III strategy reduce demand for existing hazardous waste facilities of all kinds, but production and waste processing plants alike would emit less air and water pollution as a result of progress toward Type II practices on a consistent basis and Type III practices where feasible. Reducing pollution at the source also minimizes cross-media transfers from air or water pollutants to hazardous waste. Traditional air and water pollution control measures require industries to install scrubbers and wastewater treatment plants to minimize the volume and toxicity of emissions and effluents. Progress in this regard has been achieved through improvements in treatment technologies that allow for the capture of smaller particulates and lower concentrations of toxic substances. These advances have helped to reduce industrial sources of air and water pollution in industrial cities throughout North America, but they also have generated new sources of hazardous waste, especially incinerator ash and treatment sludge.

WASTE AS DISSIPATIVE LOSS

Ayres uses principles of ecology and physics to explain the environmental effects of Type I and II industrial ecologies (with nonexistent or limited recycling) and the value of adopting Type III measures (involving recycling and reuse of all, or nearly all, production-related materials):

> There are only two possible long-run fates for waste materials: recycling and reuse or dissipative loss. (This is a straightforward implication of the law of conservation of mass.) The more materials are recycled, the less will be dissipated into the environment, and vice versa. Dissipative losses must be made up by replacement from virgin sources. A strong implication ... is that a long-term (sustainable) steady-state industrial economy would necessarily be characterized by near-total recycling of intrinsically toxic or hazardous materials, as well as a significant degree of recycling of plastics, paper, and other materials whose disposal constitutes an environmental problem. Heavy metals are among the materials that would have to be almost totally recycled to satisfy the sustainability criterion. (Ayres, 1994: 31)

The law of conservation of mass applies to all non-nuclear chemical reactions and states that mass or energy inputted is equal to mass or energy stored plus mass or energy outputted (Soesilo, 1995). In other words, the mass of materials that take part in a chemical reaction is the same as the mass of the products and residuals. By way of example, burning coal produces carbon-dioxide gas, water vapor, and ash which, if they could be combined, would have a mass equal to the coal in its original state (Lindsay, 1984). With regard to heavy metals and other toxic materials, "near-total recycling" (Ayres, 1994) is necessary to counter the dissipation or degradation of the original materials during production and consumption, as well as their dispersion into the environment through air emissions, water effluents, and waste streams (see Table 3). Because the combined mass of the pollutants is equal to the toxic substances before they are processed, it is theoretically possible to return a large proportion of many industrial feedstocks to their original state through recycling. Technological and economic limitations are more problematic, so research and development are critical to achieving Type III industrial processes.

The laws of thermodynamics are illustrative of this fundamental problem. The first law of thermodynamics states that matter and energy can be neither created nor destroyed, consistent with the law of conservation of mass (Daly & Cobb, 1989). However, the second law of thermodynamics declares that whenever matter or energy is processed and used, the amount of useable materials decreases due to entropy. Entropy, the qualitative degradation of matter, occurs as particles are rearranged or dissipated during their use. Daly and Cobb liken this physical reaction to an hourglass whereby sand in the top chamber (low-entropy matter) loses its ability to fall to the bottom once it has already done so because the transformation from top to bottom changes the sand into high-entropy matter. Returning to the example of burning coal, the reconcentration of heat and gas back into a useable form of energy (i.e., turning the hourglass upside down) would itself require the use of energy, thereby limiting or even nullifying the benefit of such recycling. Thus, a fundamental redesign of production processes is often necessary so that they use fewer materials more efficiently in the first place. Daly and Cobb argue that a fundamental rethinking of neo-classical economic theory is also necessary so that it recognizes and incorporates the problem of entropy into production decisions.

TABLE 3
Examples of Dissipative Use

Substance	Tonnes (millions)	Dissipative Uses
HEAVY METALS		
Copper sulfate	0.10	Fungicide, algicide, wood preservative, catalyst
Sodium bichromate	0.26	Chromic acid (for plating), tanning, algicide
Lead Oxides	0.24	Pigment (glass)
Lithopone	0.46	Pigment
Zinc Oxides	0.42	Pigment (tires)
Titanium Oxide	1.90	Pigment
Tetraethyl lead	?	Gasoline additive
Arsenic	?	Wood preservative, herbicide
Mercury	?	Fungicide, catalyst
OTHER CHEMICALS		
Chlorine	25.9	Acid, bleach, water treatment, PVC solvents, pesticides, refrigerants
Sulfur	61.5	Sulfuric acid, bleach, chemicals, fertilizers, rubber
Ammonia	24.0	Fertilizers, detergents, chemicals
Phosphoric acid	93.6	Fertilizers, nitric acid, chemicals (nylon, acrylics)
Sodium Hydroxide	35.8	Bleach, soap, chemicals
Sodium Carbonate	29.9	Chemicals (glass)

Source: Adapted from Ayres (1994: 33)

INCENTIVES AND IMPEDIMENTS TO SUSTAINABLE INDUSTRIAL ECOSYSTEMS

Manufacturing and processing industries, of course, are always keenly interested in improving economic efficiencies, so in one sense they have a vested interest in adopting technologies and techniques that conserve materials and avoid or minimize the need for waste management. Tables 4 and

TABLE 4

Hidden Labor Costs Associated with Pollution Treatment

Time to fill drums or storage tanks with waste
Time to properly label waste drums
Time to move waste drums within the plant
Time to load waste drums for shipment
Time to pump out drums or empty a storage tank
Time to schedule waste transportation
Time to fill out waste manifests
Time to file and record manifests
Time to cut checks for waste disposal and transportation firms
Time for waste information training
Time to approve waste disposal invoices
Time to supervise personnel engaged in waste-related activities
Time to select disposal facilities, transporters, consultants, labs
Time to inspect disposal site or sites
Time to obtain waste samples
Time for learning regulatory compliance requirements
Time for all other waste-related activities

Source: Allen (1995: 267), adapted from Waste Advantage, Inc. (1988).

5 depict the many hidden costs associated with pollution control that could be prevented or reduced through pollution prevention. Yet, even these economic realities have not led industries to develop Type II and III technologies and practices on a consistent basis. In 1983, the National Research Council organized a committee of experts from academia and industry to examine factors related to waste generation and possibilities for its reduction (NRC, 1985). That same year, scientists with the Office of Technology Assessment issued a similar analysis (Office of Technology Assessment, 1983). The National Academy of Science (NAS) industrial ecology colloquium in 1992 made comparative findings (Jelenski, et al., 1992). They identified four incentives for pollution prevention which are presently built into the American regulatory approach and which also apply to Canada:

  1. increasing costs of disposal;

TABLE 5

Fifty Environmental Compliance Activities: Hidden Compliance Costs

1. Emergency planning	26. Scheduling waste shipments
2. Emergency notification	27. Handling rejected waste shipments
3. Community right-to-know reporting	28. Air quality permits
4. Toxic chemical release reporting	29. Approve invoices
5. Waste generation reports	30. Hire consultants
6. Apply for construction permits	31. Local reporting requirements
7. Apply for operating permits	32. Worker safety requirements
8. Compliance scheduling	33. Hazardous substances transportation requirements
9. Conduct testing and monitoring	34. Waste export reports
10. Underground tank requirements	35. Report waste information to management
11. Self-monitoring	36. Mailing waste manifests
12. Waste generator surveys	37. Modeling requirements
13. Record-keeping requirements	38. Selection of laboratories for waste analysis
14. Contingency planning	39. Waste sampling
15. Episode planning	40. Non point-source discharge permits
16. Pollution incident prevention planning	41. Point-source discharge permits
17. Employee waste training	42. Read and understand new regulations
18. Federal inspections	43. Attend regulatory seminars
19. State/provincial inspections	44. Waste cleanup activities
20. Noncompliance reporting	45. Inspect waste disposal sites
21. Fire Marshall inspections	46. Inspect waste transporters
22. Completing waste manifests	47. Inspect laboratories
23. Disposal facility selection	48. Evaluate bids and proposals
24. Waste transporter selection	49. Manifest exception reporting
25. Waste container labeling	50. Supervise waste activities

Source: Allen (1995: 268), adapted from Waste Advantage, Inc. (1988)

2. prospects for incurring substantial financial liability for remedial (clean-up) activities, even where the generator may not
   have been directly responsible for improper disposal;

3. the risk of third-party liability; and

4. the unpredictability of adverse public reaction or opposition.

NAS and the other groups also outlined deficiencies in regulations as they relate to minimizing waste. One problem is that these regulations have allowed for a heavy reliance on land-disposal, a method that poses longer-term environmental risks than others. Cheaper fees—about one-half the cost of incineration—account for much of the tendency to landfill. Another limitation is that industries tend to select proven production technologies over less known alternatives that may result in less pollution. Also, as a production process matures, firms are even less likely to adopt new methods. A third limitation has to do with confidentiality. When a firm finds a cost-effective way to reduce waste, it can better retain competitive advantage by not divulging information to other firms that could adopt the same process without having to invest the resources to figure it out for themselves. Pollution prevention programs attempt to facilitate corporate exchange of at least generic waste reduction information; however, confidentiality remains an inherent limitation.

POLLUTION PREVENTION IN CANADA AND THE UNITED STATES

The rhetoric of pollution prevention is a relatively recent phenomenon that permeates the environmental strategies of governments as well as virtually all related interest groups, even those representing industry. The Responsible Care program organized by the Canadian Chemical Producers Association (CCPA) and its American counterpart, the Chemical Manufacturers Association (CMA), is a notable example of the latter. But a major precedent for the approach has a somewhat longer history. Through their work with the International Joint Commission (IJC), the two countries have agreed to these principles since 1972, at least within the Great Lakes ecosystem, when they signed the Great Lakes Water Quality Agreement. In 1987, the Canadian and American governments amended the bilateral agreement to call for the "virtual elimination" of persistent toxic substances, a goal which IJC has continued to support through a policy to ban or sunset their manufacture, use, and disposal.

GOVERNMENT PROGRAMS

One of the Canadian and Ontario governments' key pollution prevention efforts is waste exchange. The federal program publishes a bimonthly bulletin that lists industrial wastes being sought or offered for re-use across the country. It lists materials under the following eleven categories: solvents; other organic chemicals; oils, fats, and waxes; acids; alkalis; other inorganic chemicals; metals and metal-containing sludges; plastics and rubber products; textiles and leather; wood and paper products; and laboratory materials and miscellaneous. Environment Canada has estimated that the program has facilitated nearly 450,000 tonnes of exchanges. The Ontario program has a staff of three full-time people and facilitates about 100,000 tons of waste exchanges annually (CEC, 1996; EPA, 1994).

The Ontario Ministry of Environment (MOE) also operates a Pollution Prevention Pledge Program, a voluntary initiative that encourages industries to reduce toxic emissions and advertises success stories by giving awards to companies of varying size that establish innovative recycling programs. The agency also has established Memoranda of Understanding with the Canadian Motor Vehicle Manufacturers Association (CMVA) and CCPA regarding pollution prevention. The CMVA agreement has led to 42 projects at 13 facilities that reduce nearly 4,000 tonnes of toxic emissions annually (MOEE, 1995). The agreement with CCPA led in 1992 to reductions of over 2,300 tonnes of emissions involving 306 chemicals (MOEE and CCPA, 1995). The Ontario pollution prevention program has over 150 participating facilities and has been responsible for over 52,000 tonnes of toxic emissions reductions since 1993 (Ontario MOE, 2001c).

The United States government's efforts with pollution prevention began when Congress passed the Pollution Prevention Act of 1990. The law does not give EPA regulatory authority to address the problem, but rather serves as a legislative basis for a preferred hierarchy of environmental management that emphasizes waste reduction at the source as a priority and waste disposal only as a last resort. EPA Pollution Prevention Strategy of 1991 seeks to institutionalize a "pollution prevention ethic" within the agency, particularly with regard to enforcement actions. The federal government does not operate a waste exchange program, but there is a private national network (which also lists information from the Canadian exchanges) as well as four private regional and two state-run programs. The national and regional programs across North America are estimated to have facilitated a total of over nine million tons of industrial waste exchanges since they began operating, some dating back to the mid 1970s.

EPA operates an on-line bulletin known as the Pollution Prevention Information Exchange System, which facilitates voluntary pollution prevention, including hazardous waste minimization (EPA, 1992). Rather than facilitating waste exchanges as in the Canadian program, the EPA database is used by firms to communicate ideas for pollution prevention. The program's chief problem has been the issue of confidentiality. As we saw earlier, there is an inherent contradiction between freely communicating successful pollution prevention strategies and retaining a strategic, cost-efficient position in the market.

INDUSTRY PROGRAMS

CCPA and CMA have been attempting to assist the chemical industry in its efforts to respond to environmental pressures and to act in more environmentally responsible ways. To accomplish this task the two groups have worked in concert to develop an environmental strategy known as Responsible Care. The program requires CCPA and CMA members to agree to a series of guiding principles, management practice codes, and self-evaluations. It includes six codes of conduct with which member firms must comply: community awareness and emergency response; research and development; manufacturing; transportation; distribution; and hazardous waste management. In addition, members are required to conduct annual self-evaluations based on the principles. The hazardous waste management code is designed to address all issues related to hazardous waste, including minimization. Section Two of the code, hazardous waste avoidance — material recovery, states that:

> The underlying principle of hazardous waste management is to avoid the generation of hazardous waste. Recovering the value of materials is preferred to their classification, treatment, and disposal as wastes. The hazardous waste management system shall:

2.1 require consideration of hazardous waste management needs at the initial stages of product research and development or process design and/or modification;

2.2. continually identify waste sources, evaluate opportunities for hazardous waste elimination and reduction, and hazardous material recycle, recovery or re-use, and take appropriate implementation action. (CCPA, 1992: 35)

In fact, industry surveys have found considerable voluntary movement toward hazardous waste reduction, though the trend is very uneven with most activity found in larger firms. In a Carnegie Mellon University survey of 450 American corporations, an impressive 100 per cent of company representatives responded that pollution prevention is an important aspect of business strategy, and nearly 80 per cent believed that it could improve economic performance (Gottlieb, Smith, & Roque, 1995). But private-sector notions of what constitutes pollution prevention are more troubling. Slightly over 50 per cent and 20 per cent, respectively, identified "waste treatment" (including off-site transfers) and "pollution control" as forms of prevention. Forty per cent were unable to accurately recognize "reduction at the source" as being an important environmental strategy. This reflects an on-going battle over definitions, with industrialists insisting they should receive credit for off-site recycling, and with government regulators and environmentalists only recognizing on-site or "closed-loop" recycling, in addition to reduction at the source, as pollution prevention. An external audit conducted in 1985 and 1992 of 29 chemical companies with active pollution prevention programs found that 87 per cent of the firms' waste reduction projects involved process, operations, and equipment changes (Dorfman, et al., 1992). The petrochemical and other large-scale sectors account for most of the present success in corporate pollution prevention. Both Canada and the United States have reported that small and medium-sized firms have much more room for improvement in this regard as compared to larger companies (CEC, 1996).

POLLUTION PREVENTION AND THE ENVIRONMENTAL MOVEMENT

Greenpeace (1992) characterizes most of these programs as examples of "greenwashing" that are intended to repair industry's image as a major polluter. Regarding Responsible Care, they first criticize the lack of public access to the annual self-evaluations of CCPA and CMA members. Second, they see no criteria for what constitutes a safe product. Related to this point is the organizations' failure to publicly recognize the inherent toxicity of their business, even when they do manage to handle their feedstocks, products, and wastes appropriately. This is particularly the case with regard to the chemical industry. Third, they argue the waste minimization code amounts more to end-of-pipe measures than prevention (Greenpeace, 1992). Another criticism of American pollution prevention efforts to date is that many of the industry-reported chemical reductions are due to either changes in emission estimation procedures or plant closings (Allen, 1995).

Regarding individual corporate programs, Greenpeace points out the numerous hazardous waste-related accidents many companies have caused, contaminating surface waters and underground aquifers across North America and the world. These types of accidents have continued to occur, they argue, despite the chemical industry's involvement in the Responsible Care program. Great Lakes United, a binational environmental organization, and Pollution Probe, a Canadian anti-toxics group, have both called for "zero discharge" as the only sensible long-term goal for industries and regulatory agencies. Both groups also criticize Canada and the United States for failing to implement the provisions of the Great Lakes Water Quality Agreement.

THE INTERNATIONAL JOINT COMMISSION AND "VIRTUAL ELIMINATION"

Hazardous waste regulation has come a long way during the 25 years of its evolution as formal policy. But, although the Great Lakes Water Quality Agreement between Canada and the United States is now 25 years old, neither country has made much progress on its implementation. Also, by signing the 1987 amendments to the agreement, the two countries agreed to "virtually eliminate" persistent toxic substances (PTSs) through "a comprehensive, binational program to lessen the uses of, and exposure to persistent toxic chemicals found in the Great Lakes environment" (Environment Canada and EPA, 1996: 3). PTSs are defined as any chemical with a half-life greater than eight weeks or that bioaccumulates in living tissue.

The International Joint Commission (IJC), originally established in 1909, has become increasingly involved in assisting Canada and the United States with boundary water issues (Bloomfield & Fitzgerald, 1958; Tupper & Bailey, 1967), up to and including the implementation of the Great Lakes Water Quality Agreement of 1972 (Morchain, 1973). The binational agency has also commented on the importance of hazardous waste issues relative to the strategy for virtual elimination of PTSs. A 1994 IJC Virtual Elimination Task Force report concluded:

> The assessment and containment/remediation of hazardous waste sites must be considered in a strategy for virtual elimination of persistent toxic substances [PTSs] from the Great Lakes Basin Ecosystem.
>
> Existing land disposal methods cannot guarantee protection of groundwater resources in the long run. Once an aquifer has been contaminated by PTSs, the resource is, for most intents and purposes, lost for generations.
>
> Synthetic organic chemicals, particularly chlorinated organics, are a likely source for many of the chemically induced reproductive failures, birth defects and abnormalities in wildlife and possibly humans. These compounds are prevalent in hazardous waste sites, and chlorinated organics are a part of everyday life, not only for industry but for individuals as well. If we cannot control the fate of these chemicals, then it is time to assess how essential they are to a healthy and productive life, essentially to ask, do their benefits outweigh the risks? (IJC, 1994: vii)

IJC has also determined that both Canada and the United States currently have sufficient legal authority to implement the virtual elimination strategy. The Canadian Environmental Protection Act (CEPA) and the American Toxic Substances Control Act (TSCA) give regulatory agencies the power to severely restrict and even ban the use and disposal of particular chemicals. Yet IJC's Virtual Elimination Task Force has concluded that there is:

> a broad consensus that the governments have not fully acted on their authority. The implementation of laws in the United

States and Canada has been a failure, from the standpoint of developing a comprehensive and effective virtual elimination strategy. Despite progress that has resulted from existing laws, goals such as zero discharge have been overlooked and practically forgotten. TSCA has become, at best, a tool to screen the introduction of new chemicals. It has only been used to limit the use and manufacture of PCBs. CEPA has been incredibly slow and cumbersome, and seemingly ineffective. (IJC, 1993: 43)

More recently, the Canadian Commissioner of the Environment and Sustainable Development, Office of the Auditor General has issued findings that indicate this lack of progress continues to the present. In her 2002 report, Commissioner Gélinas reported that the federal government:

still has not completed the scientific assessment process for all the substances on its own priority lists; still has not imposed on major sources of emissions the controls needed to reduce the release of toxic substances into our air and water; and still does not know whether the tools it has to manage toxic substances actually reduce the risk to Canadians. (Office of the Auditor General of Canada 2002: 1)

In response to these kinds of criticisms, Canada and the United States developed a draft *Strategy for the Virtual Elimination of Persistent Toxic Substances in the Great Lakes Basin* in 1996. Both countries agree to "seek" 50 to 90 per cent reductions in the use, generation, or release of 13 Level I Substances by at least the year 2005. In 1985, IJC's Great Lakes Water Quality Board identified 11 of these as the most critical to address because of their toxic and bioaccumulative properties and their persistence in the Great Lakes environment. Both governments also commit to "promote prevention and reduced releases" of sixteen other Level II Substances (Environment Canada and EPA, 1996: 7). The strategy follows the framework outlined in *Agenda 21: A Global Action Plan for the 21st Century*, adopted at the 1992 United Nations Conference on Environment and Development. Both countries and other nations committed, "where appropriate," to:

undertake concerted activities to reduce risks for toxic chemicals, taking into account the entire lifecycle of the chemicals.
These activities could encompass both regulatory and non-
regulatory measures, such as promotion of the use of cleaner
products and technologies; emission inventories; product
labeling; use limitations; economic incentives; and the phasing
out or banning of toxic chemicals that pose an unreasonable
and otherwise unmanageable risk to human health and the
environment, including those that are toxic, persistent and
bioaccumulative and whose use cannot be adequately controlled. (Environment Canada and EPA, 1996: 3)

The American and Canadian governments are making important
progress in the implementation of virtual elimination of PTSs by com-
mitting to specific reductions in 12 of the more dangerous ones. Yet, in
relation to a petrochemical industry that produces approximately 14,000
separate chemical feedstocks and products, this represents a relatively small
step. Both countries would also seem to have considerable flexibility in the
Agenda 21 provisions on toxic substances, given that the most stringent
strategies (chemical bans and clean technology) are only examples among
others like product labeling and emission inventories. The phase out of
PTSs is a critical component of an overall strategy for advancing to sustainable Type II and III industrial ecosystems that rely more on pollution
prevention than waste treatment and disposal. These kinds of approaches
to environmental management are also necessary pre-conditions to achieving fairness and justice (particularly intergenerational equity) with regard
to industrial facilities of all kinds, including and especially hazardous waste
facilities.

Conclusion

This chapter has explored many of the various problems associated with
hazardous waste. The inequitable distribution of hazardous waste facilities,
described conceptually in Chapters 1 and 2, has been demonstrated empirically and associated with race and class. The debate over the appropriate
geographic scale to measure the relationships between race, class, and
waste notwithstanding, communities that are targeted for new hazardous

waste facilities often feel threatened by the risks and other burdens associated with such land uses. The problem of fairness figures prominently in disputes over facility siting, particularly when local residents are racial minorities or low income (social equity). Other dimensions of equity and justice come into play as well, such as when there is a spatial disjoint between benefits and burdens (geographic equity) or when an area is disproportionately burdened by numerous industrial hazards (cumulative equity). Intergenerational equity, the balancing of present economic benefits and future environmental burdens is yet another dimension of the problem. Procedural equity is required to ensure that all voices are heard in hazardous waste decision-making, including the communities targeted for new facilities.

Structural limitations of hazardous waste laws and regulations, described in Chapter 1, also contribute to environmental injustice. Industries in Canada and the United States are not required to limit their generation of toxic wastes, regardless of the quantity or severity of these substances. Instead, cradle-to-grave management systems are imposed, but they come into effect only after the waste has already been generated. The second half of the present chapter has demonstrated the difficulties and opportunities associated with limiting the emission of pollutants within production. Federal, provincial, and state governments operate voluntary pollution prevention programs to facilitate recycling and reduction, but no public authority in either country can mandate these kinds of activities. Many in the scientific and engineering communities have pointed to the need for research and development to support technological advances that could help reduce pollution through production design changes that approximate Type III industrial ecosystems. Already, there are indications that wastes contaminated with metals could be recycled about as economically as exploiting virgin ores. Process changes within the chemicals industry could achieve still further progress toward pollution prevention.

Given the nature of environmental injustice in its many distributive, procedural, and structural forms, how should we interpret hazardous waste facility siting? Chapters 4 and 5 in Part II review ten commercial hazardous waste facility siting cases in two regions on the Canada-United States border. Chapter 4 focuses on the Niagara region on the New York-Ontario border, and Chapter 5 examines the Detroit and Sarnia areas on the Michigan-Ontario border. The cases reveal a number of interesting issues related to environmental equity and justice. Stakeholders on varying sides of the disputes are each shown to have their own personal interests and corresponding conceptions of fairness. The result is a complex mix of competing arguments and evidence from different perspectives with which facility siting review boards must contend in order to make final decisions that are not only fair, but also practical. The cases presented in Part II show that often this is quite a difficult balancing act, particularly given the indeterminacies of law when applied to locally contingent circumstances. Moreover, different stakeholders bring widely ranging expectations of fairness, equity, and justice to facility siting proceedings.

Note

1. Minority population was defined as all persons except non-Hispanic whites.

The Niagara Region, Detroit, and Sarnia

Introduction

The Great Lakes Region on the Canada-United States border is a highly industrial area encompassing one province (Ontario) and eight states (Illinois, Indiana, Michigan, Minnesota, New York, Ohio, Pennsylvania, and Wisconsin) as shown in Figure 12 (see p. 124). According to the International Joint Commission (IJC, 1994), there are 4,503 hazardous waste sites in the region, 98 per cent (4,421) of which are located in the United States, 2 per cent (82) of which are located in Canada, and 94 per cent (4,249) of which are closed and no longer accepting new waste (see Figure 13, p. 130). I conducted the field work for this study in two partly industrial regions within the Great Lakes area: the Niagara region on the New York-Ontario border and the Detroit and Sarnia communities on the Michigan-Ontario border. As shown in Figure 13, Detroit and Niagara Falls, New York have among the highest number of hazardous waste sites per square mile (over 0.20) found in the Great Lakes region. The Canadian portions of both study regions have much lower concentrations of facilities. Lambton County, Ontario (including the Sarnia area) has 0.01 to 0.05 hazardous waste sites per square mile and the Regional Municipality of Niagara, Ontario has less than 0.01. The lower density of sites in Ontario, as compared to the Great Lakes states in the United States, stands in contrast to the province's rather heavy annual discharge of industrial pollution, ranked first in Canada and third in North America (CEC, 2002).

FIGURE 12

The Great Lakes Basin

The high degree of present and historic industrial activity in the Great Lakes area generally and in the Niagara and Detroit/Sarnia regions specifically is an obvious advantage for an analysis of hazardous waste management. Also, both study regions include presently operating or proposed off-site treatment, storage, or disposal facility (TSDF) sites on both sides of the international border. The Niagara region is heavily industrialized along both sides of the Niagara River frontier, especially in Niagara Falls, New York where proposals were advanced for expanding two hazardous waste facilities in the early 1990s. Across the river in Niagara, Ontario, the Ontario Waste Management Corporation (OWMC) attempted to site a new facility in two separate communities during the 1980s and early 1990s.

Ontario's only currently operating commercial hazardous waste landfill and incinerator is located just outside of Sarnia where there are numerous petrochemical facilities and where a proposed additional incinerator was to be located in the early 1990s. Across the international border in the Detroit, Michigan area, six separate proposals for new hazardous waste facilities were developed for construction and operation in various locations of the

"Motor City" during the 1980s and early 1990s. Together, these ten cases comprise the sample of data used to investigate the relationships between hazardous waste facilities and environmental justice in Canada and the United States (see Table 6).[1]

The methodology employed in Part II draws from various research techniques commonly used in studies of law and society. Blacksell, et al.(1986) have pointed to the importance of the geographical imagination on legal studies as a way of understanding the connections between law and society in terms of spatial patterns and processes. Blomley (1989, 1994) and Clark (1985, 1986, and 1989) have both used legal and quasi-legal case studies involving interjurisdictional conflicts (among communities and between various levels of government) in Canada, the United States, and other countries to examine the politics of legal interpretation. Lake and Johns (1990) have applied this approach to the analysis of hazardous waste facility siting in the United States and its relationship to environmental law. Following a similar approach, I use an interpretive case study method (Lijphart, 1971) to review and compare Canadian and American facility siting disputes with an emphasis on their local, regional, and national settings (Eckstein, 1963).

For each of the ten facility siting cases, I reviewed government files including hearing transcripts, arguments, and evidence submitted by parties to the proceedings as well as government agency decisions in order to document the power struggles reflected in the events. I also conducted interviews with community stakeholders, public officials at the state/provincial and local levels, and industry representatives to "ground truth" the information elicited from the government case files and data. The combined information provides a rich body of evidence from which to analyze the environmental justice implications of hazardous waste facilities from a variety of points of view within and across communities on both the American and Canadian sides of the Great Lakes Region.

While the cases are not necessarily representative of all such cases in Canada or the United States, or even of the Great Lakes Region, they do reveal noteworthy issues with each country's approach to hazardous waste management. The ten cases also reflect diversity in proposed facility types such as, for example, expansions of existing facilities as well as new developments at "greenfield" sites; corporate-sponsored and also government-sponsored projects; small designs with only one facility component (e.g., a treatment facility) as well as large developments with as many

TABLE 6

Hazardous Waste Facility Siting Disputes
in the Niagara, Sarnia, and Detroit Areas

Facility	Community	Pre-Existing Site	Facility Type
CECOS 6/87-3/90	Niagara Falls, NY (urban)	HW Landfill	Landfills
CWM 4/89-11/89 6/90-6/93	Lewiston, NY (suburban)	HW Landfill	Landfill; Incinerator
OWMC 1/80-11/81 11/81-2/95	Niagara Peninsula, ON (agricultural)	Greenfields	Landfill; Incinerator; Solidification; Treatment
Laidlaw 12/89-10/93	Moore, ON (agricultural)	HW Landfill; Incinerator	Incinerator
EMS 6/82-10/82	Sumpter, MI (suburban)	Municipal Landfill	Landfill
ERES 9/82-12/82	Pontiac, MI (suburban)	Municipal Landfill	Incinerator
Stablex 12/82-9/83	Groveland, MI (suburban)	Quarry	Landfill
NCS 12/87-5/88	Detroit, MI (urban)	Treatment Facility	Treatment
City Env. 2/89-9/89	Detroit, MI (urban)	Municipal Incinerator	Treatment
EDS 8/90-2/01	Romulus, MI (suburban)	Greenfield	Underground Injection

as four facility components at one location (e.g., a landfill, incinerator, treatment facility, and solidification plant); and "successfully" and unsuccessfully sited facilities. Also, the affected communities varied from case to case in terms of whether they were urban or rural and also in the racial and socioeconomic characteristics of residents (e.g., white working-class and middle-class rural and urban communities; First Nations reservations;

Facility	Opposition	Concerns	Outcome
CECOS 6/87-3/90	City; County; Local Group; Ontario Govt.	Cumulative and Spatial Equity; Hydrogeology	Denied
CWM 4/89-11/89 6/90-6/93	City; County; School Board; Local Group; Ontario Govt.	Cumulative & Spatial Equity; Hydrogeology	Landfills Approved & Built; Incin. Withdrawn
OWMC 1/80-11/81 11/81-2/95	City; Regional Municipality; Local Group; Laidlaw	Spatial Equity; Intrusion on Private Sector	Denied
Laidlaw 12/89-10/93	Local Groups; Walpole Island	Cumulative & Spatial Equity	Withdrawn
EMS 6/82-10/82	Township	Hydrogeology	Denied
ERES 9/82-12/82	Township; School Board	Hydrogeology & Proponent	Denied
Stablex 12/82-9/83	Township	Hydrogeology & Design	Denied
NCS 12/87-5/88	Local Group	Cumulative Equity	Approved; Never Built
City Env. 2/89-9/89	Unorganized Residents	Cumulative Equity	Approved; Never Built
EDS 8/90-2/01	City (After Initial support)	Zoning; Spatial Equity	Built; Later Approved

urban African American neighborhoods). Moreover, their location on the Canada-United States border makes the cases interesting not only in terms of comparison with one another, but also with respect to national differences, cross-boundary disputes and related matters.

Note

1. This collection of ten cases constitutes all of the formally proposed facility siting cases in the Niagara and Detroit-Windsor/Sarnia regions for which public hearings were conducted since the early 1980s when facility siting boards and official hearing proceedings were instituted in Michigan, New York, and Ontario.

4
The Niagara Region

Introduction

The Niagara Region on the Canada-United States border has been the setting for a number of extraordinary industrial-environmental conflicts, particularly with respect to hazardous waste. As discussed in Chapter 2, the Love Canal contamination in Niagara Falls, New York transformed the way North Americans think about hazardous waste and forced major environmental policy changes. But Love Canal is by no means the only hazardous waste issue facing the Niagara region. This is especially true of the New York side of the border area which has been dominated by chemical sector production and waste disposal dating back to large wartime efforts and strong early postwar growth. This local industrial history has surfaced in several other contamination discoveries that have been classified as Superfund cleanup sites.

In all, there are 132 contaminated sites in Niagara County, New York (Olsen, 1991, 1995), among the highest densities of inactive facilities in the Great Lakes basin, as shown in Figure 13 (NY DEC, 2000). Further, the national and state-wide reforms originally conceived with Niagara Falls in mind have come back full circle, forcing the community to serve as a host for wastes from throughout North America so that production may continue unabated however badly industry fails to internalize its own noxious by-products. Capacity assurance policies, for example, have led state environmental officials and private waste management firms to seek approval for expansions of existing facilities in Niagara County repeatedly throughout the 1980s and 1990s. This irony has been at the heart of recent efforts to remediate not only contaminated sites, but also the geographic inequity of being the only community in the state targeted for new com-

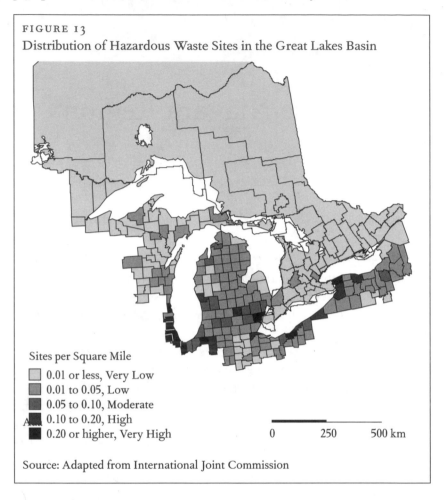

FIGURE 13

Distribution of Hazardous Waste Sites in the Great Lakes Basin

Sites per Square Mile

☐ 0.01 or less, Very Low
☐ 0.01 to 0.05, Low
☐ 0.05 to 0.10, Moderate
☐ 0.10 to 0.20, High
☐ 0.20 or higher, Very High

0   250   500 km

Source: Adapted from International Joint Commission

mercial hazardous waste capacity; Niagara County is also the single jurisdiction in the state with an active commercial hazardous waste landfill despite the relatively even spatial distribution of hazardous waste genera-tion in New York (NY DEC, 1989, 1995). This issue is discussed further in the last section of this chapter. The Chemical Waste Management (CWM) facility has its own interesting history as the site of significant Manhattan Project activities from World War II which left radioactive wastes that are still on-site.[1]

In many respects, the industrial history of Ontario's Niagara region is very similar to that of neighboring New York State. The municipalities of Niagara Falls in New York and Ontario take full advantage of the tourism benefits of the waterfalls and have developed highly commercial riverfront districts (Pitegoff, 1991). Also, both regions exploit hydroelectricity from the Falls and have built a number of industries along the river. In addition, each side has rural, largely agricultural hinterlands. It is in these outlying areas that Niagara, Ontario's experience with hazardous waste has become most pronounced. The Niagara peninsula communities of South Cayuga and West Lincoln were the sites of a 15-year dispute over attempts to build a large integrated hazardous waste facility with a landfill, incinerator, and physical/chemical treatment capacity on previously agricultural and presently undeveloped land. Rural agricultural communities seem to be unlikely candidates for such a development, but the region's proximity to industrial waste generators in the Hamilton and Toronto areas, as well as its thick clay deposits, made it a prime choice in the eyes of the provincial government, specifically the Ontario Waste Management Corporation (OWMC).

An additional historical contingency is that the proposed facility site was near a small and seemingly harmless light industrial district that was found to be the source of a serious PCB contamination. By the time it was discovered in 1985, the toxic plume had already migrated down to the bedrock and had entered an underground aquifer that served as a drinking water source for the nearby town of Smithville (Ketcheson, 1995; O'Neill, 1995; Smithville Phase IV Bedrock Remediation Program, 1995). Residents were forced to abandon their now useless water system, and the province paid for a new one that pumps water from Lake Ontario (Macdonald, 1991; Packham, 1995). Area citizens' experiences with this incident, as well as basic fairness issues related to becoming a provincial (and even continental) sink for industrial sources, influenced local opposition to the disposal facility in much the same way as occurred in Niagara, New York in response to the Love Canal tragedy.

The similarities and differences between the two halves of this international region make it an interesting point of comparison to uncover community resistance to hazardous waste and its environmental justice implications. Not only does the area offer a binational view, it also provides a regional and local setting in which to explore the relationships between communities targeted for waste disposal and government agencies at the provincial/state or federal levels. Thus, this chapter proceeds with a discussion of hazardous waste and facility siting policies in Ontario and New York with a review of facility siting case studies from both sides of the Niagara region. Hearing transcripts, arguments, and evidence submitted by parties to the proceedings, siting board decisions, and interviews with stakeholders are used to document the community power struggles reflected in these quasi-judicial cases. I trace the developments and analyze them in terms of environmental justice considerations such as distributive and procedural equity, as well as the structural and historical dimensions of hazardous waste management in Niagara.

Following a discussion of hazardous waste facility siting laws in New York and Ontario and disputes over particular locational decisions within the Niagara region, the cases are then analyzed in terms of three critical factors: defining facility need, deciding facility size and type, and promoting fairness in facility siting. Stakeholder groups had significant differences of opinion on these issues, differences which shaped the disputes in various ways. The first two issues (facility need and facility size/type) were to a large degree technical matters that led parties to the proceedings to argue over projections and predictions about waste generation rates and risk assessments, among other things. The third issue (fairness) was related to the first two in the sense that the technical matters structured the distributions of benefits and burdens associated with hazardous waste. Whether a facility is needed and, if so, how large and of what type it should be are important questions that formed much of the basis for how stakeholders viewed the overall fairness of the proposals. Ultimately, however, differences of opinion over fairness issues had to do with whether one's loyalties were tied to the promotion of "good" government, a strong economy, community concerns, or some variation of one or more of these different, yet sometimes overlapping, concerns.

Hazardous Waste Facility Siting in New York

Facility siting policies and practices have varied within the Niagara region, especially, of course, along the international border. In New York, hazardous waste siting is handled pursuant to the state Environmental Conservation Law (ECL) of 1987, as amended (Sections 27-1102, 27-1103, and 27-1105). Among other things, the law requires a hearing with an administrative law judge to run the process and a siting board that makes a final recommendation to approve or deny. The ultimate decision rests with the State Commissioner of the Department of Environmental Conservation (DEC). New York State has also attempted to use a public authority, the

Environmental Facilities Corporation (EFC), to site a hazardous waste incinerator in Cayuga County in the central portion of the state, though the proposal was dropped in 1983 after three years of planning. Intense local opposition and problems securing ownership of the desired property caused DEC to shift to a regulatory approach relying on private sector proposals and pre-emption of local control under the authority of ECL, as amended in 1987 (Heiman, 1990; Rabe, 1994).

NEW YORK'S "GEOGRAPHIC EQUITY" POLICY

In part, the 1987 amendments — Section 27-1102(2)(f) — required DEC to develop a comprehensive hazardous waste facility siting plan that would promote "equitable geographic distribution," due to concerns about Niagara County's disproportionate share of disposal capacity and contaminated sites in need of cleanup. DEC developed drafts of the facility siting plan for public comment in June 1988 and August 1989 but has not produced a final plan or implemented any of its intended provisions (Olsen, 1991, 1995). This lack of action became a central issue for Niagara area voters in the 1990 campaign for state governor when the region's Republican State Senator Daly publicly criticized then Governor Cuomo for failing to deal with the problem (Glynn, 1990). The two politicians aired their views in letters mailed to all Niagara County residents and in op-ed pieces in the *Buffalo News* (Daly, 1990; Murray, 1990).

THE CHEMICAL WASTE MANAGEMENT (CWM) PROPOSALS

The conflict between Cuomo and Daly never resolved the thorny question of how to interpret (and thus make determinate) the geographic equity provisions of ECL as a matter of policy, but it did raise the political stakes of individual facility siting cases in Niagara. These included Chemical Waste Management's (CWM) June 1990 proposal to build two hazardous waste incinerators with a total capacity of 100,000 tons per year at their existing landfill site in Lewiston, New York just north of Niagara Falls (Gerrard, 1994). At the time, Lewiston was a small community of approximately 15,000 people with a mostly white population (98.9 per cent) and a higher than average median household income ($40,327) as compared to the State of New York overall ($32,965), according to the 1990 census. In June 1993, three years later, CWM rescinded its proposal after fierce public opposition in the nearby local communities of Lewiston and Porter.[2] In a negotiated agreement, the community agreed not to object to a 47.1-acre landfill expansion if CWM would scrap its incinerator plans for at least ten years, even though the same landfill had as recently as November 1989 received approval for another 22-acre expansion (New York State Department of Environmental Conservation, October 1989; New York State Facility Siting Board, November 1989).

For the residents of Niagara County, New York generally, and the Town of Lewiston especially, the prospect of a hazardous waste incinerator clearly was seen as more of a threat than the expansion of the existing CWM landfill. After all, a landfill is only open for a given period of time and then capped and closed, whereas an incinerator operates for an indefinite period of time. But this difference in reaction to a landfill versus an incinerator is not evidence of a benign acceptance of landfills. In the earliest CWM case, the 1989 22-acre landfill expansion, party status was denied to all opposition groups who applied on the basis that their stated issues were neither "significant" nor "substantial" (New York State Facility Siting Board, July 1989). The Town of Lewiston and Niagara County both sought to participate in the proceedings because of concerns about the risks from increased truck traffic caused by the facility expansion. The Lewiston-Porter School District opposed the facility because of its close proximity to the site. The Province of Ontario sought party status because of concerns that CWM's proposed landfill design would be potentially insufficient in preventing surface runoff to, and thus contamination of, nearby streams that feed into the Niagara River and from there, Lake Ontario.

Beginning in 1990, when groups opposed to CWM's incinerator proposal were faced with essentially a choice between an incinerator or yet another expansion of the existing landfill, they had to recognize certain realities. Given their most recent experience with opposing a CWM landfill expansion (in 1989) as well as the 1990 siting board denial of a request to expand the existing nearby CECOS hazardous waste landfill (discussed in the next section), intervenor groups had limited options. In the context of the state's interest in maintaining capacity assurance for hazardous waste disposal, there seemed to be no way that it would deny a request to expand what has become New York's only operating commercial hazardous waste landfill now that the CECOS landfill is closed (Dolen, 1996). Besides, there were major concerns that if a negotiated agreement was not reached, the community might end up with both an incinerator and landfill expansion.

THE CECOS PROPOSAL

In June 1987, prior to the CWM siting controversies, CECOS International, a hazardous waste landfill operator in nearby Niagara Falls, New York, requested a 20-acre expansion to its existing 385-acre site. At the time, Niagara Falls, New York had a population of just over 61,000 people with a mostly white population (82.1 per cent white; 15.4 per cent black; 2.5 per cent other). Unlike Lewiston, Niagara Falls had a lower median household income ($20,641) as compared to the state-wide average ($32,965), according to the 1990 census. In March 1990 the siting board denied the permit, after an initial approval in August 1989, because of poor hydrogeology and lack of short-term need. Interestingly, the risk assessment score changed from 196.2 in the first decision to 213.0 in the final decision, just under and then over the "scientific" threshold of 200.0. The initial decision had to be reexamined to allow for additional hearings based on changes in DEC's Draft Siting Plan which were also made in August 1989. While the Initial Draft Siting Plan completed in May 1988 projected that the state would require capacity for about 2.2 million tons of landfilled hazardous wastes over the next 20 years (NY DEC, August 1989), the Revised Draft Siting Plan projected less than half of that (931,000 tons). Thus, the basic question of whether the CECOS facility was needed at all became an open question (Pearlstein, 1990).

Residents of the LaSalle neighborhood (also the home of Love Canal) where the CECOS facility is located bitterly fought the project through a local citizens' group known as LaSalle and Niagara Demand (LAND). LAND joined a consolidated party of opposition groups known as "Citizens Organizations" to act as a formal "intervening" party to the proceedings (Intervenor Concerned Citizens Organization, 1988).[3] The City of Niagara Falls became an intervenor group because the portion of the existing facility being proposed for expansion was within its city limits. The City consolidated with the County of Niagara and the Niagara County Board of Health as one intervenor group (City of Niagara Falls, et al. 1989). The Province of Ontario became an official party to the proceedings as an intervening party as well because of its own concerns about the facility's potential to leach into the Niagara River and ultimately into Lake Ontario (Terris and Hecker 1988). In fact, the existing landfill was already leaking (New York State Facility Siting Board, December 1993; Dickey, 1995; Tarnawskyj, 1995).

Facility Siting and The Ontario Waste Management Corporation

Facility siting in Ontario is subject to similar regulatory provisions as found in New York, though policy implementation has taken a very different form. Procedurally, siting decisions are made on the basis of an initial review by what was at the time the Ontario Ministry of Environment and Energy (MOEE) and an administrative hearing before the Ontario Environmental Assessment Board (EAB) pursuant to the Ontario Environmental Protection Act (OEPA) and the Environmental Assessment Act, among other provincial statutes. Proposed expansions of the Laidlaw landfill near Sarnia, Ontario's only existing commercial hazardous waste facility (other than transfer stations), have been handled similarly to those in New York. The Sarnia facility, which is now owned by Safety-Kleen, has the highest volume of toxic discharges and transfers of toxic materials in Canada and is ranked ninth in North America (CEC, 2002). Laidlaw sold its waste management services and merged its hazardous waste services with Rollins Environmental in the late 1990s. What these cases had in common was that they were all proposed by private industry and reviewed by government-appointed review boards. But the province has also pursued a public-sector approach to siting in one and then another community on the Niagara peninsula. OWMC's first choice was the town of West Cayuga, about ten kilometers west of the Regional Municipality of Niagara. The agency's final selection was West Lincoln Township in the Regional Municipality of Niagara, a largely white (94 per cent) jurisdiction with a population that was just under 400,000 people and with a median household income of $40,050, as compared to the Ontario average of $44,432, according to the 1991 Canadian Census.

The South Cayuga Proposal

From 1980 until 1995, Ontario hazardous waste policy and politics focused on the Ontario Waste Management Corporation (OWMC), which was at the time a provincial crown corporation created to site, build, and operate a 63-acre hazardous waste landfill, incinerator, and treatment facility with a capacity of 300,000 tonnes per year. OWMC's first siting proposal, announced in 1980, was in the Niagara peninsula town of South Cayuga. The choice was made for the practical reason that the province already owned the land. This fact and the Ministry of Environment's decision to waive the

Ontario Environmental Assessment Act requirement for an environmental assessment were met with immediate skepticism by area residents. They were not swayed by OWMC's chair, Dr. Donald Chant, who argued that the facility was too urgently needed to wait for the completion of an environmental assessment. Chant had been chosen for the position because of his academic credentials as a professor of zoology at University of Toronto and his environmental record as the founder and former chair of Pollution Probe. These initial decisions, however, began eating away at his and OWMC's badly needed credibility.

While no formal environmental assessment was to be conducted for the South Cayuga site pursuant to the Environmental Assessment Act, Chant insisted that public hearings and a series of environmental studies would be carried out pursuant to the Ontario Environmental Protection Act. A full environmental assessment would have required an analysis of alternatives to the project, including other possible locations. But the South Cayuga studies did review the hydrogeology and flood histories of the location. The decision proved to be a critical one: in November 1981 OWMC announced that it would reject the site because of results indicating a high potential for flooding and ground water contamination. Chant also chose this time to initiate a complex siting process to find an environmentally acceptable location. This time, a formal environmental assessment and public review process would be carried out pursuant to the Consolidated Hearings Act, in addition to several other statutes.

THE SEARCH FOR A "SUITABLE" LOCATION

The post-Cayuga site selection process ostensibly began with consideration of all areas of the province as potential host communities. But in January 1983, OWMC announced that it had narrowed its search to the Golden Horseshoe region, which stretches from the Toronto area westward around Lake Ontario and east and south to the Niagara peninsula. One of the justifications for this decision was that 70 per cent of the province's hazardous waste is generated there, from industries concentrated in Toronto, Hamilton, and Niagara Falls. By minimizing the distance from waste generators to waste facilities, the risk of accidents in transport would be minimized. This would also serve to hold down transport costs, an important factor to OWMC since one of its central goals was to "minimize financial cost to OWMC and to the people of Ontario" (EAB, 1994).

FIGURE 14
OWMC Hydrogeology Mapping

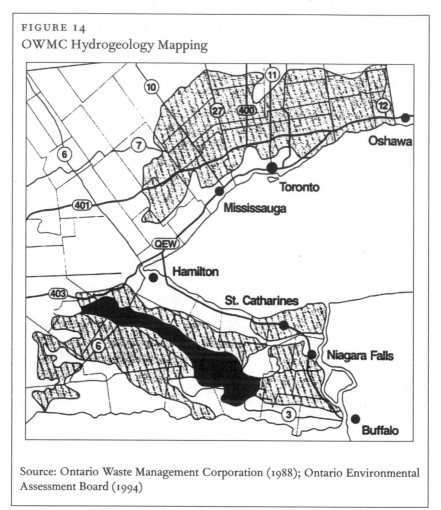

Source: Ontario Waste Management Corporation (1988); Ontario Environmental Assessment Board (1994)

The other justification was that the Golden Horseshoe area was well suited for a landfill because of its naturally thick clay deposits, a geological feature that would inhibit underground leaching. This commitment to "natural containment" was a part of OWMC's other goals of minimizing "risk to human health" and "impact to the environment" (EAB, 1994). OWMC produced a map that depicted the most hydrogeologically suitable locations for the facility (see Figure 14). The most ideal area (Zone 1) is highlighted in black and the second best areas (Zone 2) are shaded in grey, the difference in the two zones having to do with the average depth and permeability of natural deposits of clay. The hydrogeology in Zone 2 was

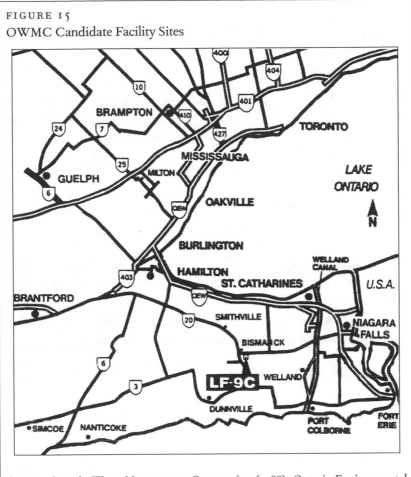

FIGURE 15
OWMC Candidate Facility Sites

Source: Ontario Waste Management Corporation (1988); Ontario Environmental
Assessment Board (1994)

determined to be more variable than Zone 1 on average, but site-specific
soil conditions within both areas were thought to be potentially suitable.

The next phase of the process was to identify several possible specific
locations within the Golden Horseshoe area based on the hydrogeological mapping. OWMC began this task in January 1983 and announced 20
candidate areas in May. After nearly a full year of analysis, the list was
narrowed to eight sites in March 1984 (see Figure 15). OWMC then spent
the 18 months deciding which of the eight options would be its pick. Only
two of the eight sites were situated in Zone 1, and both are in the Township

of West Lincoln, so municipal and regional-municipal government officials were not terribly surprised by OWMC's September 1985 announcement that West Lincoln was its preferred location, LF-9C specifically (Boggs, 1995; Packham, 1995). OWMC spent the next few years developing an environmental assessment and preparing for public hearings before the Ontario Environmental Assessment Board (EAB). Meanwhile, their opponents prepared themselves to fight the facility. Aside from OWMC, there were 17 parties to the hearing, three of whom were full-time members that participated throughout the rest of the siting process — Ontario's Ministry of Environment and Energy (MOEE), a group of three local opposition groups (the so called Tri-parties), and Laidlaw Environmental Services.

LOCAL OPPOSITION IN WEST LINCOLN

MOEE fully supported the OWMC decision and the environmental assessment with no reservations, but local groups disagreed vehemently. The Tri-parties — the Ontario Toxic Waste Research Coalition, The Township of West Lincoln, and the Regional Municipality of Niagara — represented community and environmental interests and opposed the facility for reasons of public health and environmental concerns about the mostly agricultural West Lincoln area. They also objected for reasons of equity that it would be unfair to ask a quiet agricultural community to bear the burden of such a large facility for the benefit of industries in Toronto, Hamilton, Niagara Falls, and other North American jurisdictions (Boggs, 1995; Packham, 1995). Laidlaw Environmental Services Corporation also opposed the facility, not because of environmental concerns, but rather on the basis that hazardous waste management should be market driven rather than governmentally controlled (Rombough, 1994). This perspective was also reflected in Laidlaw's December 1989 announcement that it would seek approval to build its own rotary kiln incinerator to complement an existing liquid hazardous waste incinerator and landfill near Sarnia, Ontario. This development came just as the OWMC hearing was about to start.

THE ENVIRONMENTAL ASSESSMENT

OWMC released its environmental assessment in November 1988 seeking approval to build and operate an integrated hazardous waste facility consisting of an incinerator, physical/chemical treatment plant, solidification plant, and landfill at its preferred location in West Lincoln Township. The document was 22 volumes and about 7,000 pages in length. The estimated total development cost (including planning and construction) was $500 million, but the province had already spent nearly $100 million and was nowhere near having the necessary approvals to even begin construction, suggesting early on that cost overruns would be likely. The environmental assessment justified the proposal on the need for off-site disposal capacity and reviewed alternatives (OWMC, 1988). In this regard, it also explained and evaluated OWMC's site selection choice. The environmental assessment as well as several government and consultant reports comprised OWMC's evidence to support the project in the ensuing public hearings before EAB. Each of the intervenor groups presented their own evidence and arguments as well. The hearing took over three years to complete, beginning in February 1990 and ending in September 1993. By the time it was over, OWMC had spent over $140 million on its siting efforts (Regional Municipality of Niagara, 1994).

The facility would have had a total annual capacity of 300,000 tonnes, with the first phase being about half that size. Several legal requirements were necessary to achieve such a reality, including 11 separate statutory approvals. The first was pursuant to EAA Section 5(1)(a) and Sections 12(2)(c), (d), and (e) which require an EAB approval for the project as defined in an environmental assessment and consistent with terms and conditions negotiated with MOEE, as Ontario's environmental regulatory agency (EAB, 1994). For these requirements, OWMC sought approval for the physical/chemical treatment and solidification plants with an annual capacity of 240,000 tonnes, two incinerators with a total annual capacity of approximately 60,000 tonnes, and a landfill for storage of treatment and incineration residuals. Pursuant to OEPA Section 27, OWMC sought approval to build and operate the first phase of the facility which would have comprised one-half of the overall project—physical/chemical and solidification treatment plants with 120,000 tonnes of annual capacity and the first incinerator with about 30,000 tonnes of annual capacity. OWMC also sought several other approvals pursuant to various sections of the Ontario Water Resources Act, the Lakes and Rivers Improvement Act, the Conservation Authorities Act, and the Expropriations Act.

Summary of Cases in the Niagara Region

Siting boards denied permits in two of the three facility siting cases in the Niagara region and in the third gave a partial approval after a negotiated agreement between the proponent and the affected community. The compromise between CWM and local residents in Niagara, New York was that the existing landfill could be expanded, but only if the company would agree not to seek approval for an incinerator for at least ten years, or before 2003. The other two facilities were rejected because of hydrogeological concerns in the CECOS case in New York and cost-effectiveness considerations with regard to OWMC in Ontario. The OWMC decision took 15 years to make, during which time the crown corporation abandoned its first locational choice due to poor hydrogeological conditions and chose its second site based on what it considered ideal conditions in this regard.

How is it that so much effort on the part of facility proponents went unrewarded? The following three sections will review the cases and analyze them in terms of key decisions that the various stakeholders made along the way. The definition of facility need, for example, was a fundamental issue that proponents had to prove successfully in order to realize their plans. Likewise, the selection of particular facility characteristics such as location, size, and type was critical. Finally, siting boards considered issues of fairness in terms of process and outcome in their final decisions. Each of the stakeholder groups had its own arguments and evidence about these issues and attempted to convince decision-making officials as to the veracity of their claims. Ultimately, siting boards had to consider the opinions and justifications of all parties with regard to each of the issues in question in order to reach their own conclusions (see Table 7).

Defining Facility Need

Defining facility need was one of the more fundamental issues over which stakeholder groups disagreed regarding each of the proposals. The definition of need differed somewhat between the two halves of the Niagara region. In terms of appearances, there seemed to be a notable difference in governmental strategy between evaluating facility proposals submitted by private-sector firms (as in the case of the Niagara, New York proposals) and evaluating proposals submitted by other public-sector

TABLE 7

Summary of Cases in the Niagara Region

Community & Existing Site	Proponent & Proposal	Opposition Groups & Issues	Outcome & Reasons
Niagara Falls, NY (urban): HW Landfill	CECOS: Landfill (6/87-3/90)	City, County, Local Group, Ontario: Spatial & Cum. Equity Hydrology	Denied: Hydrogeology
Lewiston, NY (suburban): HW Landfills	CWM: Landfill & Incinerator (4/89-11/89) (6/90-6/93)	City, County, School Board, Local Group, Ontario: Cum. & Spatial Equity, Hydrogeology	Landfills Approved & Built; Incin. Negotiated
S. Cayuga & W. Lincoln, ON (agricultural): Greenfields	OWMC: Landfill, Incinerator, Treatment Facilities	City, Regional Munic., Local Group, Laidlaw: Spatial Equity & Private Sector Intrusion	Denied: Cost-effectiveness

agencies (as in the case of the Niagara, Ontario proposals). The Ontario government, through OWMC, certainly had greater discretion over the demonstration of this point as compared to New York officials who were resigned to evaluating the arguments and evidence of private-sector facility proponents. Ultimately, however, the stakeholder disputes over this matter revolved around waste generation projections, which Ontario and New York government officials and industry groups interpreted as a justification for facility need, whereas local and regional opponents saw a greater need for waste reduction and pollution prevention efforts to reduce waste at the source.

NIAGARA, ONTARIO

The Ontario government was intimately involved in defining and characterizing facility need, starting with the creation of OWMC. From the beginning, the crown corporation's mission was to site, build, and operate a large, integrated hazardous waste facility with an incinerator, landfill, and related treatment plants because the private sector was not thought to be providing adequate hazardous waste disposal capacity in Ontario. In 1980, Progressive Conservative Environment Minister Harry Parrot announced that: "We can and do fully accept the responsibility as a government for the operation of a [hazardous waste facility] site" (Ontario Ministry of the Environment, quoted in Harrison, 1986). This statement came just before OWMC unveiled its plans for the South Cayuga site. The justification for Parrot's decision was that the province's only existing hazardous waste facility near Sarnia (then owned by Tricil, later part of Laidlaw, and now owned by Safety-Kleen) was insufficient. In addition, there had been several private-sector proposals that were never realized, either because of proponent withdrawal or failure to secure EAB approval. Ontario's political climate has changed several times during the life of the OWMC dispute; however, government support for a public-sector approach that would protect the public from the "vagaries of the hazardous waste marketplace" continued until EAB denied the application for approval in November 1994 (Ontario Environmental Assessment Board, 1994).

Laidlaw used its own presence in the Ontario hazardous waste management market as justification for opposing the OWMC project. It rejected OWMC's claim that there were deficiencies in the private-sector provision of this service. The company, in fact, operated the only commercial toxic waste landfill and incinerator in the province. Tricil as well as Laidlaw representatives insisted that the private sector would respond to any existing or future waste capacity needs if only OWMC would get out of the way. In addition, Laidlaw sought approval to build a rotary kiln incinerator, the same technology that OWMC was planning to use for its West Lincoln facility, to complement its liquid injection incinerator and landfill near Sarnia in southwestern Ontario near the Michigan border. The rotary kiln technology was seen as important by both Laidlaw and OWMC because it could handle wastes (such as PCBs and contaminated solids and sludges) that the Sarnia facility could not. But in October 1993, just over a month after the OWMC hearings were completed, Laidlaw announced that it was withdrawing its incinerator proposal because of "insufficient market need and the availability of alternative technologies" (Laidlaw, 1993).

The Tri-parties and other opponents of OWMC approached the issue of facility need from a very different point of view. Rather than emphasizing the private sector's ability to respond to market deficiencies, these locally concerned activists disputed OWMC's projections of facility demand. The Tri-parties argued that the OWMC numbers were exaggerated because of a failure to account for the waste reducing effects of pollution prevention programs and on-site disposal. They also argued that the facility would create excess capacity, which would hold down the cost of disposal and hence discourage efforts at waste reduction and pollution prevention. OWMC argued that its status as a crown corporation would allow it to resist the pressures of market supply and demand that supported the opponents' arguments. It maintained that it would work with MOEE to develop a pricing policy to encourage pollution prevention rather than one that would subsidize waste generation. The Tri-parties also disagreed with MOEE suggestions that future changes in regulations and policies would stimulate higher than anticipated waste generation rates.[4]

In its final decision, EAB generally supported OWMC regarding the role of government and facility need. The Board concluded that

> ... there are compelling policy reasons for a publicly-owned
> and operated facility that will: i) provide secure capacity; ii)
> protect Ontarians from the vagaries of the [hazardous] waste
> marketplace; iii) be able to manage all types of waste; and iv)
> have the capacity to manage contingency/unforseen wastes.
> (Ontario Environmental Assessment Board, 1994)

Clearly, the board disagreed with Laidlaw's interpretations on the value of crown corporations in the provision of waste management services. With regard to OWMC's hazardous waste projections, and thus the issue of need, EAB shared the Tri-parties' concerns that the government numbers may have been too high; however, the board ultimately found that the need for off-site disposal capacity was sufficiently large to warrant consideration of the facility. The EAB decision on this matter reveals its concern with balancing the concerns and arguments of interested parties on the question of facility need. Nonetheless, even with compelling evidence that OWMC waste generation projections may have been inflated, the board revealed a fundamental commitment to capacity assurance as a matter of overall policy. Ironically, even though EAB failed to consider this point more fully, its denial of the facility application prompted the minister of environment in the final days of Bob Rae's New Democratic Party (NDP) government to announce that OWMC would have a new mission to promote pollution prevention without the responsibility of facility siting (MOEE, 1995). Nonetheless, the crown corporation did not have the opportunity to realize its lofty new vision since Mike Harris's Progressive Conservative Party government assumed power and eliminated OWMC altogether (Fletcher, 1998).

NIAGARA, NEW YORK

Facility need was also a point of contention in Niagara County, New York with respect to the CECOS and CWM facility proposals. While neither of the facilities were to be government owned or operated, as in the case of OWMC, the state had previously attempted to site a hazardous waste incinerator through a public authority (EFC) in Cayuga County in the central portion of the state (Heiman, 1990b). Because of EFC's failure to successfully site the facility, proposals for both of Niagara County's off-site waste management facilities, CWM and CECOS, were for private ownership. But while the role of New York's DEC was limited to reviewing the initial proposals and environmental reviews, the state still had a strong interest in maintaining its in-state capacity assurance for hazardous waste treatment and disposal (Olsen, 1991, 1995). This is not markedly different from Ontario MOEE's support of the OWMC facility.

New York State's support of the CWM facility is also demonstrated by the siting board's determinations regarding risk. While five of the eight board members agreed on a total risk score of 182.4, the other three issued a minority opinion that the certificate of approval should be denied based on what they considered a more appropriate score of 200.9, just over the threshold limit of 200.0. Both estimates were far higher than CWM's conclusion that the risk score should be 149.0. Interestingly, each of the five siting board members who expressed the majority opinion were New York State commissioners (considered ex-officio members), including the chair, who was a commissioner of DEC. The three ad hoc members, who were chosen for their expertise in environmental science and engineering rather than their positions in state government, argued that the population density in the area (nearly 4,000 persons residing or working within a half mile of the site) was too high to permit a hazardous waste facility in the vicinity.

The minority opinion made reference to a number of "incompatible" structures that were proximate to the proposed facility (e.g., the Lewiston-Porter School with 2,700 students; United States Army and National Guard training stations; several residences; and a restaurant). The minority opinion concluded that CWM should consider alternatives to the proposed facility and implied that it was not needed:

> The Minority disagrees with the ... findings of the Majority in that the applicant did not answer the question of reasonable alternative sites to this location for hazardous waste treatment, storage and final disposal. While the applicant currently operates three hazardous waste landfills that are as large or larger than this proposed site, no evidence was presented to show that either or all of these sites could not handle the waste materials expected to come to the proposed site. The question of whether rail, water or air transportation could be utilized at these other sites was not offered for discussion. Alternatives to landfilling were not adequately presented for study. These items should have been adjudicated. (New York State Facility Siting Board, Minority Opinion, December 1993a: 3)

The majority opinion of the siting board saw fit to make much more definitive statements regarding need in its majority decision:

> The proposed ... facility constitutes a critical environmental management resource for New York State. Under federal law, each state must demonstrate the continuing capacity to manage all of the hazardous waste generated within its borders. New York State has no other commercial land burial facility for hazardous waste and therefore this project is needed if the State is to be able to meet the requirements of the Superfund Amendments and Reauthorization Act (SARA) for hazardous wastes that cannot be disposed of through other means.
>
> Because this new resource is so valuable, it is crucial that its useful life be extended as long as possible. (New York State Facility Siting Board, December 1993b: 5-6)

These statements reveal a difference of opinion over facility need, not only among stakeholders, but also among siting board officials. The minority members clearly wanted to address alternatives to the proposed landfill expansion to a greater extent than did the ex-officio or majority members. Interestingly, however, each of the alternatives specified involved transporting waste to undetermined existing facilities in other locations rather than reducing or preventing waste at the point of production. As with the EAB decision regarding OWMC, the overall siting board opinion revealed a fundamental commitment to capacity assurance. Its reference to the Superfund statute indicates an overall concern that the CWM landfill expansion was needed to ensure compliance with SARA.

In the CECOS case, differences in risk estimates occurred not among members of the siting board, but between the initial approval in August 1989 and the final decision to deny the certificate of approval in March 1990 after a redetermination of facility need. In the initial decision, the board unanimously agreed on an estimate just below the 200.0 threshold. But after reopening the hearing to address additional issues related to facility need, it reassessed its risk estimate and increased it to over 200.0 based on potential contamination of ground and surface waters. The siting board concluded:

> Even assuming the accuracy of [CECOS's] analyses, the record demonstrates that the leachate from [the proposed facility], in and of itself, would be capable of creating a threefold exceedence in the ambient standard for PCBs in the Niagara River. State water quality standards are set at levels designed to protect receiving waters for their best usage. We therefore conclude that this potential exceedence is a sufficient basis to find that the [proposed facility] presents severe problems with respect to water contamination. This conclusion is further reinforced by the fact that ambient conditions in the Niagara River already exceed the standard for PCBs. (New York State Facility Siting Board, March 1990: 3)

The board also expressed concern about the population density of the area, which was 1,200 persons per square mile within a half mile of the facility. Given that the reason for reopening the hearing was to reassess the issue of need, it seems surprising that issues of risk were so prominent in the final decision. Ultimately, the board found that short-term need could be met sufficiently by the CWM landfill, but chose not to make a finding with respect to long-term need since the revised risk score was over 200.0.

> In light of the fact that the Board has concluded that this project does not qualify for a siting certificate on grounds

unrelated to the need issue, it would serve no public purpose
to render a determination on evidence that presents a snapshot
of the need issue at a period in time when the picture is subject
to major changes, the effects of which are difficult to project.
(New York Facility Siting Board, March 1990: 9)

In the case of CECOS, the problem of determining facility need was
complicated by competing and shifting assessments of risk. In the end,
it is difficult to isolate the precise reason for the ultimate permit denial.
Was it based on the March 1990 reassessment of risk that exceeded the
200.0 threshold (after the August 1989 risk assessment below 200.0)?
Alternatively, was it more a function of the November 1989 decision to approve an expansion of the nearby CWM landfill? Given the political as well
as scientific and technical nature of risk assessment, in addition to the siting
board's decision not to specify a conclusion regarding need, these questions
remain unresolved.

Selecting Facility Location, Size, and Type

As with the definition of facility need, decisions about locating facilities of
particular sizes and types became contentious and related to one another in
the Niagara area cases. In general, large facilities, rather than smaller ones,
are advantageous from the viewpoint of provincial and state agencies as
well as industrial interest groups because they provide greater treatment
and disposal capacity. Similarly, integrated facilities that provide multiple
forms of treatment and disposal (e.g., an incinerator, treatment facility, and
landfill) in one location are also often considered preferable. Communities
targeted for large facilities, however, see all the more reason to oppose
them because of the volume of waste they will receive, often from distant
regions. This was the case in all of the Niagara proposals, each of which
involved huge landfills, and two of which involved incinerators as well. In
the OWMC case involving a landfill, treatment facility, and incinerator,
it is difficult to determine which of the facility components, if any, were
most objectionable to the Ontario community since they were never given
a choice. In the CWM case which also involved a landfill and incinerator,
the community made a choice between the two, apparently deciding that a
landfill expansion would be preferable to a new incinerator.

NIAGARA, ONTARIO

Decisions about facility location, size, and type became heated and inter-
twined in the case of OWMC. Starting with its first hazardous waste facility
proposal in South Cayuga and continuing throughout its plans for West
Lincoln, OWMC expressed a commitment to a centralized, fully-integrated
facility with an incinerator, physical/chemical treatment plant, solidification plant, and landfill.[5] Moreover, no matter which site was ultimately
chosen, there was a clear preference for each of the facility components to
be located together rather than separately and for a site featuring "natural
containment" in the form of a thick clay deposit underneath. This meant
that one community would host all of the facility components (i.e., with a
large capacity) and that all its attendant risks and other burdens would be
concentrated there. In a 1985 interview about OWMC's West Lincoln and
South Cayuga siting decisions, Donald Chant stated:

> We've always said that if we could have it, we wanted a cen-
> tralized facility. They're safer to operate. It minimizes interfa-
> cility transport. Another reason which is less tangible is that to
> go to an area and give them only the landfill is seen as giving
> them only the dump. No benefits are attached to that. All of
> the action, all of the good things in terms of employment and
> local cash flow, come from the treatment facilities. (Quoted in
> Harrison, 1986: 143)

In its 1993 Written Argument in Chief to EAB, OWMC reiterated that
it had decided on a centralized, fully-integrated facility "early in its planning process," but that it had continued to "re-visit" the issue in its systems
analyses, each time concluding that the initial decision was correct (EAB,
1994). The Tri-parties interpreted OWMC's decision-making quite differently. They argued:

> The "systems study" was never anything but window dressing
> for a system that was selected in 1982 and sited by 1985 ...
> OWMC never fairly considered systems alternatives because
> it had already sited its preferred system, the integrated,
> centralized facility on a clay plain. (Ontario Environmental
> Assessment Board, 1994: 3-5)

A preferable approach according to the Tri-parties was a geographically dispersed system of facility components, each designed to meet specific regional waste capacity needs with different kinds of facilities. To design such a system, however, required data on waste quantities categorized both by "treatability" and geographic area. While OWMC had explored alternatives to an integrated centralized facility, it did not match them with treatability categories (e.g., incineration, physical/chemical treatment, solidification, landfilling) or specific geographic areas. Instead, OWMC simply estimated future waste generation for the province and considered different locations, some geographically dispersed, and others integrated at a single site. It did not consider whether particular types of facilities in separate regions of the province, combined with increased pollution prevention efforts, could meet projected capacity needs for each area.

The Tri-parties also criticized OWMC's systems analysis for failing to adequately assess salt mine disposal as an alternative to landfilling. The main advantage of salt mines, they argued, is their ability to contain chloride residues from solidified wastes, a problem that landfills cannot necessarily prevent even with "natural containment" provided by thick clay deposits. Another advantage from a local perspective is that there are no salt mines in the Niagara region, thus undermining the viability of at least OWMC's choice of location if not the need for the project. The Tri-parties submitted that:

> … it is very likely that a thorough and competent systems study would have shown that the most suitable repository for the waste residues from an OWMC-type facility is an existing salt mine at either Goderich or Windsor. (Ontario Environmental Assessment Board, 1994: 5-21)

EAB's final decision on site selection and facility size sided partly with OWMC and partly with the Tri-parties. Nonetheless, its interpretations of these issues proved to be critical in denying the application for approval to build the facility. With respect to the evaluation of alternatives to the West Lincoln site, the board agreed with both parties to some extent but ultimately ruled in favor of OWMC on this particular point. It stated:

> We accept the proposition that the better approach to analysing alternative waste management systems is to begin

by organizing the waste according to geographical origins and treatment categories. However, that, per se, does not cause us to conclude that OWMC's systems analyses were fatally flawed. (Environmental Assessment Board, 1994: 5-19)

EAB's findings on OWMC's review of the salt mine alternative had much more serious implications for the proposed facility. The environmental assessment had rejected the salt mine option on economic considerations since its capital and annual operating costs would be $27 million and $4 million, respectively, as compared to those of the landfill approach, $5 million and $3 million. EAB pointed out that OWMC had found "the cost factors present[ed] the most significant differences among the alternatives," yet had not included chlorides management in its landfill costs. This was a serious omission given that chlorides management added an estimated $35.7 to $40.9 million in capital costs and $7.9 to $9.4 million in annual operating costs. Worse yet, these estimates were based on the initial plan for only one rotary kiln, so the addition of the second incinerator would increase chlorides management costs to an estimated $370 million over the life of the facility.

In the end, it seems that EAB chose to consider all stakeholder positions in its final determinations regarding facility location, size, and type. With regard to the question of centralized versus dispersed locations for the various facility components, the board found merit in the Tri-parties' arguments that a more sophisticated analysis of waste projections by geographic areas and treatability categories would have been a useful planning technique. In the absence of such information, however, EAB chose not to deny OWMC a construction permit, at least on this point. Were it not for cost-effectiveness considerations related to chlorides management and the unresolved question of whether to dispose of treatment residues in the proposed landfill or in salt mines, EAB appears to have been willing to approve the facility proposal.

NIAGARA, NEW YORK

One of the main differences between the experiences with hazardous waste facility siting in Niagara, New York and Niagara, Ontario is that the New York State government had little control over the location of the facilities whereas the Ontario provincial government was directly in charge. Instead of directing a state-wide search for "suitable" locations as happened in the case of the West Lincoln, Ontario OWMC proposal, New York had to rely on its commercial waste management firms to choose potential facility sites. The result was that "natural" containment was less of a siting priority in New York than in Ontario, which rested its choice of West Lincoln as its proposed site on favorable hydrogeological conditions in the area. Instead, New York, pursuant to federal RCRA requirements, mandates the use of synthetic liners to minimize risk of leaching through "engineered" containment, making "ideal" hydrogeological conditions less of an issue for site selection. This is not surprising given that Ontarian provincial and Canadian federal regulations do not require synthetic liners for hazardous waste landfills.

Ontario's formal opposition to the CECOS and CWM facility proposals coincided with its own attempts to successfully site the OWMC facility in West Lincoln. In its opposition to the 1989 expansion of the CWM landfill, attorneys for the Province of Ontario recognized this point as well as its concerns regarding hydrogeology:

> Ontario is not opposed, in principle, to the landfilling of hazardous waste. Ontario itself has a hazardous waste landfill and is in the process of considering approval of another. The issue is whether the design of [the CWM landfill expansion proposal] will provide adequate protection of human health and the environment from contamination of groundwater and surface waters by the hazardous wastes stored in the facility.
>
> CWM has not provided sufficient data to demonstrate that its analysis of the hydrogeological conditions at the proposed site ... is adequate. (Terris & Hecker, June 1989: 2)

Local groups opposed to CWM landfill expansions were more concerned with traffic as well as the facility's proximity to what the minority members of the siting board for one of the expansion proposals had termed "incompatible" structures. Especially troubling, in this regard, was that CWM is located within a quarter of a mile from the Lewiston-Porter School. In its opposition to CWM, the acting superintendent of the school system offered several reasons why the siting board should deny the 1989 landfill expansion because of its impact on the community generally and school specifically:

> Foremost, is the adverse affect [sic] the existing facility is having on the quality of life in the Town of Lewiston, Town of Porter, and the Lewiston-Porter School District. CWM has advised the School Board that a minimum of fifty trucks per day will pass the school campus going to and from the site.... This creates an adverse impact upon the Lewiston-Porter School District.... The traffic issue cannot be stressed enough. There is the potential for accidents and for hazardous waste spills which could seriously affect the children and staff on the campus. In addition, the noise, fumes, and distractions created by the truck traffic intrude on the activities taking place in the school. The safety and welfare of all our students, employees, and visitors is of paramount importance to the Lewiston-Porter School District. (Yates, June 1989: 1)

Groups opposed to the CECOS landfill expansion expressed quite similar objections about the location of that facility. Among their concerns were:

> Demographics (population density near the site, population adjacent to transport route, and population growth projections); Climatological conditions at the site; Proximity to incompatible structures; Proximity to utility lines; Seismic risk; and Consistency with local planning and ordinances. (Pearlstein, August 1989: 12)

In terms of community reactions to various types of facilities, an illustrative case to consider is CWM's negotiated agreement with local opposition groups allowing a 47-acre landfill expansion as long as the company agrees not to seek approval for an incinerator until at least the year 2003. Local opposition to the landfill was clearly diminished once it was divorced from the incinerator proposal. In this regard, the community seems to have been more concerned by the prospect of an incinerator than a landfill. But, as stated previously, intervening parties were concerned that continued opposition to the landfill would be futile since CWM was by then the only operating commercial hazardous waste landfill in the State of New York. In this regard, the community's reaction to landfills versus incinerators was more a recognition of its own limitations than a tacit approval of one over the other. In addition, not all local residents were in agreement with the settlement (though there is no indication as to how many) as shown in this passage from the hearing report in which the administrative law judge paraphrased a concerned resident's objection:

> One speaker, Lisa Aug of Niagara Falls, said the agreement did not represent the feelings of community residents, although it was signed by the governments of Lewiston, Porter, and Niagara County. She said local elected officials had been "muzzled" by [CWM], and that the DEC had "written off" Niagara County except as a "dump" for hazardous waste. (Buhrmaster, October 1993: 3)

This sentiment, though it was not outwardly expressed by citizens who were involved in the negotiated agreement once reached, does reflect the kinds of concerns that led the New York Assembly to write geographic equity provisions into the state hazardous waste statute. The proposals to expand the only two commercial hazardous waste landfills in the state rather than find new locations, as well as the plan to add an incinerator to one of the facilities, flew in the face of everything the geographic equity concept stood for.

Promoting Fairness in Facility Siting

Niagara, Ontario

Perhaps the most central concern of the Tri-parties in their opposition to OWMC had to do with the basic fairness issue of asking West Lincoln Township to live with the environmental and social burdens of hazardous waste management from industries throughout Ontario and other North American jurisdictions. For this reason, one of the group's proposed conditions, should the project receive EAB approval, was that the OWMC facility not be allowed to accept wastes from outside the province. Their other two conditions of approval had to do with containing leachate by means of landfill engineering requirements and reducing odors through operating restrictions. Clearly, these local participants in the public review process viewed geographic equity as an important consideration, since they were only willing to accept the facility with a spatial limit on the sources of waste and some assurance of reducing burdens on the host community.

EAB addressed procedural equity concerns by providing intervenor funding to defray the legal and administrative costs of OWMC's opponents. Approximately $500,000 was provided to the two full-time intervening parties, the Tri-parties and Laidlaw, as well as other persons and entities involved in particular aspects of the hearing. These funds were no doubt critical in allowing individual community residents to question the reasonableness and viability of the OWMC proposal. However, local participants clearly saw more to procedural equity than the provision of official party status before EAB. The Tri-parties charged that serious procedural problems were present well before the EAB hearing even started, particularly during the earliest portion of site selection. They stated that:

> the original identification of the Golden Horseshoe, as [OWMC's] choice of candidate region ... was arbitrary, lacking in adequate supporting data, neither traceable nor replicable, nor in compliance with the Environmental Assessment Act. (Ontario Environmental Assessment Board, 1994: 7-5)

While EAB supported local interests with regard to issues of cost-effectiveness, it disagreed with the Tri-parties on equity grounds perhaps more than any other. With respect to the question of whether to prohibit the facility from accepting wastes from outside Ontario, the Board simply stated that "it would not be appropriate to impose a Condition that would prohibit the OWMC facility from accepting such wastes" (EAB, 1994:xi). With respect to the Tri-parties' other two conditions regarding engineered containment in the landfill and odor controls for the facility generally, EAB referred to OWMC's decision to provide a $35,000 annual budget for a Community Monitoring Committee of five to nine local residents and a technical consultant to monitor potential problems with leachate and odors. The board made no findings against OWMC's choice of the Golden Horseshoe area and West Lincoln as site selections or any other procedural factors.

Niagara, Ontario communities seem to have been extremely lucky that EAB denied the OWMC permit. While opposition groups were surely benefited in a procedural equity sense by the provision of intervenor funding, the board did not find much merit in local claims regarding spatial equity.

Had it not been for economic considerations related to the cost of chlorides management and OWMC's failure to adequately assess the option of salt mine disposal of chlorides residuals, EAB appears to have been fully willing to approve the facility for location in West Lincoln Township.

> The Board felt that a salt mine system has the potential to be preferred, and it could not find that OWMC's proposal for managing hazardous wastes would provide the greatest benefit to the people of Ontario.
>
> On other matters, the Board found that there is a need for additional off-site hazardous waste treatment and disposal capacity in Ontario. It also found that, in general, OWMC's choice of technology for the treatment of such wastes ... was appropriate. Further, if a centralized, fully-integrated system was the preferred waste management system, West Lincoln would be the preferred site. The Board felt that OWMC had adequately characterized the risks and impacts expected with its facility and proposed to take extensive measures to minimize risks and impacts, consistent with the *Environmental Protection Act*. As a result, the Board did not consider the residual risks and impacts to be of such magnitude that it would have denied approval, had it accepted the environmental assessment. (Ontario Office of Consolidated Hearings, 1994: 1)

OWMC also had the right to revise its proposal after a thorough analysis of the salt mines alternative, but decided instead simply to abandon the idea in February 1995.

NIAGARA, NEW YORK

As in the case of OWMC, one of the more central concerns of Niagara, New York residents and communities related to the issue of fairness. Despite New York's geographic equity policy, CWM is the only operating commercial hazardous waste landfill in the state and CECOS, though its landfill is now closed, still receives liquid hazardous wastes in its waste water treatment facility. In its 1987 revisions to ECL, the state legislature required that NY DEC make:

> [A] determination of the number, size, type and location by
> area of the state of new or expanded [hazardous waste] facili-
> ties ... consistent with ... an equitable geographic distribution
> of facilities. (McKinney Supp., 1991)

New York DEC's Draft Siting Plan identifies counties in three regions in
the state that account for the bulk of hazardous waste (93 per cent) generated in New York (see Figure 16). In 1993, the Western Region, which
includes Niagara County, generated 54 per cent, as compared to 23 per cent
for the Central Region and 23 per cent for the Eastern Region (NY DEC,
March 1995). While the intent of the legislation and the Draft Siting Plan
was to develop off-site hazardous waste capacity in each region, the results
to date are that the Western Region, and Niagara County specifically, still
have the only commercial facilities in the state.

With respect to the CECOS and CWM facility siting cases specifically,
fairness and equity concerns had little bearing on the proceedings or the
siting board decisions. In each case, opposition groups argued that the proposals ran counter to the geographic equity policy and, therefore, should
not be approved. The "toxic legacy" of Love Canal, they submitted, was
indicative of Niagara County's existing hazardous waste burden and was
therefore reason enough to deny the certificates of approval. But to the
extent these issues were even considered, the siting boards reduced them
to "psychological" or "psychosocial" issues that ultimately had no impact
on their decisions to approve or deny the proposals. The siting board's
conclusion and recommendation regarding equity in the initial approval of
the CECOS proposal are illustrative of this point.

> The [CECOS] application and the prospect of the facility be-
> ing built was shown to have an adverse psychological impact
> on a significant, though unquantified, proportion of persons in
> the community. This impact was not demonstrated in terms of
> the traditional measures of stress, but was shown to be char-
> acterized by feelings of *powerlessness and inequity* due to the
> proposed expansion of hazardous waste activities at CECOS
> ... *This psychological effect is not a sufficient basis for denial
> of the permit* or certificate, but it does provide a basis for the
> imposition of mitigative permit conditions.

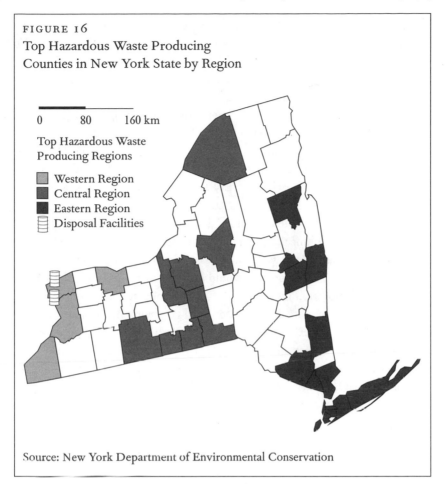

FIGURE 16

Top Hazardous Waste Producing
Counties in New York State by Region

0   80   160 km

Top Hazardous Waste
Producing Regions

▢ Western Region
▢ Central Region
▢ Eastern Region
▢ Disposal Facilities

Source: New York Department of Environmental Conservation

CECOS should be required to increase and intensify its community outreach and educational programs. A specific plan with a schedule for implementation of such expanded programs should be prepared by CECOS subject to approval of [DEC] staff, or the Siting Board and Commissioner may prescribe specific elements of such a plan within their discretion. (Pearlstein, August 1989: 137-38; emphasis added)

Of course, because the initial approval was later overturned, these issues eventually became moot. Nonetheless, the preceding statements show a lack of regard for community concerns about fairness, even in the context of a geographic equity law specifically written into ECL and a draft policy developed by New York's DEC but never implemented. The siting board's recommendation that CECOS should "intensify" its outreach and education efforts fails to comply with the original intent of the legislation, which was to promote geographic equity of facility sites, not "psychosocial" sensitivity of the same waste management corporations operating new hazardous waste facilities in the same places. Ultimately, NY DEC found the geographic equity policy difficult to implement without an OWMC-style governmental site selection process. The State of New York had used such an approach unsuccessfully in the early 1980s and was unwilling to try this again (Eismann, 1995).

NY DEC also attempted to add a dimension of procedural equity to siting by giving technical assistance grants to communities facing the prospect of new hazardous waste facilities so that they could hire their own technical experts. This approach would have been roughly similar to the Ontario intervenor funding program. The agency recommended such a program so as to facilitate the efforts of local governments in their own decision-making (NY DEC, 1988), though this, too, was never implemented and no funds were ever allocated for it. In the end, Niagara, New York communities saw no relief through either geographic equity or procedural assistance from the existing disproportionate burdens of hazardous waste that they presently face.

Notes

1. Interestingly, the early history of the CWM site (Model City) is tied to that of Love Canal: The Niagara region of Ontario lies just over the river from New York State. The two sites were to have been connected by a canal designed to divert water from the upper to lower Niagara River for hydroelectric power, thus creating an industrial district that William T. Love himself was the first to call Model City. What came to be known as Love Canal was his aborted first attempt at digging the southern section. It was only later filled with hazardous waste (McGreevy, 1994).

2. Residents Organized for Lewiston-Porter's Environment, Inc. (ROLE) served as the main community opposition group and also participated in negotiations toward the final community agreement with CWM. R. Nils Olsen, Jr., a professor of law at the University of Buffalo served as the chief negotiator. The Lewiston-Porter School District (under a quarter of a mile from the site) and the Niagara County Government were also officially opposed.

3. The Citizens' Organizations, aside from LAND, included the Campaign to Save Niagara, the Ecumenical Task Force of the Niagara Frontier, Inc., Evershed

Restoration Association, Great Lakes United, and the Society to Oppose Pollution in Towns.

4. OWMC and MOEE used the possibility of a future Ontario "land ban" as their main example of such a policy or regulatory change. The restriction has been in place in the United States since 1984 and requires limits on toxicity levels before hazardous waste can be placed in a landfill. Instead, current Ontario landfill restrictions impose "physical stability" requirements to inhibit underground leaching. Such a change, OWMC and MOEE predicted, would increase the universe of wastes in need of treatment and incineration, thereby heightening the need for additional facility capacity in Ontario (Radcliffe, 1994, 1996). To date, the province has not enacted a land ban regulation, though on December 18, 2001, MOE issued a discussion document that proposes such a policy.

5. OWMC defined a "centralized" system as one full-service facility and a "decentralized" system as more than one full-service facility. By "fully-integrated" they meant that each of the facility components would be on a single site as opposed to a "partially-integrated" system, which would locate the components on two or three separate sites.

5
Detroit and Sarnia

Introduction

The Detroit and Sarnia areas lie on the Michigan-Ontario border between the southern end of Lake Huron and the mouth of Lake Erie (see Figure 12). The Detroit metropolitan area includes the City of Detroit and also Wayne, Oakland, and Macomb counties. The area is located in the southeastern portion of the State of Michigan. Sarnia is part of Lambton County and is located in the southwestern part of the Province of Ontario. Both communities are heavily industrialized, with metals processing and auto industries in Detroit and petrochemical plants in the Sarnia area. Poor air and water quality have long been critical environmental issues and sources of conflict between industries and residents. Two of the industries with the largest generation of toxic materials in North America are located in the Michigan side of the region, including fourth-ranked Nortru, Inc. and eighth-ranked Michigan Recovery Systems, Inc. in Romulus (CEC, 2002). The Detroit metropolitan area is home to 14 of Michigan's 19 commercial hazardous waste treatment, storage, and disposal facilities (TSDFs), six of which are in the City of Detroit (Mohai & Bryant, 1992). Ontario's only commercial hazardous waste facility is across the border in the Sarnia area. Additionally, the transboundary nature of the problem has made it an international issue and drawn the attention of the International Joint Commission (IJC). Both the Saint Clair and Detroit rivers are on IJC's list of "Areas of Concern" due to the long history of industrial activity in the area.

The area faced especially tough environmental problems from 1971 to 1978 when Dow Chemical Canada faced a lawsuit for destroying the commercial fishing industry in Lake Saint Clair by having discharged mercury into the Saint Clair River at their Sarnia plant over a 20-year period. In 1985, a highly publicized Dow Chemical Canada spill of dry-cleaning fluid created so-called "toxic blobs" in the Saint Clair River. Walpole Island, a Canadian First Nation territory, has long suffered the effects of spills and discharges into the Saint Clair River because of its down-stream location in the river delta (Nin-Da-Waab-Jig, 1983, 1984, 1986). Since then, the island's Ojibwe residents have been forced to curtail their hunting and fishing practices and adjust their diets to store-bought food and bottled water (Williams, 1995).

The City of Detroit's municipal waste incinerator, which began operating in 1988, has been another source of controversy on both sides of the border, particularly since it was built with no scrubbers. In 1988, the United States Department of State and the Canadian Secretary of State for External Affairs issued requests to IJC that it investigate air pollution problems in the region (IJC, 1992). Both made specific references to the Detroit incinerator and also to a proposal to burn liquid hazardous wastes in the kiln of a Detroit-area cement plant. IJC released findings and issued recommendations on air quality in the Detroit-Windsor/Port Huron-Sarnia Region in 1992 and 1993. On the Michigan side of the border, the report identified 1,678 incinerators in the three counties of the Detroit metropolitan area and Saint Clair County, including Port Huron. The majority (94 per cent) were small facilities (mostly for apartment buildings) and the remainder were moderate to large facilities (mostly on-site units for industrial plants). In the Ontario counties of Essex (including Windsor) and Lambton (including Sarnia), IJC identified nine incinerators, six of which are small biomedical units and three of which are large industrial facilities. One of three large facilities is a commercial incinerator owned and operated by Safety-Kleen (previously owned by Laidlaw) and the other two are on-site industrial units.

The Detroit and Sarnia areas were the settings for several hazardous waste facility siting disputes during the 1980s and 1990s. In the following section, Laidlaw-Sarnia's attempts to site a new incinerator are discussed in relation to the company's dispute with the Ontario Waste Management Corporation (OWMC). Laidlaw eventually withdrew its proposal so the facility was never built. The chapter continues with reviews of six facility siting cases in the metropolitan Detroit area. Two were located in the City of Detroit, two in the city's Wayne County suburbs, and two in the Oakland County suburbs. Together, the Detroit area cases involved two landfills, two treatment facilities, one incinerator, and a deep-well injection facility. Only two of the proposals received approvals initially (both were treatment facilities in the City of Detroit), but neither have been built. The deep-well injection system was built without being subjected to public hearings (as each of the other cases were), though a protracted series of legal disputes over the matter eventually led to formal public review proceedings and the facility was ultimately granted permission to begin operations.

The Laidlaw-Sarnia Case and OWMC

Laidlaw's proposal to build a new hazardous waste facility at their existing location in Moore Township just outside of Sarnia, Ontario was, as shown in Chapter 3, at least indirectly tied to the OWMC siting proposals. In December 1989, when Laidlaw announced its intentions to seek approval to build a rotary kiln incinerator (the same technology as the proposed OWMC incinerator), the OWMC public hearings were about to begin. As an official party to the OWMC proceedings, Laidlaw's opposition to competing for business with the crown corporation was already in full public view and only became more so when the West Lincoln hearings began in February 1990. As well, during public hearings for its own proposal in August 1993, the company continued to express its opposition to the OWMC facility.

Moore Township is a small rural community that, around the time of the dispute, had a population just over 10,000 people and an above average median household income of $52,553 as compared to the Province of Ontario generally ($44,432), according to the 1991 Canadian census. It lies on the outskirts of the City of Sarnia, Ontario, a highly industrial jurisdiction similar to Niagara Falls, New York in terms of its concentration of chemical plants. The Laidlaw facility site has been used for industrial waste disposal since 1960 and for hazardous waste incineration since 1968 (Laidlaw, 1990). The property has had several ownership changes since this time. The previous owner, Tricil, Ltd., purchased the facility in 1980 and sold it to Laidlaw in 1989. The facility is now operated by Safety-Kleen.

THE ENVIRONMENTAL ASSESSMENT BOARD (EAB) HEARING

In August 1993, the first of what was to be a series of public hearings on Laidlaw began, chaired by a representative from Ontario's Environmental Assessment Board (EAB). The company used the opportunity to state its case for the proposal and to introduce its own environmental assessment, emphasizing its compliance with the Ontario Environmental Assessment Act (EAA). A representative from the province's Ministry of Environment and Energy followed with a statement which concluded that Laidlaw had addressed the requirements of EAA in a "reasonable, rational and traceable planning framework" (EAB, August 1993). In addition, ten separate groups and individuals made statements as to their concerns about the new incinerator; seven of these requested full-time party status and one requested part-time status.

In July 1993, just before the public hearings were to begin, Laidlaw issued a written argument to Ontario EAB and prospective intervenor groups, including OWMC. The company's long-standing disagreements with the crown corporation came through clearly in its arguments and conclusions regarding the merits of the proposal and why it was needed. The document cautioned that while a rotary kiln incinerator would be most useful for burning some of the wastes that were already going to the Laidlaw facility, OWMC's proposal would only duplicate, rather than add to, treatment capacity. In response, OWMC made a statement reminiscent of Ontario's remarks about the CECOS and CWM proposals in Niagara, New York that it was "not in opposition to the proposal, in principle" (EAB, August 1993: 39). Nonetheless, the crown corporation expressed concerns about how Laidlaw's proposed incinerator would affect the market for OWMC if it were to be approved and how operational and environmental safeguards would compare with those OWMC planned for its own facility.

LOCAL OPPOSITION TO LAIDLAW

Most local groups and individuals were opposed to the Laidlaw proposal, except for the Moore township government, which stated no firm preference but did ask to participate in the proceedings on a full-time basis to ensure that local safety concerns were addressed to its satisfaction. The four local groups who opposed the new incinerator and requested full-time party status were the Citizen's Environmental Action Group (CEAG), a local environmental group; the Lambton Federation of Agriculture; the Saint Joseph's Health Centre; and the Walpole Island First Nation. In addition, two individuals who were nearby residents of the Laidlaw facility expressed their opposition and requested party status in the proceedings. In general, these groups expressed concerns related to ongoing problems they had experienced with the existing facility historically, as well as the potential for increased problems brought on by the proposed new incinerator.

Laidlaw Withdraws

Just two months after what was to have been the first of several public hearings on Laidlaw, the company withdrew its proposal for a new incinerator. The announcement came after the conclusion of OWMC hearings in September 1993. In an information release, the changed plans were attributed to "insufficient market need and the availability of alternative technologies" (Laidlaw, October 1993). This justification seemed surprising given that as little as two months before in the EAB hearing the company had claimed publicly that the facility was needed. Laidlaw's reversal on the issue of need seemed to refer as much to OWMC as it did to its own proposal, insomuch as insufficient need for additional capacity was a direct challenge to the Ontario government's assumption that the OWMC facility was necessary to ensure adequate capacity:

> The reality is that rotary kilns operating within the North American environmental services sector are running at an average of only 70 per cent of available capacity. The time has come and gone when Ontario's needs require a 20,000-tonne-capacity rotary kiln in the province. The service can be provided in other ways. (Laidlaw, October 1993)

Hazardous Waste Facility Siting in Michigan

In the State of Michigan, hazardous waste siting is conducted pursuant to the Michigan Hazardous Waste Management Act (Act 64 of 1979). As with the State of New York's facility siting cases in Niagara County, Michigan uses a regulated market strategy that relies on private waste management firms to propose particular projects in specified locations. The Michigan

Department of Environmental Quality (MI DEQ) has the responsibil-ity of reviewing hazardous waste facility siting applications and requiring proposal modifications if it deems them to be necessary or desirable. Until October 1995, this responsibility rested with the Michigan Department of Natural Resources (MI DNR). MI DEQ either denies the application or submits a draft construction permit to the Site Review Board (SRB) which is responsible for overseeing public hearings, reviewing arguments and evidence from parties to the proceedings, and making a recommendation to approve or deny the proposal.

The SRB includes ten members, two representing the local area and eight who are "permanent" members pursuant to 1987 amendments to Act 64. Prior to 1987, the board reflected local interests to a greater extent in that it consisted of four local members and five permanent members. That year, the composition of SRB was changed so that one local member is appointed by the municipal government of the town or city where the facility is to be located, while the other is appointed by the county govern-ment. The state governor appoints the eight permanent members, one of whom serves as a non-voting chairperson. The others include a geologist, a chemical engineer, a toxicologist, a representative from a manufacturing industry, two representatives from the public, and a municipal government representative (from a community other than the location of the proposed facility). Other groups and individuals may attend the public hearings and are allowed to make statements and submit evidence to SRB, but, unlike what happens in New York and Ontario, they are not given party status. In 1991, shortly after his inauguration, Governor Engler made a more sig-nificant change to hazardous waste siting by giving the authority for final determinations to MI DNR, now MI DEQ. SRB now has only an advisory role in such matters.

Since 1979 when the original hazardous waste facility siting provi-sions were put into law under Act 64, SRB has conducted hearings for seven separate commercial hazardous waste proposals. The first, in 1981, regarded an incinerator in the western part of the state on the shore of Lake Michigan, outside of this study region. The other six were in the Detroit metropolitan area and are reviewed in the following sections. They include a Wayne County landfill (EMS), reviewed from June 1982 to October 1982; an Oakland County incinerator (ERES Corporation), reviewed from September 1982 to December 1982; an Oakland County treatment facil-ity and landfill (Stablex Corporation), reviewed from December 1982 to

October 1983; a treatment facility in the City of Detroit (NCS), reviewed from December 1987 to May 1988; and another City of Detroit treatment facility (City Environmental), reviewed from July 1988 to September 1989. In addition, a sixth Detroit-area deep-well injection facility (EDS) was constructed in Wayne County in October 1993 after three years of planning and with approval from local officials. The SRB did not review the case initially, however, because of a loophole in Act 64 that exempts deep-well injection systems from the review process if no other facilities are involved. The action resulted in a series of lawsuits that came to an end in 1996 when EDS proposed to build another deep-well system at a nearby location, also in Romulus. The new proposal included an adjacent storage facility, thus triggering the SRB process and other reviews.

ENVIRONMENTAL MANAGEMENT SYSTEMS (EMS)

In June 1982, SRB began reviewing the Environmental Management Systems (EMS) proposal for a hazardous waste landfill in the Wayne County community of Sumpter Township. Wayne County includes the City of Detroit and stretches to the south. It had a population just over 2,000,000 and a lower than average median household income of $27,997 as compared to Michigan state-wide figures ($31,020).[1] The county's racial makeup was 57.4 per cent white, 40.2 per cent black, and 2.4 per cent other. Sumpter Township is a largely white (85.3 per cent), suburban community with a population just over 10,000 and a slightly higher than average median household income of $34,929. The proposed facility would have been an 80-acre hazardous waste landfill expansion of an existing 160-acre municipal waste landfill. The original landfill had been in operation for an unknown period of time but was known to have been accepting wastes for more than 20 years at the time of the public hearings in 1982 (SRB, August 1982).

SRB heard testimony from MI DNR and the applicant, EMS, as well as local residents and government representatives from Sumpter Township. MI DNR had already issued a draft construction permit and took the position that the proposed facility and location met all the technical requirements of Act 64. EMS spoke to the suitability of the site in terms of the "natural" containment provided by 20 feet of clay deposits and of the technical sophistication of the design with its synthetic liner and leachate collection system. All other testimony came from local government officials and residents who were decidedly negative toward the proposal.

Several representatives of the Sumpter Township government and their technical consultants expressed concerns about the suitability of the site in terms of hydrogeology and also about ongoing problems with the existing landfill. The various officials testified that well monitoring data from the existing facility showed evidence of styrene and sulfate contamination. In addition, core samples from the natural clay deposits at the site were found to be sufficiently high in moisture content as to hinder their ability to prevent leaching and ground water contamination. They were also concerned about high ground water levels in the area (less than one foot below the surface in places), the presence of numerous private wells, and the potential for flooding. Finally, they questioned the fairness of the process, in particular the "contractual relationship" that would occur between MI DNR and EMS should the facility be approved. The township supervisor suggested that, if granted, the permit should be a "three-way" agreement, with the community acting as the third party. Numerous local residents made statements throughout the hearings, generally expressing ongoing frustrations with the existing facility and the potential for increased problems if the new facility were to be approved. Truck traffic and odor problems were the most commonly mentioned difficulties.

In October 1982 after four months of hearings, SRB met one final time to issue their decision, which was to deny a permit by a vote of six to three. Because the proceedings took place before the 1987 amendments to Act 64, the panel included four local members and five permanent members (rather than two and seven). This was probably critical to the outcome given that all four local members voted to deny the permit and three of the five permanent members voted for approval. The reasons for the decision included unresolved concerns about a "poor record of performance" at the existing landfill and the potential for flooding. Central to the permit denial was the matter of the high water table, which would put the landfill in direct contact with ground water, a violation of Act 64 (R299.6415).

ENERGY RECOVERY SYSTEMS (ERES) CORPORATION

In September 1982, SRB initiated hearings regarding an Energy Recovery Systems Corporation (ERES) proposal for a hazardous waste incinerator in the Oakland County community of Pontiac Township. Oakland County is a suburban jurisdiction within the Detroit metropolitan area and lies to the northwest of the City of Detroit. The county had a population just over

1,000,000 and a higher than average median household income of $43,407 as compared to the state generally ($31,020), and a racial makeup of 89.6 per cent white, 7.1 per cent black and 3.3 per cent other. Pontiac Township is located to the north of the City of Pontiac, within the Pontiac metropolitan area, which had a population just over 71,000,000, a lower than average median household income of $21,962, and a racial distribution of 51.5 per cent white, 42.2 per cent black and 6.3 per cent other.

The proposed incinerator site was a 50-acre tract of vacant land adjacent to an existing municipal waste landfill. SRB heard from six State of Michigan legislators and a number of local residents, each of whom was vehemently opposed to the proposed facility. Their comments ranged widely but generally focused on local nuisance issues such as noise and odors as well as risk-related concerns about emissions from the stack, the possibility for ground and surface water contamination, and truck traffic. Local government officials from Pontiac Township, two nearby villages, and a school board voiced their opposition to the proposal and submitted resolutions to that effect as evidence for SRB review. A representative of the American Lung Association's Southeast Michigan Chapter expressed opposition because of the potential toxicity of emissions. The most positive reaction came from the Oakland County Health Division, which supported the proposal as a way of dealing with the problem of "hazardous waste materials which are indiscriminately entering [waste water treatment facilities] via sewers, landfills and illicit dumpings" (SRB, October 1982).

In December 1982, SRB issued a seven-to-one decision to deny the permit. All four local members voted against the facility as did three of the four permanent members. The decision was not based on direct evidence that the facility would be unable to comply with Act 64 or otherwise pose an unreasonable risk to the community or the environment, as occurred in the EMS verdict, but on the basis that ERES had failed to submit a satisfactory analysis of risk related to transportation, ground and surface water contamination, fires and explosions, and overall environmental impact. In addition, the board concluded that ERES had "failed to provide adequate information to indicate that it possesses the level of technical and managerial expertise needed to safely operate a facility of the size and complexity being proposed" (SRB, December 1982). In effect, the decision to deny the facility was based as much on an insufficient application for permit (from the proponent) as it was on the insufficiencies of the proposed facility itself.

STABLEX CORPORATION

SRB first met to review the Stablex facility siting proposal in December 1982. The applicant was seeking approval to build a landfill and stabilization/treatment facility in the suburban Oakland County community of Groveland Township to the north of Pontiac, Michigan. Groveland Township had a mostly white (97.1 per cent) population of just under 5,000 and a higher than average median household income of $48,288 as compared to the State of Michigan generally. Stablex was proposing to convert a 200-acre quarry into a landfill and treatment facility. The first stage of the project would have involved a 50-acre landfill, but the applicant's long-term plan was for up to a 184-acre landfill.

The proposal was particularly controversial because it would not have included a synthetic liner, which Stablex argued would be unnecessary given its patented process of solidification. The "sealosafe" solidification process used calcium alumino silicate (typically flyash from coal plants) and cement mixed with chemically pre-treated hazardous wastes. The British company had developed and applied the process at landfills in England and later at a facility in the Montreal area. The proposal was not new to area residents since the company had originally sought approval for the facility in 1978 when EPA issued Stablex an unusual regulatory waiver from the general requirement for synthetic liners in all hazardous waste landfills. Because the case was first proposed before the 1979 passage of Act 64 and the establishment of SRB, it was initially handled as a civil proceeding and went through a variety of appeals. In May 1981, the Michigan Court of Appeals denied Stablex's request for a construction permit and ordered an SRB review.

During public hearings before SRB from December 1982 to October 1983, local government officials and residents of Groveland Township expressed numerous concerns about the Stablex facility. Town officials took issue with the landfill's incompatibility with the site's existing E1 (extraction) zoning, the population density in a three-square-mile vicinity (4,136 persons per square mile), a lack of hydrogeological assessments, a lack of emergency planning, and the "untested" nature of the "sealosafe" process (at least within the United States). A number of area residents spoke to each of these concerns as well as to the problem of odors and the potential for accidents between waste haulers and school buses. Many of the complaints implied a lack of trust in the company, particularly given its previous attempts to avoid the SRB process and the various competing appeals between the company and the township that had ensued.

In September 1983, SRB took a preliminary poll of members and denied the construction permit by a vote of six to three. Each of the four local members voted for denial as did two of the five permanent members. The decision was based on incompatible hydrogeology (the site was on top of an aquifer with no natural barrier), a conflict with local zoning, potential harm to local recreation in nearby streams and lakes, insufficient engineering plans, and a lack of proof that the "sealosafe" technology is safe without a synthetic liner. The decision was adopted in October 1983 by a five-to-two vote (one local member and one permanent member were not present).

NATIONAL CHEMICAL SERVICES (NCS)

SRB hearings on a National Chemical Services (NCS) proposal for a hazardous waste treatment facility in the City of Detroit began in December 1987. Detroit's population was just over 1,000,000 with 75.6 per cent black, 21.6 per cent white and 2.8 per cent other. Its median household income ($18,742) was much lower than the Michigan state-wide average ($31,020). The facility was proposed for siting in the highly industrial southwestern part of the city in the neighborhood of Delray. The area had a population just under 4,000 and was 61 per cent white, 29 per cent black and 10 per cent other. The City of Detroit's Master Plan has addressed this aspect of Delray's environment in terms of a long-standing dilemma regarding the "incompatible" needs of residents and industries in the context of urban decay and deindustrialization:

> The City now advocates retention of Delray as a community, including housing, schools, churches, the health center, and commercial and retail services.... Many changes may be needed. In Delray, the general "goal" of accommodating reindustrialization within existing industrial corridors is not entirely feasible because of the current inter-mixtures of land uses. (City of Detroit, 1985)

At the time of the public hearings, NCS already operated a spent acid regeneration facility at the 7.2-acre site and was seeking approval to build a series of tanks to chemically treat 72,000 gallons per day of metal-bearing wastes as well as spent acids. Members of the Delray Environmental Concerned Citizens Association (DECCA) as well as many individual neighborhood residents opposed the facility expansion on the grounds of pollution problems from the various industries in the area. Especially troubling was a permit application submitted by a cement company in the Delray neighborhood (Peerless Cement) so that it could begin burning paint sludges, thinners, and solvents in its kiln. In January 1988, after a year of public hearings regarding NCS, MI DNR rejected Peerless's permit application, diffusing at least one of the community's frustrations. With respect to the NCS facility specifically, community opponents expressed the usual concerns regarding truck traffic, air emissions, and the threat of spills, fires, and explosions. The existing NCS facility's record of perform-ance was not specifically referenced as a cause for concern.

The City of Detroit was not officially opposed to the NCS proposal but stopped short of supporting it. In a written statement to SRB, the Detroit Health Department expressed the need for "proper" waste management fa-cilities "to protect the overall public health and the environment" (Detroit Health Department, April 1988). The document never defined what a proper facility might be or whether the NCS proposal might be able meet that test, but it did go on to state the following position:

> The safeguards designed into this facility's operation appear, in theory, to reduce the public health risk to the neighborhood to minimal levels under normal operation. However, we are still unable to lend our full support to the siting of this facility in this particular location due to the concerns for the public health and safety in the immediate neighborhood. (Detroit Health Department, April 1988: 1)

In May 1988, SRB voted to approve the NCS proposal with a vote of seven to one. All five permanent members voted to grant the permit as did two of the four local members. Of the two remaining local members, only one voted against the facility and the other was not present. Even the one member who voted for denial explained his decision as an act of solidarity with the community given its opposition, but expressed the belief that the company "would live up to [its] agreement" to operate the facility safely (SRB, May 1988: 12). Despite the SRB approval, however, NCS decided not to expand its facility due to a lack of market demand (Burda, 1997).

CITY ENVIRONMENTAL

SRB hearings on the proposed City Environmental, Incorporated, chemical treatment facility began in February 1989. The company was proposing to site the plant on the city's near east side one block from Detroit's highly controversial municipal waste incinerator. The neighborhood had a population just under 6,000 and was 73 per cent black, 25 per cent white and 2 per cent other. City Environmental's parent company, City Management Corporation, hauled garbage and incinerator ash on a contractual basis for the municipal incinerator. City Environmental also operated hazardous and municipal waste landfills throughout the State of Michigan. Their proposal was for a treatment facility to process up to 100,000 gallons per day of corrosive and metal-bearing wastewaters.

The City of Detroit made no objections to the City Environmental proposal, but area residents voiced a number of concerns during the public hearings. Ongoing problems with the Detroit incinerator were heavily emphasized as evidence that the company, given its relationship to City Management, could not be trusted to operate a safe hazardous waste facility. The municipal incinerator has been in operation since 1988 and has drawn criticism ever since, not only from Detroit area residents, but also environmental groups and the Province of Ontario. With respect to the City Environmental proposal itself, area residents' concerns were very similar to those expressed during the NCS proceedings. The most common problems they feared related to truck traffic, air emissions, and the threat of spills, fires and explosions.

In September 1989, SRB voted in favor of granting City Environmental a permit with an eight-to-one vote. The only vote to deny the permit was made by one of the two local members. This was the first SRB proceeding to operate pursuant to the 1987 amendments to Act 64 that changed the composition of the board from four local and five permanent voting members to two local and seven permanent members. It has been eight years since the SRB granted City Environmental permission to begin construction, but it has not done so and has no present plans to that effect. As with NCS's decision not to expand its existing treatment facility, as well as Laidlaw's decision to withdraw its proposal for an incinerator, the City Environmental case reflects a lean market for hazardous waste facilities. One reason for this has to do with increased capacity and competition in the industry, partly from expansions of existing commercial hazardous waste facilities and additionally from the blending of liquid hazardous wastes with fuel oil to burn in cement kilns and other industrial boilers (Hanke, 1993). A second reason is the increased practice of on-site pre-treatment of wastes in the chemical industry and other sectors. The most common form of this involves the removal of water from liquid wastes so as to reduce volume, though toxicity and other hazardous characteristics generally increase with this method (Bouck, 1993). A third aspect of the present hazardous waste market is that current practices in contaminated site remediation emphasize on-site containment of wastes rather than the more costly method of off-site disposal, which was more common in the 1980s (Bouck, 1993).

Environmental Disposal Systems (EDS)

In August 1990, Environmental Disposal Systems, Incorporated (EDS) initiated plans to build a deep-well injection system to dispose of liquid hazardous wastes in the suburban Wayne County community of Romulus. The City of Romulus had a population of nearly 23,000 and a racial composition of 85.3 per cent white, 13.7 per cent black and 1.0 per cent other. The city's median household income was $31,723, slightly higher than the Michigan state-wide average. From the beginning, City of Romulus council members worked closely with EDS to develop a proposal that both the company and the city government could support. In January 1993, the city council passed a resolution in support of the facility after reaching an agreement with the company that the local government would receive 5 per cent royalties.

SRB did not have the opportunity to review the EDS proposal initially, so public input was minimal. The project slipped through a loophole in Act 64 that exempts deep-well injection if no other facilities are involved. The system was designed to allow liquid waste haulers to connect directly to the well head without the use of a storage facility, thus avoiding the siting process. The facility has the capacity to receive 400,000 gallons per day and up to 96 million gallons per year. MI DNR officials issued a construction permit in October 1991 but cautioned EDS officials that the SRB process would be advisable to protect the company's interests once the facility began operations should community opposition become an issue (Burda, 1994). EDS declined the advice and began construction in July 1993. The facility was completely built by August that same year.

Shortly after the facility's construction was complete but before it was able to begin operations, public opinion against the project started to grow rapidly. In September 1993 a candidate for city council expressed opposition to the city's agreement with EDS. In early October, several hundred residents attended a protest meeting regarding the issue and urged the council to intervene before an operating permit could be issued. One week later, the council issued a unanimous resolution to file an injunction against the company. On October 22, 1993, just two weeks before the council election, the city filed a lawsuit against EDS charging that the company had not complied with local zoning procedures and that the location was unsuitable for a hazardous waste facility. A 1997 court ruling prevented EDS from operating the facility but in 1999 the zoning issue was finally settled when an appeals court ruled that the facility was exempt from local zoning as long as it complied with state and federal environmental regulations. The City of Romulus and several environmental groups have continued to oppose the facility. The most vocal opposition came from a local group known as Romulus Environmentalists Care About People (RECAP).

In 2000, SRB ruled against the facility but their decision was not heeded by MI DEC which now holds final decision-making authority on hazardous waste siting. SRB opposed the facility on numerous grounds, the most fundamental of which was its argument that additional capacity was not needed. The board noted that hazardous waste generation was declining in Michigan and that pollution prevention could reduce the reliance on disposal facilities even further. Moreover, if allowed to operate, SRB suggested, the EDS site would "encourage" imports of hazardous waste from other American states and Canada. SRB also concluded that MI DEQ should reject the proposal because of uncertainties with the technology itself, particularly since it would be the only deep-well system operating in Michigan. The hydrogeological implications of injecting hazardous wastes underground were especially troubling to board members.

SRB was particularly concerned that MI DEQ had not reviewed social and cumulative matters sufficiently in its permit review of the EDS facility, leading to a December 2000 proposed permit. The board members argued that the cumulative impact of waste hauling to and from the facility would present an additional risk to the community that had not been addressed sufficiently. Additionally, they felt that MI DEQ should have considered the environmental justice implications of the operation, given the large proportion of blacks in the Detroit area, particularly in Wayne County. In February 2001, MI DEQ ruled against the SRB recommendations and in favor of EDS.

Summary of Cases in the Detroit and Sarnia Areas

Of the seven facility siting proposals in the Detroit and Sarnia areas, only three treatment facilities were approved, two of which were never built. Aside from the underground injection facility which was built without public hearings, siting boards approved none of the four remaining proposals involving two landfills and two incinerators. One of these was withdrawn by the proponent and the other three were denied permits.

In spite of the major efforts of facility proponents, they ultimately achieved little in the way of success. The following three sections, patterned after those in Chapter 4, will examine this question by reviewing the cases and analyzing them in terms of key decisions made by various stakeholders along the way. The definition of facility need, for example, was a fundamental issue that proponents had to prove successfully in order to realize their plans. Likewise, the selection of particular facility characteristics such as location, size, and type was critical. Finally, siting boards considered issues of fairness in terms of process and outcome in their final decisions. Each of the stakeholder groups had its own arguments and evidence about these issues and attempted to convince decision-making officials as to the veracity of their claims. Ultimately, siting boards had to consider the opinions and justifications of all parties with regard to each of the issues in question in order to reach their own conclusions (see Table 8).

Defining Facility Need

SARNIA, ONTARIO

Defining facility need was one of the most central issues that faced the Laidlaw-Sarnia decision. The company's role as an intervening party to the OWMC proposal in Niagara, Ontario was at least part of what made this the case. In an environmental assessment of its own rotary kiln incinerator proposal, Laidlaw dismissed the OWMC proposal because it considered the construction and operation of a hazardous waste management facility to be an inappropriate activity for government. The company argued that the province's West Lincoln facility would turn out badly for the public interest as well as for Laidlaw itself on the basis that OWMC would "maximize rather than minimize public sector costs" and would create "major financial

TABLE 8

Summary of Cases in Sarnia and Detroit

Community & Existing Site	Proponent & Proposal	Opposition Groups & Issues	Outcome & Reasons
Moore, ON (agricultural): HW Landfill & Incinerator	Laidlaw: Incinerator (12/89-10/93)	Local Groups, Walpole Island: Cumulative & Spatial Equity	Withdrawn: Lack of market
Sumpter, MI (suburban): Munic. Landfill	EMS: Landfill (6/82-10/82)	Township, School Board: Hydrogeology	Denied: Hydrogeology
Pontiac, MI (suburban): Munic. Landfill	ERES: Incinerator (9/82-12/82)	Township, School Board: Hydrogeology & Proponent	Denied: Hydrogeology & Proponent
Groveland, MI (suburban): Quarry Site	Stablex: Landfill (12/82-9/83)	Township: Hydrogeology & Design	Denied: Hydrogeology & Design
Detroit, MI (urban): Treatment Facil.	NCS: Treatment Facility (12/87-5/88)	Local Group: Cumulative Equity	Approved: Never Built
Detroit, MI (urban): Munic. Incinerator	City Env: Treatment Facil (2/89-9/89)	Unorganized Residents:Cum. Equity	Approved: Never Built
Romulus, MI (suburban): Greenfield	EDS: Underground Injection (8/90-2/01)	City (after initial support)	Approved

uncertainties and limited financial return for Laidlaw Environmental" (Laidlaw, 1990). A public-sector crown corporation approach, the company argued, would be "highly inflexible" due to its "depenuden[ce] upon facilities which have yet to be approved, unknown cost arrangements, and undefined role in the market place." Further, it would mean a "major reorientation for Laidlaw Environmental from [a] major to minor treatment role" (Laidlaw, 1990).

In its early statements regarding the need for its own facility expansion, Laidlaw's aversion to the OWMC project came through as well. The company argued that adding a rotary kiln incinerator to its existing facility in Moore Township near Sarnia would allow it to treat organic sludges and solids otherwise either landfilled without being treated or shipped out of province. Conversely, Laidlaw suggested that the crown corporation approach of building the OWMC facility on the Niagara peninsula would only hinder Ontario's ability to meet industries' disposal needs by disrupting the private market and corresponding profits. Laidlaw's private-sector plan would "redirect" waste, not to another facility in another region as OWMC favored, but within the existing Laidlaw-Sarnia site:

> Laidlaw Environmental [proposes] to enhance the environmental integrity of its existing operations by redirecting selected organic wastes to an environmentally preferred management option. The redirection of such wastes can only be realized to the extent that service delivery by Laidlaw Environmental to its customers and market share are not diminished.
>
> [A]dditional market share may be necessary to maintain the requisite profitability.... As a private sector proponent offering an important and necessary waste management service to government, industry and the public, it is in the public interest and it is consistent with Laidlaw Environmental's corporate mandate, to increase the type and level of service it can provide economically and at every available opportunity. (Laidlaw, 1990: 8)

In its early statements, and throughout the public hearing, Laidlaw continued to reiterate its interrelated arguments regarding the role of government and facility need. As a facility proponent it also had to address the question of whether pollution prevention could sufficiently diminish the need for existing and future waste disposal capacity. Laidlaw concluded there was "no further potential for reduction of target waste streams and no evident prospects—given limitations of market, technology and waste characteristics" (Laidlaw, 1990). Yet, in a final statement explaining the withdrawal of its proposal, Laidlaw strongly suggested that no new facilities were needed in Ontario since the province could make greater use of pollution prevention to reduce waste in need of treatment and send the remainder to existing rotary kiln incinerators in Canada and the United States:

> [U]nder existing and projected market conditions, Laidlaw Environmental could provide effective treatment services more economically by offering waste generators access to rotary kilns already in operation in the North American market and by continuing to pursue waste minimization opportunities within the province. (Laidlaw, 1993)

DETROIT, MICHIGAN

In Michigan, hazardous waste facility siting has been subject to similar kinds of proceedings as in Ontario and New York, but with different sets of circumstances. With respect to the role of government, the Detroit area proposals were similar to those in Sarnia, Ontario and Niagara, New York in that they were all subject to a regulated market approach with private corporations submitting proposals for government review. The Michigan cases differed in that they were heard by larger and more diverse siting boards as compared to those in the other jurisdictions, but citizens groups were not given official status as intervenor groups. Further, Michigan's SRB became less represented by community interests after 1987 revisions to Act 64 which reduced the number of "local" members from four to two and replaced them with two more "permanent" members appointed by the governor. Since 1991, the state government has had even greater autonomy over local interests in hazardous waste facility siting since SRB decisions are now only advisory and are not binding on MI DEQ, the state's environmental regulatory agency.

The siting board composition and the opinions of permanent and local members were important factors in the outcomes of Michigan facility siting cases. The City Environmental proposal was the first proposal reviewed pursuant to the new SRB makeup. Had the changes to Act 64 been made earlier, other cases may have turned out differently. Three of the four cases prior to City Environmental ended in permit denials because of unanimous opposition from local board members. The fourth such proposal, NCS, was approved because two of the three local members present at the time of the final vote were willing to grant the permit.

In light of the number of failed attempts to site new hazardous waste facilities, need was a continuing issue that drove MI DNR's support of each.
Had the proposals not been seen as necessary in light of capacity assurance
objectives with which all American states must comply, the agency would
have had far less interest in supporting them. After three unsuccessful facility siting attempts in 1982 and 1983, the need for additional capacity was
still unresolved from the state government's point of view. In a 1984 report
of hazardous waste options, MI DNR recommended the SRB membership
changes that were later written into law precisely because of a perceived
need for new facilities. The report attributed the need for new facilities
to (a) wastes from contaminated site cleanups, (b) increased compliance
from small quantity generators, and (c) ongoing waste generation from
large industries (MI DNR, 1984). After witnessing three denials and two
approvals, MI DNR issued a 1991 Hazardous Waste Management Plan in
which it continued to express interest in the siting of new facilities but also
recognized the importance of waste reduction:

> Michigan policy should support the general goal of achiev-
> ing and maintaining sufficient hazardous waste management
> capacity (at a variety of types of facilities) within the state to
> meet the needs of Michigan generators, without precluding the
> interstate transport of imports and exports. When feasible, this
> capacity should be located at multiple sites to provide stability
> in site availability.
>
> Michigan policy and studies on future management capacity
> and needs should continue to incorporate the projected impact
> of ongoing hazardous waste reduction, including the impact of
> the state hazardous waste reduction policies. (MI DNR, 1991:
> 36)

The role of local government took an interesting twist in the EDS case
in that the Romulus city council was initially in favor of the project—so
much so that members worked closely with the company in developing
the proposal—yet ended up opposing the facility and filing suit against the
company after construction was completed. Also, of all the cases reviewed
in Chapters 4 and 5, this was the only one in which state government
officials expressed reservations about a proposal (at least in terms of its
avoidance of a public SRB review) and where the official local government

position was supportive (even if only initially). MI DEQ's concern related specifically to the lack of a formal SRB, and thus community, review. The city council's initial support of EDS only changed when community concerns became obvious. Once SRB was finally able to conduct a public review of EDS, it concluded that facility need had not been demonstrated given a decline in hazardous waste generation in Michigan, though MI DEQ disagreed with the board's nonbinding decision. The facility, now owned by Michigan Recovery Systems, has become the eighth largest emitter of toxic substances throughout North America and the second largest in Michigan (CEC, 2002).

Selecting Facility Location, Size, and Type

SARNIA, ONTARIO

The Laidlaw-Sarnia case was interesting in terms of its location because of the issues it would have raised had it been approved. Groups opposed to the CWM and CECOS facilities in Niagara, New York expressed considerable frustration at being the only region of the state with commercial hazardous waste facilities. Niagara, Ontario opponents of the OWMC facility objected to having four separate facilities on one site in their rural community. As it stands, the Laidlaw-Sarnia facility is the only commercial hazardous waste facility in the province and would only have increased in size had the company continued its support for the proposal and received the necessary approvals. The OWMC process was still under way at this point, but its eventual failure to win the approval of EAB left the Sarnia area with the only commercial landfill and incinerator in the Province of Ontario. It is ironic that the Sarnia area ended up with exactly the situation that Niagara, Ontario residents feared so much with regard to the OWMC facility. Today, the facility, owned by Safety-Kleen, Inc., is the seventh largest emitter of toxic substances and the largest emitter of known or suspected carcinogens in North America and the largest in Ontario of both. Perhaps most significantly is that the facility's releases of toxic substances increased more than any other facility in North America; from 1998 to 1999, the most recent year for which North American comparative data are available, Safety-Kleen's disposal of hazardous waste (mostly zinc and compounds) increased from 152,090 kg to 15,378,584 kg, a surge of over 10,000 per cent (CEC, 2002).

Contrary to the OWMC process that led to a site selection in Niagara, Ontario, each of the Sarnia and Detroit area proposals was submitted by commercial waste management firms. In each, the role of government was limited to reviewing the applications and overseeing the public hearings. As was the case with the Niagara, New York disputes, risk became a dominant issue in the context of site selection and review. The Laidlaw-Sarnia case did not have the chance to reach this point in its EAB proceedings before the company withdrew its proposal, so we will never know how risk concerns would have ultimately played out in this case.

DETROIT, MICHIGAN

The Michigan SRB denied the EMS and Stablex landfills and the ERES incinerator based on hydrogeological concerns about the potential for leaching and ground water contamination. Such concerns were also important to the SRB recommendation that MI DEQ deny the EDS permit, even though the advice was not heeded. These outcomes were much the same as with the OWMC-South Cayuga and CECOS decisions in the Niagara region. In addition, Michigan SRB officials expressed serious concerns about the ability and willingness of private sector applicants to operate the facilities safely. In a MI DNR report issued one year after the third SRB permit denial, the agency addressed concerns about the siting dilemma:

> There are people who cite the fact that three proposed commercial facilities have been denied by site review boards and go from that experience to draw the conclusion that the process will never result in the siting of a new commercially available facility. Others contend that the fact that the site review board turned down these three applications gives evidence to the fact that the site review board process is working. They cite deficiencies in the applications and the answers provided by the applicant during the site review board meetings as the reasons for denial. (MI DNR, 1984: 39)

Because hydrogeology was central to each of the SRB decisions to deny permits, the report explored siting options that would require a preliminary assessment of environmentally suitable locations before applications are even submitted. In its 1984 report, MI DNR addressed this idea with reference to Ontario's OWMC proposal, among other issues:

> There has also been interest expressed in having the state do some prequalification of hazardous waste sites. The State could select several sites which are geologically and otherwise environmentally appropriate for a hazardous waste management facility. The trouble with this suggestion is that it results in great public controversy over possible hazardous waste sites without there ever being an applicant for the site. This problem has occurred in both Ontario and Minnesota.
>
> Also, if the state is involved in selecting potential sites, it can create even greater controversy when an applicant comes to the site review board. It will appear to the citizens the state selected the site and thus are [sic] a co-applicant for the facility. (MI DNR, 1984: 40)

Facility size and type were also important factors affecting the outcome of facility siting decisions. After having denied permits for two landfills and an incinerator, MI SRB approved the NCS and City Environmental treatment facilities. In comparison to landfills and incinerators, treatment facilities are much smaller and present fewer environmental risks since they neither involve direct contact with the land nor continuous emissions. This is not to say that either of the City of Detroit neighborhoods involved in the treatment facility proposals welcomed their presence. Local SRB members were divided over the decisions, whereas in the three prior cases, which involved landfills or incinerators, local members had been unified in their opposition to the proposals. MI DNR also expressed fewer concerns about treatment facilities as compared to landfills:

> It must also be recognized that every hazardous waste management facility is not a hazardous waste landfill and the natural geological protection which might be preferred for wastes which are to be permanently stored, such as landfilling, may not be required for processing plants which receive limited quantities and types of wastes and pose little threat to the groundwater. (MI DNR, 1984: 40)

Michigan's SRB and DEQ would later have similar disagreements about facility type under new procedural arrangements brought about by the Engler administration. While SRB was fully opposed to permitting the state's only deep-well injection facility on the grounds that the technology had the potential for unnecessary hydrogeological risks to future generations, MI DEQ deferred to separate state (MI DNR) and federal (US EPA) reviews and approved the permit. It focused its review on the adjacent storage facility that EDS initially had attempted not to build. The agency argued that SRB and public concerns about ground water contamination problems with deep-well injection operations in other parts of the country had more to do with improper storage on the ground surface than with migration from the subsurface. Their permit decision added that the EDS storage facility would have adequate controls to contain any possible spillage.

Promoting Fairness in Facility Siting

SARNIA, ONTARIO

The Laidlaw facility was opposed by community groups in two respects related to fairness. The first problem had to do with the existing facility and its location. The Sarnia-based group CEAG argued that the proposal was deficient in terms of its lack of a "real" site selection process and an "appropriate consideration of a reasonable range of alternatives to the undertaking" (EAB, 1993: 30). Unlike the OWMC process for Niagara, Ontario with which residents of the Sarnia area were very familiar, the Laidlaw siting process was simply another of many expansions of an existing land use that was becoming an increasing nuisance in the eyes of local opposition groups.

Walpole Island's Ojibwe residents voiced a second objection to the siting process because Laidlaw had excluded them from previously held consultation sessions with local residents. In addition, the company refused to offer them intervenor funding to cover the legal and administrative costs of full party status. Laidlaw offered the remuneration to CEAG and Moore Township only and had excluded Walpole Island from the public consultations and the funding on the basis that the community was located outside the "community study area" boundary. Walpole residents' interest in participating had less to do with their proximity to the facility in a strict sense than it did with the island's downriver location from the Sarnia area where not only Laidlaw, but also several other heavy industries, are located. The community has had a long history of environmental problems because of their geographic position relative to Sarnia area industries.

DETROIT, MICHIGAN

On the whole, the six Michigan siting disputes had less to do with fairness or equity compared to the New York and Ontario cases. One reason may be that commercial hazardous waste facilities are not unique to the Detroit area, where there are five already located in the northern, western, and central regions of the state. This is very different from the situation in Ontario where one area (Sarnia) hosts the only commercial hazardous waste facility and in New York State where its only two commercial facilities are both located in one county (Niagara County). The first three suburban proposals in Michigan were opposed by local groups and also rejected by SRB largely on the basis of risk-related concerns, particularly hydrogeology. In the fourth suburban case, EDS, local residents' concerns were also dominated by questions about risk in terms of the overall safety of deep-well injection as a disposal method.

Fairness issues were not altogether missing from local objections to the Detroit area proposals. Critics of EDS's deep-well injection facility, for example, alluded to spatial equity by drawing attention to the company's plans to draw its customer base partly from Ontario and other parts of Canada. Additionally, SRB criticized MI DEQ, now responsible for final approval decisions, for not adequately considering environmental justice issues given the large black and low-income population in metropolitan Detroit, especially Wayne County. Local opponents of the two City of Detroit treatment facility proposals emphasized cumulative risk as a central area of concern. Their specific objections had less to do with the potential for leaching and air emissions from the particular facilities up for review than they did with ongoing problems related to area industries. To repeat a point from the previous section, treatment facilities are less noxious than landfills or incinerators since they do not involve dumping or burning, though the related issue of truck traffic may still be a sore point for affected communities.

To distinguish itself from other industries in the Delray community, NCS negotiated an agreement with ten separate local groups just one day before the SRB took its vote on the proposed facility expansion. The company agreed to hire 60 per cent of its employees from Delray and committed itself to $12,000 in annual donations to area schools and for a neighborhood rehabilitation program, among other concessions. In the last public hearing, the president of the local group DECCA, which had opposed the proposal initially, ended up defending NCS while calling attention to the cumulative environmental problems presented by other industries:

> This might not be much to the liking of my community, but I would like to say that since I have lived here for 36 years, I have the same concerns that you do and I have to live, breathe and live in that same area that you do. I think that it is a shame that with the organizations that we have in our community, that our people are not more knowledgeable about the differences between this company and an incineration company. This is a recycling industry. They do not burn, they recycle. And when you recycle a product, it is not profitable to lose anything that they are processing.
>
> They are the first ones ... that have offered to work with the community.... Nobody else has done that.... [I]f they are given their permits, which they probably will, at least we have a chance, avenues to work — to combat the rest of the pollution that we have there. (MI SRB, May 1988: 43)

Critics of the City Environmental treatment facility proposal were especially concerned about cumulative risks from nearby industries as well as increased truck traffic. Many of the complaints related more to the Detroit municipal incinerator across the street from the site than to the proposal itself. Curiously, the question of environmental racism did not surface even though the neighborhood has a black majority. Instead, local residents opposed the facility on the grounds that it was yet another noxious industry that they would prefer not to have in their vicinity. Unlike NCS, City Environmental did not negotiate a community agreement, so changed opinions were not forthcoming. MI SRB approved the facility's construction permit in spite of local opposition. But just like NCS, City Environmental decided not to build its facility (Burda, 1997).

The following chapter compares each of the cases from Part II, Chapters 4 and 5, in regard to the environmental justice implications of hazardous waste. It focuses on distributive and procedural equity considerations and evaluates the extent to which they were considered in the facility siting proceedings, as articulated by intervenor groups. The findings are summarized in a series of tables in Chapter 6 as well as in Table 9 in the introduction to Part III.

Note

1. All populations, racial percentages, and median incomes here and in the following discussion of cases in Michigan are taken from the 1990 United States Census.

PART III

INTERPRETATIONS

Environmental Justice and Hazardous Waste

Introduction

The facility siting disputes reviewed in Part II reveal a fundamental contradiction in hazardous waste policy between capacity assurance objectives and pollution prevention initiatives. The environmental justice implications of hazardous waste play out in locational conflicts in ways relating not only to community concerns about equity, but also to broader policy questions about whether to regulate disposal methods only or to regulate production by requiring specific reductions in waste generation. Off-site disposal fulfils an industry need and thus benefits the same corporations that generate waste, while communities that serve as hosts for proposed new sites are asked to receive the burdens, often against their will. This is no doubt central to the spatial equity concerns that dominated so many of the disputes. Also, American states and Canadian provinces absorb the costs of facility siting processes, which in one of the border region cases lasted 15 years. Most of the disputes involved repeated shorter proceedings with different waste management firms in separate locations. This public sector subsidy of locating new hazardous waste facilities for off-site disposal is, again, for the direct benefit of industries that generate hazardous waste (see Table 9).

Disjoints between the economic benefits of industrial production and the environmental and social burdens pollution creates are not the only problems with hazardous waste policy generally, or capacity assurance objectives specifically. By not requiring industries to prevent, or at least

TABLE 9
Summary of Cases in the Niagara, Sarnia, and Detroit Areas

Facility	Community	Opposition
OWMC Landfill, Incinerator, Treatment Facility 1/80 - 2/95	Rural Niagara Greenfield Sites	Local Governments Local Groups Laidlaw
EMS Landfill 6/82 - 10/82	Suburban Detroit Munic. Landfill	Local Government
ERES Incinerator 9/82 - 12/82	Suburban Detroit Munic. Landfill	Local Governments
Stablex Landfill 12/82 - 9/83	Suburban Detroit Quarry Site	Local Government
CECOS Landfill 6/87 - 3/90	Niagara Falls, NY; Existing HW landfill	Local Governments Local Group Ontario Govt.
NCS Treatment Facil. 12/87 - 5/88	Downtown Detroit Existing Facility	Local Group
City Env. Treatment Facil. 2/89 - 8/89	Downtown Detroit Garbage Incinerator	Unorganized Residents
CWM Landfill & Incinerator 4/89 - 6/93	Suburban, Niagara Falls, NY; Existing HW Landfill	Local Governments Local Groups Ontario Govt.
Laidlaw Incinerator 12/89 - 10/93	Sarnia, ON; Existing HW Landfill & Incinerator	Local Groups Walpole Island
EDS Underground Injection; 8/90 - 2/01	Suburban Detroit Greenfield Site	Local Government (but initial support)

Facility	Concerns	Siting Board Findings
OWMC Landfill, Incinerator, Treatment Facility 1/80 - 2/95	Wastes should stay in industrial areas; Facility too large; Private sector	None of the concerns were considered sufficient to deny permit; Rejected based on cost
EMS Landfill 6/82 - 10/82	Incompatible hydrogeology	True; Permit denied
ERES Incinerator 9/82 - 12/82	Hydrogeology; Insufficient proposal	True on both counts; Permit denied
Stablex Landfill 12/82 - 9/83	Hydrogeology; Design (no liner)	True on both counts; Permit denied
CECOS Landfill 6/87 - 3/90	TSDFs should go to other areas (geo equity law); Too many existing hazards	Insufficient basis to deny permit; Denied based on revised risk assessment after CWM preliminary approval
NCS Treatment Facil. 12/87 - 5/88	Too many existing hazards	Minimal risk; Permit approved
City Env. Treatment Facil. 2/89 - 8/89	Too many existing hazards	Minimal risk; Permit approved
CWM Landfill & Incinerator 4/89 - 6/93	TSDFs should go to other areas (geo equity law); Too many existing hazards	Insufficient basis to deny; Landfill approved; Incinerator withdrawn until 2003
Laidlaw Incinerator 12/89 - 10/93	Too many existing hazards; Walpole Island should not be excluded from process	Proposal withdrawn before board decision
EDS Underground Injection; 8/90 - 2/01	Shipments from Canada unfair; Hydrogeology	Siting board denied; DEQ approved under revised process

reduce, the wastes they generate as a function of doing business, the state misses the opportunity to break the cycle of unchecked growth and its result, externalized noxious residuals. American and Canadian cradle-to-grave hazardous waste management systems are impressive in their sophistication at tracking and regulating the various kinds of hazardous wastes that industries generate and/or manage. But even this is not enough to deal with the need for off-site waste management in a way that avoids the siting of new facilities and expansions of existing ones. Pollution prevention is clearly the only way to address these systemic aspects of the hazardous waste problem. Intervenor groups representing community and environmental interests generally have advocated the analysis of how such measures might reduce or obviate the need for new or expanded facilities. None of the siting board decisions recognized such an examination as being necessary for the determination of facility need, though to do so would have gone a long way toward promoting justice in facility siting.

Chapter 6 interprets the findings about hazardous waste sites from Part II by using the conceptual, theoretical, and empirical discussions from Part I. I argue that the hazardous waste facility siting problem is a function both of linear production systems that fail to adopt technologically feasible recycling and recovery strategies and of a lack of research and development to advance pollution prevention possibilities even further. Questions of environmental equity and justice have predominated in many hazardous waste siting disputes and are quite difficult to resolve to the satisfaction of both community and industry interests in most cases. An environmentally just hazardous waste policy requires fairness in facility siting in order to meet with the approval of local residents who feel systematically targeted for waste facilities. The general lack of success in approving new or expanded facilities suggests that communities have begun to demand no less. But social or spatial equity in waste location will not solve the problem on its own. A sustainable industrial ecosystemic approach that makes an analysis of how pollution prevention would reduce or even obviate the need for new or expanded facilities is also necessary to promote procedural fairness in facility siting.

6
Towards Environmental Justice and Hazardous Waste

Introduction

I have attempted to demonstrate that hazardous waste presents many difficulties to society, particularly in communities with actual or planned hazardous waste facilities, and that differing concepts of fairness are central to the disputes that often arise. The environmental justice implications of facility siting heighten the controversies by adding debates about equity and justice to the complexities of how and where best to deal with industrial wastes. Distributive and procedural justice concerns about hazardous waste facilities came through to some degree in all of the facility siting cases reviewed in Part II. The particular details of each related most especially to in-state or in-province waste generation and disposal practices, resulting in variations as to the specific equity and justice issues that became most salient.

In Ontario, the role of the Ontario Waste Management Corporation (OWMC) predominated in all discussions of hazardous waste management and policy. Even though the province's only commercial facility, then and now, is located in the Sarnia area, OWMC's proposals for a large integrated facility, at one and then another greenfield site in Niagara, were at issue in other waste management decisions. This included Laidlaw's proposal to build its own rotary kiln incinerator at its existing Sarnia location; in that case the company objected to the very notion of allowing a government agency to compete with private firms in the waste management market.

The Ontario context was very different from that in Michigan and New York. There, regulated market strategies were used to determine what kinds of facilities should go where, and the private sector was relied upon to submit proposals. New York had previously tried a public-sector strategy similar to OWMC's when it used a public utility to site a facility in central New York, but the state later abandoned this plan in the face of intense public opposition. Michigan explored a similar idea in planning documents after siting boards rejected three Detroit-area private-sector proposals in a row, but dismissed it as a potentially more troublesome strategy from the state government's point of view, making specific reference to Ontario's long ordeal over OWMC as supporting evidence.

Spatial and Social Equity

Ontario

In Ontario, spatial equity was especially at issue with regard to the OMWC proposals in Niagara. West Lincoln residents, as well as local and regional governments, opposed the project on the basis that since they are a rural-agricultural, rather than urban-industrial, community and since the wastes bound for the proposed facility are mostly generated as production residuals in the Toronto, Hamilton, and Niagara Falls regions (70 per cent), then one or more of those cities should bear the responsibility for treatment and disposal. Also, since OWMC's siting approach was to locate all four facility components at one location, the community and regional response was particularly negative (see Table 10).

The Tri-parties, a local intervenor group, argued in favor of a geographically dispersed facility strategy with each component in a separate location based on a waste analysis to determine which communities generate the most of particular kinds of wastes. The group's version of spatial equity clearly posited that communities which generate waste should have to deal with it themselves rather than send it somewhere else and that the government's environmental policy response should uphold this view. Admittedly, their plan would likely have created serious problems of its own. After all, geographic equity is but one element of distributive equity, which is itself only part of the question with respect to environmental equity. Also, a perfectly equal distribution of hazardous waste across

TABLE 10
Spatial and Social Equity in Ontario

Ontario Proposals	Location/ Pre-Existing Site	Community Arguments	Siting Board Findings
OWMC Landfill, Incinerator & Treatment	Rural Niagara (W. Lincoln) (S. Cayuga) Greenfields	Waste should stay in industrial areas	Good idea, but not a sufficient basis to deny
Laidlaw Incinerator	Rural Sarnia (Moore Twnshp) Landfill & Incinerator	Walpole wanted official status over Laidlaw objections	No action before proposal was withdrawn

space would hardly constitute justice. Nonetheless, the data analysis they proposed would have certainly added to the government's knowledge and understanding of the province's waste management needs in particular regions. Such an approach, combined with increased attention to and information on pollution prevention and on-site treatment and disposal, which the group also supported, could prove to be very beneficial in the determination of particular types of waste capacity shortfalls. Also, any charge of spatial inequity would be muted with this kind of strategy since it would place the disposal facilities more proximate to waste generators.

The Tri-parties' three conditions for approval, were the siting board to have allowed the project to go forward, were clearly designed to make for the fairest result, in a spatial sense, of what they saw as an unjust situation. Two of the points, engineered containment and odor control, had been addressed to the extent possible through negotiations with OWMC. The crown corporation agreed to certain operating conditions to allay local residents' fears in case the project was approved. The third community request, a restriction on out-of-province wastes, met with no serious response by OWMC or the siting board. Given the size and expense of the proposed facility, it is understandable why neither body was willing to entertain this point more fully. Such a restriction would have limited potential customers and associated revenues to the point that the facility might never escape operating cost overruns. But the need to subsidize Ontario waste management with shipments from other jurisdictions as a necessary precondition for a cost-effective facility seems to call the entire project into question.

Given that the original justification for the idea was to deal with Ontario's hazardous waste problem, why should the facility's purpose be equally to rectify other jurisdictions' capacity shortfalls and to deal with pollution from within the province?

Ontario also relies on its only existing commercial hazardous waste landfill and incinerator near Sarnia. Local opposition to expanding that facility by adding a rotary kiln incinerator, the same technology as OWMC planned to use, was very present, though to a somewhat lesser degree than in West Lincoln. Part of the difference may have to do with the duration of the siting proceedings. The OWMC process lasted 15 years, nearly ten of which were focused on West Lincoln Township specifically. By comparison, the Laidlaw process lasted less than four years, since the company withdrew its proposal just after the OWMC public hearings ended. Had the company continued to pursue the process, local opposition may well have increased as it did in the West Lincoln case. Another difference is that the facility has been in use as an industrial waste disposal site since 1960, so to some degree the community may have become used to it. Today, the facility is owned and operated by Safety-Kleen and has experienced the largest increase in releases and transfers of toxic substances of any facility in North America from 1995 to 1999, the most recent period for which comparative data are available (CEC, 2002). Ontario transfers more chemicals around the province for the purpose of disposal than any other North American jurisdiction.

Local government opposition was not an issue in the community where the facility is located since Moore Township stated no position on it and participated only to ensure the safety of the community, whatever the decision on this specific siting question. Opposition to the Laidlaw facility was greater in Walpole Island, a First Nations community located approximately 50 kilometers down river from the facility. At the time the company withdrew its proposal, it was involved in a bitter dispute with area residents over the question of whether the Walpole Heritage Centre could act as an intervenor party to the proceedings. Laidlaw argued the community is too far from its plant to have a legitimate grievance in the case, whereas Walpole representatives claimed the Saint Clair River would transport hazards from the facility downstream and directly affect their local environment. This dispute over the likely spatial distribution of burdens presented a variation on spatial equity concerns which are typically most pronounced in the communities where the facilities are located.

TABLE 11
Spatial and Social Equity in New York State

New York Proposals	Location/Pre-Existing Site	Community Arguments	Siting Board Findings
CECOS Landfill	Niagara Falls HW Landfill	New TSDFs should go to other areas according to law	Not the Board's decision even if true; Denied on other basis
CWM Landfills & Incinerator	Suburban Niagara Falls HW Landfill & Incinerator	New TSDFs should go to other areas according to law	Not the Board's decision even if true; Approved

NEW YORK AND ONTARIO COMPARED

Spatial equity was at least as central an issue in the New York siting cases as in Ontario or Michigan, given the state's concentration of active and inactive hazardous waste facilities in Niagara County and other areas of western New York, as well as the intended remedy of the problem, the "geographic equity" provisions of the state's hazardous waste law (ECL). After abandoning a public-sector plan for an off-site hazardous waste facility in central New York, the state's only other proposals for additional disposal capacity were for expansions of the two existing facilities in Niagara (CECOS and CWM). The result was intense local opposition to both plans based largely on spatial inequity in much the same way that West Lincoln responded to the OWMC facility proposal in Niagara, Ontario (see Table 11).

The basis for the spatial injustice allegations differed somewhat between Niagara residents of New York and Ontario. Local opponents of OWMC argued that it would be spatially inequitable to ask a non-industrial community to host one of what would have been the province's two commercial hazardous waste facilities. They argued that salt mines near Windsor (and Sarnia) would provide a more suitable location for land disposal of chloride residuals than a landfill in West Lincoln. Other facility components should go to one or more of the communities that generate most of the waste (Hamilton, Niagara Falls, and Toronto) and would restrict out-of-province wastes from places like Niagara Falls, New York. This perhaps classic NIMBY response would, of course, place the facility nearly anywhere but in their own area, though one of the suggested communities (Niagara Falls, Ontario) was within the borders of the Regional Municipality of Niagara. Their salt mine suggestion would have placed still more of a spatial burden on the southwestern region of the province, the only area of Ontario that presently receives hazardous wastes on a commercial basis.

By contrast, the vision of spatial equity in Niagara, New York was that the state should remedy the existing concentration of hazardous waste in their area by siting new facilities in other regions. This, too, might be regarded as a typical, though somewhat different, NIMBY reaction: nearly anywhere other than this area would do as a viable alternative waste site location. Also, the local responses in New York as compared to Ontario seemed to contradict one another to some extent. While residents of Niagara, New York may have felt inordinately burdened by their historic and existing concentration of hazardous waste sites, their local industries were and are major contributors to the generation of toxic production residuals. In addition, it should be noted that New York State's geographic equity legal provisions were not intended to target rural areas similar to West Lincoln for new waste sites. Rather, the policy would have attempted to reduce demand on existing Niagara area facilities (and the need to expand them) by building any new hazardous waste capacity in industrial communities from the eastern and central regions of the state, which together generate nearly half of New York's hazardous waste (Eismann, 1995; Olsen, 1991, 1995).

MICHIGAN COMPARED

In the state of Michigan, spatial equity was not nearly as central to the facility siting disputes as it was in New York and Ontario. The only case that involved such a controversy was the EDS deep-well injection proposal in Romulus. The most central community concern had to do with the company's attempts, in concert with initial local government support, to avoid the SRB process and public hearings. But local residents were also angered by news that EDS planned to receive perhaps as much as half of its waste shipments from a Canadian transport company that previously shipped its waste to a cement kiln that burned hazardous waste in Alpena, Michigan in the northern part of the state (see Table 12). When the EDS facility proposal finally underwent an SRB review, the board ruled against the company on a number of procedural and distributive grounds, including

TABLE 12

Spatial and Social Equity in Michigan

Michigan Proposals	Location/Pre-Existing Site	Community Arguments	Siting Board Findings
EDS, Deep-Well Injection	Suburban Detroit Greenfield	Waste shipments from Canada unfair, social equity concerns	Approved by DEQ through a revised approval procedure

environmental justice concerns related to the majority African American population in Wayne County, Michigan.

Part of the explanation for what might be regarded as a relative lack of concern about spatial equity in Michigan relative to that in New York and Ontario may be the spatial distribution of existing commercial hazardous waste facilities. Five are located in areas of Michigan other than the southeastern region, so the prospect of having new ones in the Detroit area may have been less of a political obstacle for facility proponents to overcome than in the CECOS, CWM, and OWMC cases. Also, although the Detroit area hosts a large proportion of the state's hazardous waste generators, it also has the largest share of the state's commercial hazardous waste disposal facilities (14 of 19), six of which are located within the City of Detroit. This fact and the obvious social equity implications related to Detroit's largely racial minority (76 per cent) and low-income population make it all the more surprising that equity and justice concerns were not more salient in more of the Detroit area disputes.

Four of the six Detroit-area facility siting proposals were located in white communities in the suburbs rather than in the central city where the two remaining facilities would have been sited. These two, City Environmental and NCS, are the ones in which one would expect to find that evidence of social inequity, based on race and class, would be presented as at least part of local groups' objections to facility location plans. The absence of such evidence and arguments can be explained partly by the type of proposals, both of which were for treatment facilities, rather than landfills or incinerators. Another factor may have been that three suburban Detroit siting processes had already occurred, suggesting that white middle-class communities in Michigan are as likely to face the prospect of a new facility as are the state's racial minority or low-income communities.

Also, unlike New York and Ontario, each of which has only one area where a commercial hazardous waste site can be found, these kinds of facilities are located in four separate regions of Michigan.

Notwithstanding these explanations, given the percentage of the state's commercial hazardous waste facilities located in Detroit (32 per cent) and its metropolitan area (74 per cent), as well as the fact that siting boards rejected each of the three suburban proposals but approved the two central city proposals, it still seems surprising that social equity was not made an issue in the proceedings. The timing of the two cases within the City of Detroit (late 1980s) may also partially account for the lack of attention to racial and other social issues, since three important developments in the struggle for environmental justice had yet to take place: (1) the Michigan Coalition conference (1990), which was an important impetus for (2) the EPA environmental equity report (1992), and (3) the establishment of a local environmental justice group in the Detroit area (Bullard, 1994). A final factor was that MI DNR reduced the number of local siting board members from four to two prior to the NCS and City Environmental proposals in order to increase the chance of permit approvals. This could have reduced the extent to which area residents' concerns might otherwise have been raised and articulated during siting board meetings.

Cumulative and Intergenerational Equity

MICHIGAN

While social and spatial justice may not have been prominent issues in the Detroit area disputes, community concerns about cumulative and intergenerational justice were quite visible in each (see Table 13). Local opponents of the NCS and City Environmental proposals in the City of Detroit focused almost exclusively on cumulative risk as the basis of their arguments and positions. The type of facility involved in both cases (treatment and storage rather than disposal) was at least part of the reason for this since it poses less risk to communities than do incinerators or landfills. Aside from the usual concerns about truck traffic and the potential for accidents at the treatment facilities, most of the complaints from City of Detroit residents had more to do with the burden of existing industrial activity in the neighborhoods most affected. In other words, it was not the potential risk from the proposed

TABLE 13

Cumulative and Intergenerational Equity in Michigan

Michigan Proposals	Location/Pre-Existing Site	Community Arguments	Siting Board Findings
EMS Landfill	Suburban Detroit Munic. Landfill	Incompatible hydrogeology	Incompatible hydrogeology; Denied
ERES Incinerator	Suburban Detroit Munic. Landfill	Incompatible hydrogeology	Incompatible hydrogeology; Denied
Stablex Landfill	Suburban Detroit Quarry	Incompatible hydrogeology	Incompatible hydrogeology; Denied
NCS Treatment Facility	Central Detroit Treatment Facility	Too many existing toxic hazards	Minimal risk; Approved
City Env. Treatment Facility	Central Detroit Munic. Incinerator	Too many existing toxic hazards	Minimal risk; Approved
EDS, Deep-well Injection	Suburban Detroit Greenfield	Uncertain hydrogeology	Approved under revised procedure

facilities themselves that bothered these central city Detroiters most about the projects, but the addition of any further industrial burden in either neighborhood, however remote the possibility of serious problems should the siting board approve them. NCS managed to turn at least some of its local opposition into reluctant support by reaching a community agreement that addressed some of the residents' concerns.

In the case of larger and more complicated facilities such as incinerators, landfills, and underground injection facilities, community opposition is harder to overcome than in the case of treatment and storage units. Michigan's siting board rejected the first three proposals (two landfills and an incinerator) because of hydrogeological problems with the locations. In these cases, intergenerational equity was at least an implicit justification for these decisions, as well as the community opposition to each of the facilities. What makes this criterion of equity and justice most different from all of the others is the depth of concern siting board officials seem to have

TABLE 14

Cumulative and Intergenerational Equity in New York State

New York Proposals	Location/Pre-Existing Site	Community Arguments	Siting Board Findings
CECOS Landfill	Central Niagara Falls HW Landfill	Too many existing toxic hazards	Not the Board's decision even if true; Denied on other basis
CWM Landfills & Incinerator	Suburban Niagara Falls, HW Landfill & Incinerator	Too many existing toxic hazards	Not the Board's decision; Negotiated

regarding the potential for creating new "Love Canals" sometime in the future. Michigan decision makers were most concerned about the potential for ground water contamination, perhaps hundreds of years from now, in their denial of permits for the first three suburban facilities. SRB felt much the same way when it denied the EDS proposal for a deep-well injection system in Romulus, even though MI DEQ approved it under a revised approval procedure.

NEW YORK

Cumulative equity was central to local objections to the CECOS and CWM facilities, particularly as it related to spatial equity (see Table 14). Western New York's disproportionate share of hazardous waste includes corresponding cumulative risks and other burdens whether one considers presently active facilities only, or all facilities, including those that are closed and no longer accepting wastes. Additionally, the concentration of petrochemical plants in Niagara County makes this a heavily industrialized community with many pollution-related risks. Of course, the very existence of industries in the chemicals sector necessitates a certain amount of hazardous waste disposal capacity, so the relationship between production and disposal seems clear in Niagara, New York. The accumulation of these already spatially disproportionate risks serves only to worsen the effect on this community, but as in the Michigan cases, New York's siting board decisions had little to do with cumulative risk, despite local concerns to this effect, but instead focused on the hydrogeological suitability of the locations.

TABLE 15

Cumulative and Intergenerational Equity in Ontario

Ontario Proposals	Location/Pre-Existing Site	Community Arguments	Siting Board Findings
OWMC Landfill, Incinerator & Treatment	Rural Niagara (W. Lincoln) (S. Cayuga) Greenfields	Centralized TSDF will bring too much waste	Not the Board's decision even if true: Denied on other basis
Laidlaw Landfill & Incinerator	Rural Sarnia area HW Landfill & Incinerator	Too many existing toxic hazards	Proposal withdrawn

By contrast, intergenerational risk was a determining factor in the CECOS case, at least after the second siting board decision, because of hydrogeological concerns about the location. It seems encouraging that siting boards in New York, Michigan, and Ontario are so reluctant to approve hazardous waste landfills in places that have potential flooding or ground water problems. But the CECOS case also shows that risk assessment is at least as much a political process as it is a scientific one. In the first siting board decision, before the decision to expand the nearby CWM landfill in lieu of an incinerator, the need to expand CECOS seemed more pressing (e.g., capacity assurance). The result was a risk ranking just under the magic limit of 200. But the second CECOS decision came after the siting board approved the CWM landfill expansion, so the board slightly increased the risk score to just over 200. As long as capacity assurance is the prime justification for defining facility need, it is very convenient to allow it to trump other factors such as cumulative risk or equity.

ONTARIO

In the Province of Ontario, cumulative risk issues were somewhat different in the OWMC case as compared to the Laidlaw case. For local opponents of the OWMC facility, cumulative risk overlapped with spatial inequity, much the same as was the case across the Niagara River in New York State. In a sense, what the Tri-parties wanted as a means of achieving spatial equity—siting the facility in industrial locations—could well have generated cumulative equity concerns in those other communities similar to what happened in Niagara, New York. But siting boards in Ontario, as in Michigan and New York, gave little notice to cumulative risk in their decision-making. In its final decision to reject the OWMC proposal due to cost-effectiveness considerations, Ontario's EAB also rejected area residents' concerns about disproportionate spatial and cumulative burdens as a justification for denying the permit (see Table 15).

Laidlaw's Sarnia area opponents were very concerned about cumulative risk but, unlike OWMC's critics, they did not link the issue to that of spatial equity. Because this case ended prematurely when the proponent withdrew its application, it is hard to compare it with others. However, given that the existing commercial landfill and incinerator near Sarnia are the only ones in the province, as well as the prospect for still further expansions, it would seem just as reasonable for this community to make the link between spatial and cumulative equity as it is for Niagara residents on both sides of the border. The problem has become even more critical now, given the large increases in hazardous waste disposal at the same facility in recent years.

Even Walpole Island residents' spatial equity concerns were tied more to procedural equity questions related to whether they would receive intervenor party status than they were to cumulative equity. For them, the cumulative risk of any facility that generates or manages toxic waste located upriver from them was as problematic as the next. Like the opponents of NCS and City Environmental in central Detroit, local concerns about Laidlaw's plans had to do with existing industrial hazards in the area more than the risks posed by a new rotary kiln incinerator.

Intergenerational equity was to some degree implicit in Ontario EAB's rejection of the OWMC facility. Though the official reason for their decision had to do with cost considerations, the existence of cost-effectiveness as a determining factor only arose because of OWMC's efforts to minimize risk to future generations. If it were not for the corporation's chlorides management plan, which was to pre-treat this waste stream, projected operating costs would have been much lower. A less costly chlorides plan may well have led to a different outcome. It is interesting to note in this regard that the nearby CWM facility in Niagara, New York takes a much simpler approach to chloride wastes by releasing them into the Niagara River (Spira, 1995). OWMC did explore the option of disposal in an underground injection facility, though Ontario MOEE was unwilling to support the plan (Ontario EAB, 1994).

Procedural Equity and Beyond

Procedural equity has been the prime justification for implementing administrative and public reviews of facility siting proposals. Involving the public, particularly members of the community where the hazardous waste facility is to be located, is a necessary prerequisite to fairness in hazardous waste management and policy. But beyond the use of siting boards to review the proposals and make decisions, there are many different possibilities for facility siting procedures. Ontario differed from Michigan and New York not only with respect to the question of public or private ownership, but also with respect to support of opposition groups. Local critics of both the Laidlaw and OWMC proposals were able to apply for provincial intervenor funding to support their efforts. By contrast, neither Michigan nor New York offers such funds, making the job of opposing facility proposals all the more difficult for community groups and local governments.

Another factor is the question of siting board composition. Michigan uses a complex system that ensures representation of local and permanent members as well as distinct roles for particular kinds of experts (e.g., a chemist, a geologist, a manufacturing representative, etc.). In earlier Michigan cases, local members who represented community interests were more likely to vote against a facility than were permanent members. The decision to change the composition of the siting board to include fewer local members and to replace them with permanent members makes it much harder for community interests to control the final decision. The problem has become even more critical now that Michigan siting boards have been reduced to an advisory role and that their decisions are no longer binding. By contrast, New York and Ontario use smaller and less complicated siting board structures, and opposition groups are given a more formal role in the proceedings as are the intervening parties. Ontario intervenor groups certainly benefitted from provincial funding to support their efforts as compared to their New York and Michigan counterparts who relied on local funding, at least in cases where the official local government position was in opposition to the proposal.

Only one of the cases examined could be regarded as a "voluntary" process from the point of view of local government involvement. However, even that one (EDS) did not remain so for very long. According to Rabe (1994), voluntary site selection processes involve local communities, including the general public as well as their local representatives, as early as possible in the siting process. This can even mean a competition where two or more communities bid on hosting the facility as has occurred in Alberta, Manitoba, and Minnesota. In Ontario, even though the provincial government provided local opposition groups with intervenor funding, both the Laidlaw and OWMC processes were very much lacking in terms of fair process. OWMC's Niagara region critics clearly saw more to procedural equity than the provision of modest funding to fight a project that was chosen for them rather than with them and long after the original conception and subsequent ongoing development of the facility proposal.

Community agreements between facility operators and local governments were reached in the OWMC case, and also in Michigan (NCS) and New York (CWM), to negotiate terms agreeable to both sides. This procedural device is obviously important and potentially beneficial to communities facing at least the prospect of hosting a hazardous waste facility. But it is also limited in its capacity to fully represent local interests, particularly if negotiated toward the end of a siting process when the community is faced with an imminent siting board decision. This was the situation in each of the three cases involving community agreements. In these examples, local governments were officially opposed to the projects, negotiating with waste industry or government officials only as a last resort and in the event of a worst-case scenario (a siting board approval). This reluctance to participate in a negotiation that presumes the community will ultimately host a new or expanded facility is a good indication of the lack of local "voluntarism" so often present in hazardous waste siting, even in cases where community agreements are negotiated.

The question of voluntarism is at least implicitly addressed in recent EPA guidance on the "social aspects of siting RCRA hazardous waste facilities" (EPA, 2000). The agency sums up the problem of NIMBY and the numerous areas for industry-community and government-community conflicts over siting with "a tale of two sites," one of which represents "the best of times..." and the other, "the worst of times...." The worst-case scenario, depicted by a fictitious ABC Company, is characterized as getting it all wrong by failing to inform and enlist support from local government officials and community leaders early in the planning process. The predictable outcome, similar to many of the cases reviewed in Part II, is strong local opposition. Conversely, the XYZ Company gets it all right by virtue of their open communications with the proposed host community early in the development process, at least once a shortlist of potential sites has been narrowed for discussion. The likely result according to this idealized view is that "dialogue progresses and collaboration continues through successful permitting, construction, and operation of the facility" (EPA, 2000: 2). Clearly, the best-case scenario is more likely to result in a "successful" siting than the worst-case scenario. Ironically, communities may prefer the worst-case scenario if only because it is less likely to result in a new hazardous waste facility "in their backyards."

In many cases, then, even voluntary strategies are not enough to convince local communities to accept hazardous waste facilities. In their book *Dealing with an Angry Public*, negotiation experts Lawrence Susskind and Patrick Field (1996) suggest a framework for dealing more effectively with controversies over industrial pollution. They recommend that facility proponents (industries and government regulatory agencies) move beyond "traditional" approaches to dealing with communities and instead adopt a "mutual gains" approach involving six principles:

1. acknowledge the concerns of the other side;

2. encourage joint fact finding;

3. offer contingent commitments to minimize impacts if they do occur;

4. accept responsibility, admit mistakes, and share power;

5. act in a trustworthy fashion at all times;

6. focus on building long-term relationships.

These recommendations may seem relatively simple and obvious, but they are nonetheless a significant departure from typical industry-community relations. It is also quite likely that some industrial activities may never become mutually acceptable in particular communities. In such cases, the mutual gains approach could at the very least help facility proponents determine earlier rather than later that they will have to find an alternate location for their facility, if not a different type of facility altogether.

Even if one is to assume that a voluntary strategy is a necessary component of successful facility siting, there is still room for potential pitfalls when, for example, facility operators ignore conditions of approval after beginning their operations. The central problem is that hazardous waste facilities are unwelcome neighbors for virtually anyone, including those who are perhaps intrigued by plans for "safe," "state-of-the-art" facilities that bring badly needed local revenues through royalties on tipping fees. It is only when a facility is in place and operating that the sights, sounds, and smells of hazardous waste treatment and disposal are made clear. A Quebec industry has angered residents near its Stablex facility in Blainville because of reports that the landfill has leaked and that the company has accepted mixed wastes with traces of organics, an environmentally unsound practice that the company promised it would not use (Rabe, 1994). Alberta's voluntarily sited facility in Swan Hills was originally approved with the understanding of hazardous waste import restrictions. But the day before the EAB announced its decision on the OWMC facility in Ontario, Alberta announced that it would remove the import restrictions, allowing its cash-strapped incinerator to take in more revenues (Westell, 1994). Alberta officials were forced to shut down their facility, Canada's only commercial rotary kiln incinerator, temporarily after a series of leaks and explosions (Marsden & MacDonell, 1997). With no other means to destroy PCB wastes in this country, interpretations of capacity assurance and facility need could lead to additional incinerator proposals. If so, voluntary siting would be a definite improvement over the ten cases examined in this book.

If siting is to work in a manner that promotes equity and justice, facility operators must uphold the agreements they reach with communities, and regulatory officials must not allow breaches of faith to go unchecked. Moreover, the benefits of voluntary siting are easily overstated. If industries and governments site hazardous waste facilities only in communities willing to accept the burdens as well as the benefits of such land uses, and even if facility operators diligently uphold their end of agreements with local residents, the numerous problems associated with siting and other hazardous waste management decisions will not go away. To deal with the problem head-on requires policies that regulate production as well as disposal in order to reduce and avoid waste generation at the source rather than after the fact.

Distributive and procedural equity in facility siting and other hazardous waste management decisions are clearly important, especially to communities faced with inordinate environmental problems. But no matter how fairly we may try to distribute pollution, success in this regard will remain elusive unless and until public policies and laws directly address the industrial practices that generate it. If we are to use metaphors like cradle-to-grave in reference to our hazardous waste management systems, we should take them more seriously by extending environmental protection in both directions of the waste life-cycle to deal more effectively with the origins and destinations of toxic residuals. In order to achieve such a reality, we will have to promote pollution prevention to reduce the need for new or expanded hazardous waste facilities with at least as much regulatory muscle as we do with capacity assurance objectives, whether or not they are tied explicitly to statutory requirements.

7
Conclusion

Introduction

The environmental justice implications of hazardous waste involve a number of distributive and procedural factors that are complex and interrelated. Since the discovery of toxic contamination at Love Canal in Niagara Falls, New York, North Americans have become increasingly sensitized to the risks associated with toxic substances and wastes. Twenty-five years after the event, the anti-toxics movement has combined forces with an environmental justice movement to respond to inequities in exposure to pollution, especially those related to race and class.

Environmental policies have developed and changed dramatically during this period. In the United States and Canada, hazardous waste laws and regulations impose a number of requirements on industries that generate or handle hazardous wastes to provide cradle-to-grave management. These restrictions have provided greater protection of local environments from toxic contamination relative to the policies of two decades ago. Newer treatment, storage, and disposal facilities (TSDFs) are far better able to contain chemical and metal-laden wastes than older ones such as Love Canal and over 4,000 other inactive sites in the Great Lakes basin. But the numerous problems caused by these industrial relics have made communities highly suspicious of plans to make them hosts for new facilities, in spite of the newer "state of the art" designs.

Disjoints between the benefits of production and the burdens of toxic residuals of production tend to make communities react in a particularly negative way to proposals for new hazardous waste facilities. These distributive disparities have social, spatial, cumulative, and intergenerational aspects. Procedural inequities add to the difficulty of achieving environmental justice, particularly when facility siting proceedings are less concerned with local community and environmental interests than they are with industrial-environmental objectives that are larger than local.

The structural limitations of hazardous waste laws and regulations in both Canada and the United States make the goal of environmental justice even more elusive and indeterminant. The "end of pipe" emphasis on waste treatment and disposal over waste reduction and pollution prevention mutes the efforts of government regulators to reduce demand on existing facilities and the need for new ones. Capacity assurance objectives lead to proposals for new off-site facilities to handle projected hazardous waste streams, but there are no restrictions on the volume or toxicity of waste that industries are allowed to generate. If we are to achieve environmental justice, hazardous waste policies will have to adopt an "industrial ecology" approach that regulates production as well as treatment and disposal.

American and Canadian Hazardous Waste Policies

Hazardous waste policies in Canada and the United States have become increasingly formalized during the last 20 years. Manifests track hazardous wastes from place to place, beginning with the place at which they are generated and following through to their ultimate treatment or disposal. Regulations define the various dimensions of hazard to distinguish between various kinds of wastes. Hazardous waste facility standards impose restrictions on landfills, incinerators, deep-well injection facilities, and treatment plants. Corrective action regulations set requirements for the cleanup of facilities that are found to be leaching or otherwise threatening the environment. Capacity assurance measures have been put in place to ensure that industrial waste generators have a facility to receive the toxic residuals of their manufacturing processes.

American and Canadian hazardous waste policies are far more similar than they are different. What is different between the two countries has more to do with the style of policy-making. The American approach is legally formalistic in the sense that most of the specific requirements are statutorily driven. The Resource Conservation and Recovery Act (RCRA) has required EPA to write volumes of regulations to deal with nearly every conceivable circumstance of hazardous waste management. States are required to implement federal laws and to develop their own laws with provisions at least as strict as those out of Washington. The Canadian approach, by contrast, is to impose general requirements at the federal level and to leave the specifics to the provinces. Even provincial laws and regulations are relatively general as compared to those in the United States, with operating permits for particular facilities being the only place to find the details of specific requirements in many cases.

Facility siting often works differently between the two countries, though not necessarily. Most American states rely on the private sector to develop proposals for new hazardous waste facilities, whereas Canadian provinces have historically been more likely to establish crown corporations to provide this function, such as OWMC in Ontario. This is not always the case even in Ontario where the only operating commercial or off-site facility is owned and operated by a private-sector firm, and the failure of OWMC is likely to reduce any desire for such public-sector approaches. At present, Ontario does not appear to be in a hurry to build new hazardous waste facilities, perhaps content to rely on the Sarnia facility and the ability to export. The more recent failure to site a municipal waste landfill in Kirkland Lake would hardly make such a process desirable politically, whether using a public-sector approach or not. New York State initiated its own public-sector process to site a hazardous waste facility in the central part of the state but backed away from the plan in the face of intense community opposition. The State of Michigan explored the public-sector facility approach but decided against it on the basis that it had proved to be problematic for Ontario and other jurisdictions. In the end, all three jurisdictions had a great degree of difficulty in obtaining all the necessary approvals to build new facilities. Only two of the ten facilities reviewed in Part II were approved and built.

Community opposition was present in each of the ten facility siting cases. Local actors in the siting proceedings based their opposition on arguments responsive to problems that could or would affect nearby residents. Hydrogeological problems with the proposed sites could have led to local contamination problems at some future date. Cumulative and spatial equity, discussed further in the next section, were also uniquely local concerns in the disputes. Local residents also pointed to the possibility that pollution prevention could obviate the need for new facilities, a notion that industries and provincial/state governments found to be unrealistic, however important the need to reduce waste generation where possible. In seven of the ten cases, local governments officially opposed the proposals and presented evidence regarding these issues to support their arguments and positions. These findings are consistent with Blomley's interpretive continuum (see Figure 2) whereby local and locally concerned officials develop arguments based on instrumental forms of validity to respond to specific community needs and concerns.

Community concerns stand in contrast to those of provincial and state government officials which were based on ideological forms of validity. Their arguments and evidence emphasized the need to build new facilities as a way to provide industrial waste generators with capacity assurance so as not to hinder production and capital accumulation. This formalist approach is not statutorily driven in the Canadian context as it is in the United States, yet capacity assurance is at the very least an implicit justification for facility siting in both countries. Another indication of formalist provincial and state arguments has to do with the determination of site suitability and its relationship to facility standards in the case of landfills. RCRA requires that hazardous waste landfills in the United States use synthetic liners to minimize the risk of future ground water contamination, a form of "engineered" containment. Federal and provincial policies in Canada do not require synthetic liners but they attempt to make up for this by insisting on the selection of sites with natural deposits of thick clay to reduce contamination risks through "natural" containment. The opinions of facility proponents and regulatory agencies were more consistent with these site selection policies than they were with local concerns or needs.

Distributive and Procedural Environmental Justice

Environmental justice has a number of components described conceptually in Chapter 2 and explored empirically in Chapter 3. Distributive environmental justice refers to the social, spatial, cumulative, and intergenerational arraying of benefits and burdens associated with hazardous waste and other forms of pollution. The benefits have to do with production and the economic stimulus that comes with it in the form of revenue generation and job creation. These tend to be distributed more broadly than the risks and other burdens of hazardous waste, which are most concentrated near the facilities. Procedural environmental justice refers to the distribution of power and influence among stakeholders in facility siting processes.

Social environmental justice is a concern when racial minority or low-income communities are disproportionately burdened with the location of hazardous waste facilities relative to white or affluent areas. The empirical studies presented in Chapter 3 indicate that race is more predictive of hazardous waste facility location than class in the United States, though the results differ depending on the geographic unit of analysis and the definition of comparison groups. These factors account for the variation in results between the UCCCRJ and UMass studies. Mohai and Bryant found race to be a stronger predictive factor than class in the Detroit metropolitan area. Wayne County, including the City of Detroit, has the highest density of active and inactive hazardous waste facilities (over 0.20 per square mile) in the State of Michigan and the entire Great Lakes Basin (see Figure 13). Wayne County, and especially Detroit, are mostly non-white and low-income in population. Fourteen of 19 active commercial hazardous waste facilities in Michigan are located in the Detroit metropolitan area, six of them in the city center. The results for the other study regions in Chapters 4 and 5 found no relationship between either race or class and hazardous waste facility location. Ironically, environmental injustice social inequity arguments were made in only one of the ten cases, the EDS facility in Wayne County, Michigan. Racial minority groups in the other cases were more likely to base their claims on matters of cumulative equity and risk.

Spatial environmental justice refers to the geographic distribution of benefits and burdens associated with hazardous waste. Spatial inequities were cited by local opposition groups in five of the ten cases, though the exact basis of the claims differed from place to place. In Niagara, New York this became an issue because the state hazardous waste law includes "geographic equity" provisions to promote the location of new commercial hazardous waste facilities in other regions of the state. Niagara County is the only jurisdiction in New York where these facilities are located, despite the fact that nearly one-half of the hazardous waste generated in the state comes from other areas.

In Niagara, Ontario the OWMC case generated a different kind of spatial equity dispute. Local residents complained that they should not have to host an off-site facility, particularly such a large one, given the lack of industries that generate hazardous waste in their community. Spatial equity took yet another twist in the other Ontario case involving the Laidlaw facility. As we have seen, the Walpole Island First Nation, located 40 kilometers downriver from the site, opposed the plan for a new incinerator and sought the right to become an official intervenor group. Laidlaw opposed the request on the basis that they were not located close enough to the facility to have a direct stake. The dispute involved a difference of opinion over the spatial limit of risk, a controversy which had yet to resolve itself when the company withdrew its proposal. Still another variation on spatial equity arose in the EDS case in suburban Detroit. Local opponents of the deep-well injection facility became concerned that much of the projected business was to come from Canadian sources of hazardous waste.

Cumulative and intergenerational equity introduce a temporal dimension to claims of environmental injustice. Cumulative equity became an issue in five of the ten cases. In each of them, local concerns were with the distribution of existing sources of risk from industrial facilities, including hazardous waste facilities. These hazards were argued to accumulate over time, leading to still further disparities in risk that would be exacerbated by the addition of new facilities. These fears were especially critical in low-income, black communities in the Detroit area, which were also heavily industrialized; in these cases, cumulative equity concerns may have served as a kind of proxy for social equity concerns. Intergenerational equity claims came in five of the ten cases where concerns about hydrogeology centered on the potential for future contamination problems that might result given the risk of flooding or ground water contamination.

Generally speaking, procedural equity concerns became an issue in all three jurisdictions. In Ontario, the province reduces the salience of this issue to some degree by providing intervenor funding for opposition groups. Neither Michigan nor New York make use of this method of supporting local groups. However, only one of the ten proposals was developed with the consent of local governments, and even in that case (EDS) the local support eventually turned into opposition. Negotiated agreements between facility proponents and local communities are another way to promote procedural equity, but even in the three cases where this did occur (CWM, NCS, and OWMC) the process did not begin until very late in the game. None of the proposals could be regarded as truly voluntary.

Environmental Justice and "Industrial Ecology"

The concept of "industrial ecology" is a useful way to illustrate the structural limitations of hazardous waste regulation in Canada and the United

States. The legislative history of RCRA described in Chapter 1 shows that the debate over whether and how to regulate production as well as disposal is nothing new and that Congress's decision to establish legal authority only for disposal standards has had a lasting effect. The Canadian national and provincial governments made the same fundamental choice in strategy early on as well, focusing their debate over the allocation of power within federalism. The life-cycle and cradle-to-reincarnation approaches to industrial design described in Chapter 3 differ from the standard cradle-to-grave management in much the same way as the difference between the regulation of production and disposal.

Federal, provincial, and state governments in both Canada and the United States operate voluntary pollution prevention programs to encourage and prioritize the reduction of waste over "end of pipe" pollution control measures. Industry groups as well as environmental activists encourage these practices also. Yet, in spite of this agreement over the merits of pollution prevention, regulatory agencies have no authority to limit the volume or toxicity of industrial waste in any sector of the economy. While capacity assurance policies are used to justify the development of new hazardous waste facilities as an environmental policy priority, no similar driving force exists to insist on waste reduction. Without such a mechanism, industries have no direct incentives to prevent pollution unless it benefits them economically.

Local opponents of new or expanded hazardous waste facilities often point to the need for waste reduction as an alternative to facility siting. This was particularly true for intervenor groups involved in the OWMC proceedings (the Tri-parties). They developed a proposal to evaluate facility need by integrating the potential for pollution prevention. These measures, the Tri-parties argued, could reduce the need for particular kinds of treatment and disposal capacity for the various forms of hazardous waste from particular industrial sectors and locations. The Ontario siting board (EAB) agreed with the soundness of the proposal but stopped short of requiring that OWMC re-evaluate its proposal in this context. None of the siting boards saw fit to integrate pollution prevention into their determinations about facility need in any of the ten facility siting cases.

The Importance of Love Canal

The Love Canal story is important in its own right because of the severity of the problems it represented, the anti-toxics movement it generated, and the effects it had on environmental policy-making, especially in the United States. The location of Love Canal on the Ontario-New York State border heightened the concerns of Canadians as well as Americans. Canadians have even taken to calling the Sydney Tar Ponds in Cape Breton the "Love Canal of Canada." Public responses to hazardous waste problems in both countries have revealed an increasing distrust of hazardous waste facilities, especially when people are confronted with proposals for new ones in their local communities. There is an explicitly spatial component to the response in that acceptance of new facilities increases with distance from the location in question. The politics of not in my backyard (NIMBY) have their roots in the events at Love Canal and other stories like it.

Hazardous waste policies prior to Love Canal were fairly informal for the most part, though Congress had debated the various regulatory approaches throughout the early 1970s. The United States had added hazardous waste provisions to its federal waste statute just two years prior to the publicizing of the situation at Love Canal, but its Environmental Protection Agency (EPA) was nowhere near completing the regulations to implement any of the new requirements at the time. Congress failed to inquire into the agency's lack of progress, so the new law may as well have never been written, at least as far as legal enforcement was concerned. Love Canal was one of the principal driving forces behind renewed Congressional interest in hazardous waste policy, as the first attempts to implement the statute followed quickly, along with the creation of the Superfund program. Canadian federal and provincial hazardous waste laws had also been established prior to Love Canal but received renewed emphasis shortly afterward. This pattern had occurred before in the early 1970s when new environmental laws and regulations emerged in Canada and Ontario, partly out of fear that the emergence of tougher American laws could make Canada a North American "pollution haven" by driving heavily polluting industries, including hazardous waste management firms, to the north.

Towards Environmental Justice and Hazardous Waste

Social scientists and other scholars have generated a considerable amount of work on the issue of environmental justice in a relatively short time. The rapid growth of activist and academic interest in the various connections between environment and social justice is a good indication of the importance of this area of inquiry. While many questions remain contested and unresolved (e.g., race and class; "chicken and egg") about the precise social, spatial, cumulative, and intergenerational distributions of economic benefits and environmental burdens, it is clear that fairness and equity are central to disputes over hazardous waste facilities. These issues spill over into procedural questions about the structure of siting boards, the allocation of power and authority among interest groups, and the relative importance of capacity assurance as compared to pollution prevention.

The ten facility siting cases reviewed in Part II reveal the connections between environmental justice and hazardous waste in a number of respects. First, distributions of existing waste sites and other industrial facilities (whether actively operating or not) are fundamentally important to communities facing the prospect of new hazardous waste facilities in their local areas. Social, spatial, and cumulative equity considerations are all relevant indicators of the fairness of particular proposals. Second, communities slated to host new facilities fear the prospect of becoming new "Love Canals" at some time in the future if facility containments begin to fail. They also tend to prefer any alternative that would either obviate the need for the facility or place it somewhere, perhaps anywhere, else. This is partly a concern about intergenerational inequity where production and corresponding environmental management decisions benefit present society by risking the environmental health of people in the future. It also reflects a sense of personal loyalty and commitment to one's own community as imagined in terms of both history and destiny. Third, these local issues have been rather poorly addressed historically. National environmental and industrial needs have tended to override community desires, though NIMBY-style protests have proven to be very effective at tipping the balance of power. Still, the effectiveness of grassroots activism is highly contingent from one situation to the next.

The Great Lakes basin is an important place to explore the connections between environmental justice and hazardous waste. The area is highly industrialized and heavily polluted in places. As a binational region, it is also interesting because of the differing policy styles on one side of the border and the other. These variations refer not only to the explicit laws, regulations, and policies that federal, provincial, and state governments have imposed on hazardous waste management, they also have become relevant to the role of government in the promotion of fairness in environmental management. The composition of facility siting boards, the level of assistance provided to intervenor groups, and the question of public or private ownership of facilities have all become relevant. The cases varied from place to place, depending at least partly on whether the controlling legal authorities were American or Canadian.

If we are to deal with hazardous waste in ways that are both practical and fair, the lessons learned through activist and academic inquiries into environmental inequity and injustice are highly relevant. Distributive and procedural dimensions of the problem are especially of concern to local communities who find themselves slated to become hosts for new hazardous waste facilities. Moreover, the structural limitations of hazardous waste policies make it difficult to foster the development of more environmentally benign forms of production. The internalization of noxious externalities should not be the responsibility of communities through the development of new hazardous waste facilities. Nor should governments have to subsidize the siting process for the benefit of waste generators. Instead, governments should make industries accountable for the adoption of waste reduction techniques, rather than simply encourage them to do so. We must counter the prominence of capacity assurance as an implicit or explicit policy justification for new facilities with an expanded role for pollution prevention to reduce demand on existing facilities and the need for new ones. Without such an expanded conception of procedural equity, we will never be able to reverse existing environmental inequities and injustices related to hazardous waste and other forms of industrial pollution.

References

Allen, D. (1995). The chemical industry: process changes and the search for cleaner technologies. In R. Gottlieb (Ed.), *Reducing Toxics: A New Approach to Policy and Industrial Decisionmaking.* Washington, DC: Island Press.

Allenby, B.R., & Richards, D.J. (Eds.). (1994). *The Greening of Industrial Ecosystems.* Washington, DC: National Academy Press.

Anderson, A.B., et al. (1994, July). Environmental equity: evaluating TSDF siting over the past two decades. *Waste Age*, 83-100.

Anderton, D., et al. (1994a). Environmental equity: the demographics of dumping. *Demography* 31(2), 229-48.

Anderton, D., et al. (1994b). Hazardous waste facilities: "environmental equity" issues in metropolitan areas. *Evaluation Review* 18(2), 123-40.

Ayres, R.U. (1994). Industrial metabolism: theory and policy. In B.R. Allenby & D.J. Richards (Eds.), *The Greening of Industrial Ecosystems.* Washington, DC: National Academy Press.

Bachrach, P. & Baratz, M.S. (1962). Two faces of power. *American Political Science Review* 56(4), 947-52.

Barlow, M.& May, E. (2000). *Frederick Street: Life and Death on Canada's Love Canal.* Toronto: HarperCollins.

Beck, U. (1986). *Risk Society: Towards a New Modernity.* Trans. M. Ritter (1992). London: Sage Publications.

Beck, U. (1994, Spring). Unpopular neighbors: are dumps and landfills sited equitably? *Resources*, 16-19.

Beck, U. (1995). *Ecological Enlightenment: Essays on the Politics of the Risk Society.* Atlantic Highlands, NJ: Humanities Press.

Beck, U. (1999). *World Risk Society.* Malden, MA: Polity Press.

Been, V. (1993). What's fairness got to do with it? environmental justice and the siting of locally undesirable land uses. *Cornell Law Review* 78, 1001-85.

Blacksell, M., Watkins, C., & Economides, K. (1986). Human geography and law: a case of separate development in social science. *Progress in Human Geography* 10(3), 371-96.

Blomley, N.K. (1989a). Interpretive practices, the state, and the locale. In J. Wolch & M. Dear (Eds.), *The Power of Geography: How Territory Shapes Social Life.* Boston, MA: Unwin Hyman.

Blomley, N.K. (1989b). Text and context: rethinking the law-space nexus. *Progress in Human Geography* 113, 512-34.

Blomley, N.K. (1994). *Law, Space, and the Geographies of Power*. New York, NY: Guilford.

Blomley, N.K. & Clark, G.L. (1990). Law, theory, and geography. *Urban Geography* 11(5), 433-46.

Bloomfield, L.M., & Fitzgerald, G.F. (1958). *Boundary Waters Problems of Canada and the United States*. Toronto, ON: Carswell.

Boggs, M. (Administrator, Regional Municipality of Niagara). (1995). Personal Interview. 27 June.

Bouck, S. (1993, May). The shrinking hazardous waste universe: waste treatment and disposal will be profitable again, but for a reduced set of players. *Environmental Information Digest*, 32-36.

Bradshaw, A.D., Southwood, R., & Warner, F. (Eds.). (1992). *The Treatment and Handling of Wastes*. London: Chapman & Hall.

Bronner, S.E. (1995). Ecology, politics, and risk: the social theory of Ulrich Beck. *Capitalism, Nature, Socialism* 6(1), 67-86.

Brown, P., & Ferguson, F.I.T. (1995). "Making a big stink": women's work, women's relationships, and toxic waste activism. *Gender and Society* 9(2), 145-72.

Buhrmaster, E. (1993, October 13). *Hearing Report in the Matter of the Application of CWM Chemical Services, Inc.* Albany, NY.: New York State Department of Environmental Conservation, Office of Hearings.

Bullard, R.D. (1983, Spring). Solid waste sites and the black Houston community. *Sociological Inquiry* 53, 273-88.

Bullard, R.D. (1990). *Dumping in Dixie: Race, Class, and Environmental Quality*. Boulder, CO: Westview Press.

Bullard, R.D. (1993). Anatomy of environmental racism and the environmental justice movement. In R.D. Bullard (Ed.), *Confronting Environmental Racism: Voices From the Grassroots*. Boston, MA: South End Press.

Bullard, R.D. (1994a). Environmental justice for all. In R.D. Bullard (Ed.) *Unequal Protection: Environmental Justice and Communities of Color*. San Francisco, CA: Sierra Club Books.

Bullard, R.D. (1994b). Grassroots flowering. *The Amicus Journal* 16, 32-37.

Bullard, R.D. (2000). *Sprawl City: Race, Politics and Planning in Atlanta*. Washington, DC: Island Press.

Bullard, R.D., & Wright, B.H. (1986). The politics of pollution: implications for the black community. *Phylon* 47, 71-78.

Burda, K. (Hazardous Waste Chief, Michigan Department of Natural Resources). (1994). Personal interview. August 18.

Burda, K. (1997). Personal interview. September 11.

Butler, J.H. (1980). *Economic Geography: Spatial and Environmental Aspects of Economic Activity*. New York, NY: John Wiley & Sons.

Campbell, B., & Stanton, B. (1986, March 2). The blobs: a crisis bubbling up? *Detroit Free Press*.

Canada. (1990). *Canada's Green Plan for a Healthy Environment*. Ottawa: Minister of Supply and Services Canada.

Canadian Institute for Environmental Law and Policy. (2000). *Ontario: Open for Toxics*. Toronto, ON: CIELAP.

City of Niagara Falls, Niagara County, and Niagara County Board of Health. (1989, October 5). *Brief on Exceptions in the Matter of the Application of CECOS International, Inc.* Niagara Falls, NY.

Clark, G.L. (1985). *Judges and the Cities: Interpreting Local Autonomy.* Chicago, IL: University of Chicago Press.

Clark, G.L. (1986a). Adjudicating jurisdictional disputes in Chicago and Toronto: legal formalism and urban structure. *Urban Geography* 7(1), 63-80.

Clark, G.L. (1986b). Making moral landscapes: John Rawls' original position. *Political Geography Quarterly* 5, 147-52.

Clark, G.L. (1989). Law and the interpretive turn in the social sciences. *Urban Geography* 10(3), 209-28.

Clark, G.L., & Dear, M. (1984). *State Apparatus: Structures and Language of Legitimacy.* Boston, MA: Allen & Unwin, Inc.

Colborn, T. (1990). *Great Lakes, Great Legacy?* Washington, DC: Conservation Foundation; Ottawa, Ont.: Institute for Research on Public Policy.

Colborn, T., Myers, J.P., & Dumanoski, D. (1996). *Our Stolen Future: How We Are Threatening Our Fertility, Intelligence, and Survival: A Scientific Detective Story.* New York. NY: Dutton.

Colten, C.E., & Skinner, P.N. (1996). *The Road to Love Canal: Managing Industrial Waste before EPA.* Austin, TX: University of Texas Press.

Commission for Environmental Cooperation. (1996). *Status of Pollution Prevention in North America.* Montreal, QC: Prospectus, Inc.

Commission for Environmental Cooperation. (1997). *Taking Stock: North American Pollutant Releases and Transfers.* Montreal, QC: CEC.

Commission for Environmental Cooperation. (2002). *Taking Stock: North American Pollutant Releases and Transfers.* Montreal, QC: CEC.

Cox, K.R. (1989). The politics of turf and the question of class. In J. Wolch & M. Dear (Eds), *The Power of Geography: How Territory Shapes Social Life.* Boston. MA: Unwin Hyman.

Cox, K.R. (1997a). Spaces of dependence, spaces of engagement and the politics of scale, or: looking for local politics. *Political Geography* 17(1), 1-23.

Cox, K.R. (1997b). Representation and power in the politics of scale. *Political Geography* 17(1), 41-44.

Cutter, S.L. (1995). Race, class and environmental justice. *Progress in Human Geography* 19(1), 111-22.

Cutter, S.L., & Solecki, W. (1996). Setting environmental justice in space and place: acute and chronic airborne toxic releases in the southeastern United States. *Urban Geography* 17(5), 380-99.

Daly, H. & Cobb, J. Jr. (1989). *For the Common Good: Redirecting the Economy Toward Community and the Environment and a Sustainable Future.* Boston, MA: Beacon Press.

Davey, T. (1998, July). In media scrums, the score so far is: engineers 2, activists 10. (Editorial.) *Environmental Science and Engineering Magazine.*

Dear, M. (1981). The state: a research agenda. *Environment and Planning A* 13, 1191-96.

Dear, M. (1992). Understanding and overcoming the NIMBY syndrome. *Journal of the American Planning Association* 58(3), 288-300.

Demera, B., & Moloney, P. (2000, June 23). Vaughan mayor trashes waste proposal: we're no longer a willing host. *Toronto Star.*

Detroit. (1985). *Detroit Master Plan of Policies: Volume 3, Sector Policies*. Detroit, MI: City of Detroit.

Detroit Health Department. (1988, April 5). *Public Hearing Statement Relating to National Chemical Services*. Detroit, MI.

Dicken, P. (1998). *Global Shift: Transforming the World Economy*. 3rd ed. New York, NY: Guilford Press.

Dickey, P. (Environmental Engineer, Niagara County Health Department, Division of Environmental Health). (1995). Personal interview. June 30.

Doern, G.B., & Conway. T. (1994). *The Greening of Canada: Federal Institutions and Decisions*. Toronto, ON: University of Toronto Press.

Dolen, J. (Division of Hazardous Substances Regulation, New York State Department of Environmental Conservation). (1996). Personal interview. March 6.

Dorfman, M.H., & Wise, M. (1997). *Tracking Toxic Chemicals: The Value of Materials Accounting Data*. New York, NY: INFORM, Inc.

Dunne, M. (1999). Baton Rouge activist wins environmental award.(1999, January 27). *The Advocate*.

Eckstein, H. (1963). A perspective on comparative politics, past and present. In H. Eckstein & D.E. Apter (Eds.), *Comparative Politics: A Reader*. New York, NY: Free Press.

Eismann, P. (Deputy Permit Administrator, Division of Regulatory Services, New York State Department of Environmental Conservation). (1995). Personal interview. February 6.

Enbar, M. (1983). Equity in the social sciences. In R. Kasperson (Ed.), *Equity Issues in Radioactive Waste Management*. Cambridge, MA: Oelgeschlager, Gunn, & Hain Publishers.

Environment Canada. (1988). *Economic Profile of the Hazardous Waste Management Service Industry Subsector in Canada: Final Report*. Hull, QC: Conservation and Protection Division.

Environment Canada. (1995a). *The Canadian Hazardous Waste Inventory: Final Report*. Hull, QC.: Office of Waste Management.

Environment Canada. (1995b). *Resilog: An Exchange of Views and Information on Hazardous Waste Across Canada*. Hull, QC: Transboundary Movement Division.

Environment Canada. (2000). *Resilog: An Exchange of Views and Information on Hazardous Waste Across Canada*. Hull, QC: Transboundary Movement Division.

Environmental Protection Agency (EPA). (1992). *Environmental Equity: Reducing Risk for All Communities*. Vol.1, 2. Washington, DC: Office of Policy, Planning. and Evaluation.

Environmental Protection Agency (EPA). (1993a). *Environmental Justice Initiatives*. Washington, DC: Office of Administration and Resources Management.

Environmental Protection Agency (EPA). (1993b). *Land Use in the CERCLA Remedy Selection Process* (Memorandum from Elliott P. Laws, Assistant Administrator to EPA hazardous waste managers).Washington, DC: OSWER Directive 9355.7-04.

Environmental Protection Agency (EPA). (1993c). *Summary Report of the National Roundtable on Hazardous Waste Minimization and Combustion: November 15-18*. Washington, DC: Office of Solid Waste and Emergency Response.

Environmental Protection Agency (EPA). (1993b). *Environmental Justice Initiatives*. Washington, DC: Office of Administration and Resources Management.

Environmental Protection Agency (EPA). (1995). *National Biennial RCRA Hazardous Waste Report (Based on 1991 Data)*. Washington, DC: Office of Solid Waste and Emergency Response.

Environmental Protection Agency (EPA). (2000). *Social Aspects of Siting RCRA Hazardous Waste Facilities*. Washington, DC: Office of Solid Waste and Emergency Response.

Environmental Protection Agency (EPA). (2002). *Hazardous Waste — Treatment, Storage and Disposal — Capacity Assurance*. Washington, DC: www.epa.gov/epaoswer/hazwaste/tsds/capacity/ (last updated 24 June 2002).

Ewing, G.O. (1992). The bases of differences between American and Canadian cities. *The Canadian Geographer* 36(3), 266-79.

Fafard, P.C., & Harrison, K. (Eds.). (2000). *Managing the Environmental Union: Intergovernmental Relations and Environmental Policy in Canada*. Montreal, QC: McGill-Queen's University Press.

Fischhoff, B. (1977). Cost benefit analysis and the art of motorcycle maintenance. *Policy Sciences* 8, 177-202.

Fish, S. (1980). *Is there a text in this class? The authority of interpretive communities*. Cambridge, MA: Harvard University Press.

Fletcher, T. (1998). Facility siting and the Ontario Waste Management Corporation: environmental equity in Canada. *The Great Lakes Geographer* 5(1), 31-44.

Fletcher, T. (2002). Neighborhood change at Love Canal: contamination, evacuation and resettlement. *Land Use Policy* 19(4), 311-23.

Fong, E. (1994). Residential proximity among racial groups in US and Canadian neighborhoods. *Urban Affairs Quarterly* 30(2), 285-97.

Freeze, C., & Abbate, G. (2000, October 12). The city has declared war. *Globe and Mail*.

Frosch, R.A. (1994a). Industrial ecology: a philosophical introduction. *Proceedings of the National Academy of Science* 89(2), 800-03.

Frosch, R.A. (1994b). Industrial ecology: minimizing the impact of industrial waste. *Physics Today* 47(11), 63-68.

Gallaugher, B., & Lee, G.F. (1997). *Review of Adams Mine Environmental Assessment*. Cochrane, ON: Gallaugher Associates and G. Fred Lee and Associates for the Algonquin Nation Secretariat.

Gerrard, M.B. (1994). *Whose Backyard, Whose Risk: Fear and Fairness in Toxic and Nuclear Waste Siting*. Cambridge, MA: MIT Press.

Gibbons, A. (1991). Does war on cancer equal war on poverty? *Science* 253, 260.

Gibson, R.B., (Ed.). (1999). *Voluntary Initiatives: The New Politics of Corporate Greening*. Peterborough, ON: Broadview Press.

Gladwell, M. (1990, November 26). Public health turns to economic ills. *The Washington Post*.

Goldberg, M.A., & Mercer, J. (1986). *The Myth of the North American City: Continentalism Challenged*. Vancouver, BC: University of British Columbia Press.

Goldblatt, D. (1996). *Social Theory and the Environment*. Boulder, CO: Westview Press.

Goldman, B.A. (1996). What is the future of environmental justice? *Antipode* 28(2), 122-41.

Goldman, B.A., & Fitton, L. (1994). *Toxic Wastes and Race Revisited.* Washington, DC: Center for Policy Alternatives.

Gottlieb, R., Smith, M., & Roque, J. (1995). By air, water, and land: the media-specific approach to toxics policies. In R. Gottlieb (Ed.), *Reducing Toxics: A New Approach to Policy and Industrial Decisionmaking.* Washington, DC: Island Press.

Goudie, A. (2000). *The Human Impact on the Natural Environment.* Cambridge, MA: MIT Press.

Greenberg, M. (1993). Proving environmental inequity in siting locally unwanted land uses. *Risk Issues in Health and Safety* 23, 235-52.

Greenpeace. (1990). *The International Trade in Wastes: A Greenpeace Inventory.* Washington, DC: Greenpeace.

Greenpeace. (1992). *The Greenpeace Book of Greenwash.* Washington, DC: Greenpeace.

Gregg, A.R., & Posner, M.S. (1990). *The Big Picture: What Canadians Think About Almost Everything.* Toronto: Macfarlane, Walter, & Ross.

Handley, F.J. (1989). Hazardous waste exports: a leak in the system of international legal controls. *Environmental Law Reporter News and Analysis* 19(1), 10171-82.

Handley, F.J. (1990). Exports of waste from the United States to Canada: the how and why. *Environmental Law Reporter News and Analysis* 20(2), 10061-66.

Hanke, J. (1993, May). Hazardous waste incineration 1993: industry players ponder the recent pricing slump. *Environmental Information Digest,* 14-20.

Harris, K. (1999, September 21). Mayor complains over garbage "gag": jobs outweigh ecological issues in mining centre. *Toronto Star.*

Harrison, K. (1986). *Fairness in Facility Siting: An Evaluation of Ontario's Public Agency Approach to Hazardous Waste Management.* Dissertation. Massachusetts Institute of Technology, Boston, MA.

Harrison, K., & Hoberg, G. (1994). *Risk, Science, and Politics: Regulating Toxic Substances in Canada and the United States.* Montreal, QC: McGill-Queens Press.

Harvey, D. (1973). *Social Justice and the City.* Baltimore, MD: Johns Hopkins University Press.

Harvey, D. (1982). *The Limits to Capital.* Oxford: Basil Blackwell.

Harvey, D. (1985a). The geopolitics of capitalism. In D. Gregory & J. Urry (Eds.), *Social Relations and Spatial Structures.* London: Macmillan Press.

Harvey, D. (1985b). *The Urbanization of Capital.* Baltimore, MD: Johns Hopkins University Press.

Harvey, D. (1992). Social justice, postmodernism, and the city. *International Journal of Urban and Regional Research* 16(4), 588-601.

Harvey, D. (1996). *Justice, Nature and the Geography of Difference.* London: Blackwell.

Heiman, M. (1990a). From "not in my backyard!" to "not in anybody's backyard!": grassroots challenge to hazardous waste facility siting. *Journal of the American Planning Association* 56(3), 359-62.

Heiman, M. (1990b). Using public authorities to site hazardous waste management facilities: problems and prospects. *Policy Studies Journal* 18(4), 974-85.

Hird, J. (1993). Environmental policy and inequity: the case of the Superfund. *Journal of Policy Analysis and Management* 12, 323-43.

Hoberg, G. (1991). Sleeping with an elephant: the American influence on Canadian environmental regulation. *Journal of Public Policy* 11(1), 107-32.

Hoberg, G. (1993). Environmental policy: alternative styles. In M. Atkinson (Ed.), *Governing Canada: Institutions and Public Policy*. Toronto. ON: Harcourt, Brace, Jovanovich.

Holman, J.T. (1996). How big is your backyard? the selection of an appropriate geographic unit for implementing an environmental equity legislative proposal. Paper presented at the Association of American Geographers annual meeting. Charlotte, NC.

Honywill, B. (2000, January 27). Garbage plan in trouble for Kirkland Lake. *Toronto Sun*.

Ilgen, T.L. (1985). Between Europe and America: regulating toxic substances in Canada. *Canadian Public Policy* 11(3), 578-90.

Intervenor Concerned Citizens Organizations (1988 December 23). *Post-Hearing Reply Brief in the Matter of the Application of CECOS International, Inc.* Niagara Falls, NY.

International Joint Commission. (1992). *Air Quality in the Detroit-Windsor/ Port Huron-Sarnia Region: A Report to the Governments of Canada and the United States*. Windsor, ON: IJC.

International Joint Commission. (1993). *Council of Great Lakes Research Managers 1993 Report to the International Joint Commission*. Windsor, ON: IJC.

International Joint Commission. (1994). *An Examination of the Integrity of Five Hazardous Waste Disposal Sites in the Great Lakes Basin: A Report to the Virtual Elimination Task Force of the International Joint Commission*. Windsor, ON: IJC.

Jelenski, L.W., Graedel, T.E., Laudise, R.A., McCall, D.W., & Patel, C.K.N. (1992). Industrial ecology: concepts and approaches. *Proceedings of the National Academy of Sciences USA* 89(2), 793-97.

Jerrett, M., Eyles, J., Cole, D., & Reader, S. (1997). Environmental equity in Canada: an empirical investigation into the income distribution of pollution in Ontario. *Environment and Planning A* 29, 1777-1800.

Judd, D.R. (1997). The case of the missing scales: a commentary on Cox. *Political Geography* 17(1), 29-34.

Kasperson, R.E. (1983). Determining the acceptability of risk: ethical and policy issues. In T.J. Rogers & D.V. Bates (Eds.), *Assessment and Perception of Risk to Human Health*. Ottawa: Royal Society of Canada.

Kasperson, R.E., & Dow, K. (1991). Developmental and geographical equity in global environmental change. *Evaluation Review* 15, 149-71.

Kasperson, R.E., Golding, D., & Tuler, S. (1992). Social distrust as a factor in siting hazardous facilities and communicating risks. *Journal of Social Issues* 48(4), 161-87.

Kasperson, R.E., Renn, O., Slovic, P., Brown, H.S., Emel, J., Goble, R., Kasperson, J.S., & Ratick, S. (1988). The social amplification of risk: a conceptual framework. *Risk Analysis* 8, 177-87.

Ketcheson, D. (Smithville Phase IV Bedrock Remediation Program Manager). (1995). Personal interview. June 29.

Kovacs, W.L., & Klucsik, J.F. (1977). The new federal role in solid waste management: the Resource Conservation and Recovery Act of 1976. *Columbia Journal of Environmental Law* 3, 205-61.

Kunreuther, H. (1996). Voluntary procedures for siting noxious facilities: lotteries, auctions, and benefit sharing. In D. Munton (Ed.) *Hazardous Waste Siting and Democratic Choice*. Washington, DC: Georgetown University Press.

Laidlaw Environmental Services, Ltd. (1990). *Laidlaw Environmental Services Environmental Assessment, Part A— Primary Report*. Sarnia, ON: Laidlaw.

Laidlaw Environmental Services, Ltd. (1993 October 20). *Information Release*. Sarnia, Ontario: Laidlaw Environmental Services, Ltd.

Lake, R.W. (1987). Introduction. In R.W. Lake (Ed.), *Resolving Locational Conflict*. New Brunswick, NJ: Rutgers University, Center for Urban Policy Research.

Lake, R.W. (1993). Rethinking NIMBY. *Journal of the American Planning Association* 59(1), 87-93.

Lake, R.W. (1994). Negotiating local autonomy. *Political Geography* 13(5), 423-42.

Lake, R.W. (1996). Volunteers, NIMBYs, and environmental justice: dilemmas of democratic practice. *Antipode*. 28(2), 160-74.

Lake, R.W., & Disch, L. (1992). Structural constraints and pluralist contradictions in hazardous waste regulation. *Environment and Planning A* 24(3), 663-81.

Lake, R.W., & Johns, R.A. (1990). Legitimation conflicts: the politics of hazardous waste siting law. *Urban Geography* 11(5), 488-508.

Landy, M.K., Roberts, M.J., & Thomas, S.R. (1990). *The Environmental Protection Agency: Asking the Wrong Questions*. New York, NY: Oxford University Press.

Leiss, W. (1994). [Review of Ulrich Beck, *Risk Society*]. *Canadian Journal of Sociology*. 19(4), 544-47.

Levine, A.G. (1982). *Love Canal: Science, Politics, and People*. Lexington, MA: Lexington Books.

Lijphart, A. (1971). Comparative politics and the comparative method. *American Political Science Review* 65(3), 682-93.

Lindsay, R. (1984). Conservation of mass. *The World Book Encyclopedia*. Volume 13. Chicago, IL: World Book Inc.

Lipietz, A. (1992a). *Towards a New Economic Order: Postfordism, Ecology and Democracy*. New York, NY: Oxford University Press.

Lipietz, A. (1992b). A regulationist approach to the future of urban ecology. *Capitalism, Nature, Socialism* 3(3), 101-10.

Macdonald, D. (1991). *The Politics of Pollution: Why Canadians are Failing Their Environment*. Toronto, ON: McClelland & Stewart.

Marsden, W., & MacDonell, R. (1997, October 25). Disposal of contaminants tricky: even treatment facilities have proved to be dangerous polluters. Montreal *The Gazette*, A7.

Mazmanian, D., & Morell, D. (1992). *Beyond Superfailure: America's Toxics Policy for the 1990s*. Boulder, CO: Westview Press.

Mazurek, J., Gottlieb, R., & Roque, J. (1995). Shifting to prevention: the limits of current policy. In R. Gottlieb (Ed.), *Reducing Toxics: A New Approach to Policy and Industrial Decisionmaking*. Washington, DC: Island Press.

McGreevy, P.V. (1994). *Imagining Niagara: The Meaning and Making of Niagara Falls*. Amherst, MA: University of Massachusetts Press.

McMaster, R., Leitner, H. & Sheppard, E. (1997). GIS-based environmental equity and risk assessment: methodological problems and prospects. *Cartography and Geographic Information Systems* 24(3), 172-89.

Meyer, W.B. (1996). *Human Impact on the Earth.* New York. NY: Cambridge University Press.

Michigan Department of Natural Resources. (1984). *Hazardous Waste Management in Michigan: A Status Report and Review of Future Options.* Lansing, MI: Department of Natural Resources.

—. (1991). *Hazardous Waste Management Plan for Michigan: Report and Recommendations of the Hazardous Waste Policy Committee Submitted to the Natural Resources Commission.* Lansing, MI: Department of Natural Resources.

Michigan Site Review Board, Energy Recovery Systems. (1982, October 27). *Public Hearing: Energy Recovery Systems.* Pontiac Township, MI: Department of Natural Resources.

Michigan Site Review Board, Energy Recovery Systems. (1982, December 22). *Denial of Construction Permit.* Lansing, MI: Department of Natural Resources.

Michigan Site Review Board, Environmental Management Systems. (1982, August 24). *Public Hearing: Environmental Management Systems.* Sumpter Township, MI: Department of Natural Resources.

Michigan Site Review Board, National Chemical Services. (1988, May 5). *Public Hearing: National Chemical Services.* Detroit, MI: Department of Natural Resources.

Mitchell, R.C., & Carson, R.T. (1986). Property rights, protest, and the siting of hazardous waste facilities. *American Economic Review Papers and Proceedings* 76(2), 285-90.

Mohai, P., & Bryant, B. (1992). Environmental racism: reviewing the evidence. In B. Bryant & P. Mohai (Eds.), *Race and the Incidence of Environmental Hazards: A Time for Discourse.* Boulder, CO: Westview Press.

Morchain, J. (1973). *Sharing a Continent: An Introduction to Canadian-American Relations.* Toronto, ON: McGraw-Hill Ryerson.

National Research Council. (1985). *Reducing Hazardous Waste: An Evaluation and a Call for Action.* Washington, DC: National Academy Press.

New York State Department of Environmental Conservation. (1988, April). *Recommendations for Assistance to Localities Affected by Hazardous Waste Management Facilities.* Albany, NY: Division of Hazardous Substances Regulation.

New York State Department of Environmental Conservation. (1989, October). *Final Environmental Impact Statement for SCA Chemical Services, Inc.* Albany, NY: Division of Regulatory Affairs.

New York State Department of Environmental Conservation. (1989). *Revised Draft, New York State Hazardous Waste Facility Siting Plan and Environmental Impact Statement 4-31.* Albany, NY: Department of Environmental Conservation.

New York State Department of Environmental Conservation. (1995). *Report to the New York State Legislature on Generation and Management in New York State: 1993 Hazardous Waste Report.* Albany, NY: Department of Environmental Conservation.

New York State Department of Environmental Conservation. (2000). *New York State Inactive Hazardous Waste Disposal Site Remedial Plan: 2000 Report.* Albany: NYDEC.

New York State Department of Health. (1988). *Decision Report on Habitability: Love Canal Emergency Declaration Area*. Albany, NY: Department of Health.

New York State Department of Health. (1981). *Love Canal: A Special Report to the Governor and Legislature*. Albany, NY: Department of Health.

New York State Facility Siting Board. (1989, July). *Rulings and Memorandum to Parties*. Albany, NY: Department of Environmental Conservation.

New York State Facility Siting Board. (1989, November). *Certificate of Environmental Safety and Public Necessity*. Albany, NY: Department of Environmental Conservation.

New York State Facility Siting Board. (1990, March). *Decision in the Matter of the Application of CECOS International, Inc*. Albany, NY: Department of Environmental Conservation.

New York State Facility Siting Board. (1990, March). *Supplementary Decision in the Matter of the Application of CECOS International, Inc*. Albany, NY: Department of Environmental Conservation.

New York State Facility Siting Board. (1993a, December). *Minority Opinion in the Matter of the Application of CWM Chemical Services, Inc*. Albany, NY: Department of Environmental Conservation.

New York State Facility Siting Board. (1993b, December). *Decision in the Matter of the Application of CWM Chemical Services, Inc*. Albany, NY: Department of Environmental Conservation.

Nin-Da-Waab-Jig. (1983). *Contaminant Hydrogeology of the Walpole Island Indian Reserve*. Occasional Paper No. 1. R.N. Wallaceburg, ON: Walpole Island Heritage Centre.

Nin-Da-Waab-Jig. (1984). *Evaluation of the Domestic Water Resources on Walpole Island Indian Reserve*. Occasional Paper No. 2. Wallaceburg, ON: Walpole Island Heritage Centre.

Nin-Da-Waab-Jig. (1986). *Environmental Impacts on the Lake Saint Clair Fishery: A Case Study of Mercury Pollution and Its Effects on Walpole Island Indian Reserve*. Occasional Paper No. 11. Wallaceburg, ON: Walpole Island Heritage Centre.

Norton, B.G. (1989). Intergenerational equity and environmental decisions: a model using Rawls' veil of ignorance. *Ecological Economics* 1: 137-59.

Nozick, R. (1974). *Anarchy, State, and Utopia*. Boston, MA: Basic Books.

O'Connor, J. (1981). The meaning of crisis. *International Journal of Urban and Regional Research* 5(3):301-29.

Office of the Auditor General of Canada (2002). *Toxic Substances Revisited: Still a Long Way to Go*. News Release, 22 October 2002. Ottawa: Commissioner of the Environment and Sustainable Development.

Okie, S. (1991, April 17). Study links cancer, poverty. *The Washington Post*.

Olsen, R.N., Jr. (1991). The concentration of commercial hazardous waste facilities in the western New York community. *Buffalo Law Review* 39(2), 473-94.

Olsen, R.N., Jr. (Professor and Dean, School of Law, State University of New York at Buffalo). (1995). Personal interview. June 28.

O'Neill, K. (2000). *Waste Trading Among Rich Nations: Building a Theory of Environmental Regulation*. Cambridge, MA: MIT Press.

O'Neill, T. (Smithville Phase IV Bedrock Remediation Project Manager). (1995). Personal interview. June 27.

Ontario Environmental Assessment Board. (1993, August 10). *Public Hearing in the Matter of Laidlaw Environmental Services to Construct a High Temperature Rotary Kiln Incinerator.* Brigden Community Centre, Brigden, ON: Environmental Assessment Board.

Ontario Environmental Assessment Board. (1994, November 23). *Ontario Waste Management Corporation Application: Reasons of Decision and Decision.* Toronto, ON: Environmental Assessment Board.

Ontario Ministry of Environment. (2000). *Progress Report: Ontario Initiatives in Pollution Prevention.* Toronto, ON: Ministry of Environment.

Ontario Ministry of Environment. (2001, December 18). *Pre-Treatment Requirements for Hazardous Wastes Prior to Land Disposal (Land Disposal Restrictions) — Discussion Document.* Toronto, ON: Ministry of Environment.

Ontario Ministry of Environment and Energy. (1995, February 7). News Release. Toronto, ON: Ministry of Environment and Energy.

Ontario Office of Consolidated Hearings. (1994, November 23). Media Brief. Toronto, ON: Office of Consolidated Hearings.

Ontario Waste Management Corporation. (1988, November 28). *Environmental Assessment for a Waste Management System.* Toronto, ON: OWMC.

Oracle. (2000, August). *Adams Mine Survey Report.* Prepared for David Ramsay MPP. Cochrane, ON.

Packham, J. (Former Mayor of West Lincoln). (1995). Personal interview. June 27.

Palmer, K. (2000, June 20). Extend dump's limit, city urged: Toronto also eyes US alternatives to Kirkland Lake plan. *Toronto Star.*

Patel, C.K.N. (1992). Industrial ecology. *Proceedings of the National Academy of Sciences* 89(2), 798-99.

Pearce, D., Barbier, E., Markandya, A., Barrett, S., Turner, R., & Swanson, T. (1991). *Blueprint 2: Greening the World Economy.* London: Earthscan Publications.

Pearlstein, A.S. (1989, August 21). *Hearing Report and Recommended Decision in the Application of CECOS International, Inc.* Albany, NY: New York State Department of Environmental Conservation, Office of Hearings.

Pearlstein, A.S. (1990, February). *Supplementary Hearing Report in the Application of CECOS International, Inc.* Albany: New York State Department of Environmental Conservation, Office of Hearings.

Penn, J. (1990). Towards an ecologically-based society: a Rawlsian perspective. *Ecological Economics* 2, 225-42.

Pitegoff, P.R. (1991). Buffalo change and community. *Buffalo Law Review* 39(2), 313-40.

Popper, F.J. (1987). The environmentalist and the LULU. In R.W. Lake (Ed.), *Resolving Locational Conflict.* New Brunswick, NJ: Rutgers University, Center for Urban Policy Research.

Prouta, E. (2000, August 24). Pope, IOC asked to help stop dump. *Globe and Mail.*

Pulido, L. (1994). Restructuring and the contraction and expansion of environmental rights in the United States. *Environment and Planning A* 26, 915-36.

Pulido, L. (1996a). *Environmentalism and Economic Justice: Two Chicano Struggles in the Southwest.* Tucson, AZ: The University of Arizona Press.

Pulido, L. (1996b). A critical review of the methodology of environmental racism research. *Antipode* 28(2), 142-59.

Pulido, L. (2000). Rethinking environmental racism: white privilege and urban development in Southern California. *Annals of the Association of American Geographers* 90(1), 12-40.

Rabe, B.G. (1994). *Beyond NIMBY: Hazardous Waste Siting in Canada and the United States.* Washington, DC: Brookings Institute.

Rabe, B.G., Gunderson, W.C., & Harbage, P.T. (1996). Voluntary siting of hazardous waste facilities in western Canada. In D. Munton (Ed.), *Hazardous Waste Siting and Democratic Choice.* Washington, DC: Georgetown University Press.

Radcliffe, S. (Senior Project Coordinator, Industrial Waste Section, Ontario Ministry of Environment). (1994). Personal interview. May 19.

Radcliffe, S. (1996). Personal interview. February 14.

Rawls, J. (1967). Distributive justice. In P. Laslett & W. Runciman (Eds.), *Philosophy, Politics and Society, Third Series.* 58-82. New York, NY: Barnes & Noble, Inc.

Rawls, J. (1971). *A Theory of Justice.* Cambridge, MA: Harvard University Press.

Regional Municipality of Niagara. (1994, November 23). Press Release: *Region of Niagara Triumphant over OWMC Ruling.* Smithville, ON: Regional Municipality of Niagara.

Richards, A. (1996). Using co-management to build community support for waste facilities. In D. Munton (Ed.), *Hazardous Waste Siting and Democratic Choice.* Washington, DC: Georgetown University Press.

Richards, D.J., Allenby, B.R., & Frosch, R.A. (1994). The greening of industrial ecosystems: overview and perspective. In B.R. Allenby & D.J. Richards (Eds.), *The Greening of Industrial Ecosystems.* Washington, DC: National Academy Press.

Ristoratore, M. (1985). Siting toxic waste disposal facilities in Canada and the United States: problems and prospects. *Policy Studies Journal* 14, 140-48.

Robertson, D.B., & Judd, D.R. (1989). *The Development of American Public Policy: The Structure of Policy Restraint.* New York, NY: Harper Collins.

Rombough, M. (Environmental Coordinator, Laidlaw Environmental Services, Central Region). (1994). Personal interview. June 10.

Ruryk, Z. (2000, January 4). Firm site to mine: push on to find new dump site for city. *Toronto Sun.*

Rusk, J., & Bourette, S. (2000, October 21). Toronto scuppers garbage proposal. *Globe and Mail.*

Schoenberger, E. (1988). From Fordism to flexible accumulation: technology, competitive strategies, and international location. *Environment and Planning D, Society and Space* 6, 245-62.

Silverman, G.B. (1989). Love Canal: a retrospective. *Environment Reporter, BNR* 20, 20.

Shine, D. (2001a, May 22). Bill aims to stop Toronto garbage: US lawmaker says he sees way to ban imports. *Detroit Free Press.*

Shine, D. (2001b, March 27). Michigan could stem trash flow: bill would let local entities decide imports. *Detroit Free Press.*

Shine, D. (2001c, May 2). Canada may stop its own garbage: plan would call for ok before shipping trash. *Detroit Free Press.*

Smithville Phase IV Bedrock Remediation Program. (1995, April). *Annual Report*. Smithville, ON: Ministry of Environment and Energy.

Spira, G. (Manager of Government and Public Affairs, Chemical Waste Management, Inc.). (1995). Personal interview. June 26.

Szasz, A. (1994) *EcoPopulism: Toxic Waste and the Movement for Environmental Justice*. Minneapolis, MN: University of Minnesota Press.

Tarnawskyj, P. (Manager of Environmental Compliance and Regulatory Affairs, CECOS International, Browning-Ferris Industries). (1995). Personal interview. June 26.

Terris, B.J., & Hecker, J.M. (1988, December 23). *Post-Hearing Reply Brief of the Province of Ontario in the Matter of the Application by CECOS International, Inc.* Washington, DC: Terris, Edgecombe, Hecker, & Wayne.

Terris, B.J., & Hecker, J.M. (1989, June 16). Letter to W.J. Dickerson, Administrative Law Judge, New York State Department of Environmental Conservation, Office of Hearings. Washington, DC: Terris, Edgecombe, Hecker, & Wayne.

Tickell, A., & Peck, J.A. (1992). Accumulation, regulation and the geographies of post Fordism. missing links in regulationist research. *Progress in Human Geography* 16(2), 190-218.

Toronto. (2000). *Waste Disposal and Diversion*. www.city.toronto.on.ca/council/

Tupper, S.R., & Bailey, D.L. (1967). *One Continent—Two Voices*. Toronto, ON: Clarke, Irwin, & Company.

United Church of Christ Commission for Racial Justice. (1987). *Toxic Wastes and Race in the United States: A National Report on the Racial and Socioeconomic Characteristics of Communities with Hazardous Waste Sites*. New York, NY: United Church of Christ.

United Nations Environment Programme. (1994). *Transboundary Movements of Hazardous Waste at the Interface of Environment and Trade*. Geneva: UNEP.

United States Council on Environmental Quality. (1980). *Public Opinion on Environmental Issues: Results of a National Opinion Survey*. Washington, DC: US Government Printing Office.

United States General Accounting Office. (1983). *Siting of Hazardous Waste Landfills and Their Correlation with Racial and Economic Status of Surrounding Communities*. Washington, DC: Government Printing Office.

United States General Accounting Office. (1995). *Hazardous and Nonhazardous Waste: Demographics of People Living Near Waste Facilities*. Washington, DC: Government Printing Office.

United States Office of Technology Assessment. (1983). *Technologies and Management Strategies for Hazardous Waste Control*. Washington, DC: Government Printing Office.

VanNijnatten, D.L., & Boardman, R. (Eds.). (2002). *Canadian Environmental Policy: Context and Cases*. Toronto, ON: Oxford University Press.

Vaughan, E., & Seifert, M. (1992). Variability in the framing of risk issues. *Journal of Social Issues* 48(4), 119-35.

Wanagas, D. (2000, May 16). Councillors fail to show for hearing on $500 million contract—quorum lost: hearing held on disposal of city's garbage. *National Post*.

Westell, D. (1994, November 24). Trans-Canada faces toxic traffic: Alberta and Ontario rulings mean more hazardous waste heads west. *Globe and Mail*.

Williams, M. (Walpole Island First Nation Heritage Centre). (1995). Personal interview. August 3.

Williams, R. (1985). *Loyalties*. London: Chatto & Windus.

Willis, K.G., & Powe, N.A. (1995). Planning decisions on waste disposal sites. *Environment and Planning B: Planning and Design* 22, 93-107.

Yates, D. (Acting Superintendent of Schools, Lewiston-Porter Central School). (1989, June 20). Letter to W.J. Dickerson, Administrative Law Judge. Youngstown, NY: New York State Department of Environmental Conservation, Office of Hearings.

Young, I.M. (1983). Justice and hazardous waste. In M. Bradie, T. Attig, & N. Rescher (Eds.), *The Applied Turn in Contemporary Philosophy*. Bowling Green, OH: Bowling Green State University.

Young, I.M. (1990). *Justice and the Politics of Difference*. Princeton, NJ: Princeton University Press.

Zeiss, C. (1996). Directions for engineering contributions to successfully siting hazardous waste facilities. In D. Munton (Ed.), *Hazardous Waste Siting and Democratic Choice*. Washington, DC: Georgetown University Press.

Index